PRAISE FOR
WANNABE DISTANCE GOD

"This book is a great read. High school and collegiate runners will love this book. It describes the real deal; what it's like to try and improve in our challenging sport. But better then that, young runners will want to read about the human side of that challenge, how our parents and friends view our very intense sport that is a bit out of mainstream America, and maybe best of all, how we find this sport.

This book is different, from the young athletes point of view. There are great contrasts between people and teams, and it describes the shock and awe certain runners and teams induced in us. Running is a thinking persons' sport, and what phenomenal—though unusual—memories running leaves us.

I loaned this book to a friend and he loved it, even though he wasn't a high school or college runner. Running offers more than any other sport because it's more than just a sport, it's what we want it to be...just do it right. We are lucky to be runners."

—Bill Rodgers won both the Boston and New York City Marathons four times, ran the Montreal Olympic Marathon, and is the former American record holder in the marathon. He coauthored *Marathon Man* (2013, St. Martin's Press).

"I love *Wannabe Distance God*'s psychology of running in our own hearts. It's in you, but you have to pull it out of yourself. *Wannabe Distance God* will wake up some American youth, and it needs to be promoted at the high-school level."

—Henry Rono, in 1978, in a span of 81 days, broke the world record in the 10,000, 5,000, 3,000 Steeplechase, and 3,000 meter runs, an achievement unparalleled in the history of distance running. He is the author of *Olympic Dream* (AuthorHouse, 2007).

"If you are an athlete and particularly a runner, this is a book you will definitely want to read. If you are like most of us, searching for truth and wisdom, this is a book you will definitely want to read. It is a book not only about running but also about a man with courage enough to face himself through the years of chasing his 'ghosts' and 'gods.' The writing is spot on in clarity and razor sharp imagery that keeps the pace alive and exciting. *Wannabe Distance God* is not just a running book. It is a book about the race of a lifetime, told with candor and relentless verve."

—Billy Ray Chitwood is the author of *The Cracked Mirror: Reflections of an Appalachian Son* (2011), *Mama's Madness* (2012), *Butterflies and Jellybeans – A Love Story* (2011), and *A Bailey Crane Mystery* Series.

"*Wannabe Distance God* is a read for the soul as the writer explores the myriad feelings that relate to running, racing, relationships, and religion. While based around the quest of becoming a 'distance god,' Timmy Two-Mile shares the angst, suffering commitment, and sacrifice of those lucky enough to discover a passion and chase a dream.

The writer does a wonderful job of sharing his personal journey from both the perspective of an athlete and psychologist, taking the reader through the many stages of life.

Timmy Two-Mile, I am honored to have spent time with you in the chase pack; fourth in the Olympic Trials is only first in the chase pack! But 'we got to run'!"

—Dr. Chuck Aragon is a 3:51.6 miler, was fourth in the 1984 U.S. Olympic Trials 1500 meters, competed in the 1500 meters at the 1987 World Championships in Athletics in Rome, is the current American Record Holder in the 4 X Mile Relay (anchor leg 3:58.6), and was the first native-born New Mexican to break the four-minute mile.

"You have captured the essence of all distance runners. A must read for all runners of all abilities. Thanks for putting your thoughts on paper. Many 'Wannabe Distance Gods' become PhDs, MDs, lawyers, captains of industry, and even a few coaches."

—Joe Piane, Head Track and Field Coach, Notre Dame University

WANNABE
DISTANCE GOD:

The Thirst, Angst, and Passion of Running in the Chase Pack

A Memoir by
Timothy M. Tays, PhD

ISBN: 1479118834
ISBN-13: 9781479118830

For Renni and Gentry,
my beloved wife and son,
who teach me, ground me,
and hold my heart.

ACKNOWLEDGEMENTS

T hank you to my dad, who taught me how to tell a story; to my mom, who taught me to look beyond the face of things; to my brother Tom, who taught me tenacity; and to my sister Kat, who taught me kindheartedness.

Also, thank you to my running brothers over the years, the short list being Bryan Nelson, Jon Timothy Nelson, Ralph Clark, Joshua Timothy Dean Clark, Miltie Clark, Tim Schmidt, Shaun Trenholm, Kendall Smith, and Bruce Coldsmith. The long list is far too extensive to add here, but I thank all the young distance runners who went through the fire with me. Full stride, bros!

To my coaches, Steve Silverberg and Bob Timmons –you put me through hell, and I can't thank you enough.

And finally, to the short list of distance gods whom I never caught but always aspired to be like: Billy Mills, Bill Rodgers, Henry Rono, Chuck Aragon, Dave Wottle, Jim Ryun, Mike Boit, Mark Nenow, Paul Cummings, Matt Centrowitz (Senior), Alberto Salazar, Greg Myer, Bill McChesney, Steve Prefontaine, and Joan Benoit Samuelson.

CONTENTS

PREFACE

"*Wannabe Distance God* speaks eloquently of the sacrifices, pain, and determination many of us, if not all, go through as we attempt to choreograph our journey into a rapidly changing world and prepare for the opportunities that ultimately await us.

As I read *Wannabe Distance God,* I was humbled and powerfully reminded of the years I spent experiencing the thirst, feeling the anxiety and unaware of being a slave to my own passion as I pursued the lead pack.

The book unrelentingly shows how the perceptions society places upon us, and how the perceptions we then place upon ourselves, continually influence the pursuit of our dreams.

It reconfirmed for me that only when I pursued my personal happiness did I begin to free myself of societal and self-imposed perceptions, allowing me to truly see if my ability as a runner would allow me to run with the lead pack.

There are many lessons to be learned from reading *Wannabe Distance God.* The most significant lesson for me was how the author, all while chasing the lead pack and fighting injury, found the strength and wisdom to continue choreographing his journey into our ever-changing world and take advantage of the opportunity change ultimately presented.

It reminded me of my favorite quote that I refer to often:

'Few are those who see with their own eyes and feel with their own hearts.'—Albert Einstein

Today, as a clinical psychologist, one might say Timothy M. Tays, PhD, is running with the lead pack as he assists others to see with their own eyes and feel with their own hearts.

Onward!"

—Billy Mills, January 29, 2013

—Billy Mills is the 1964 Tokyo Olympic 10,000 meter gold medalist, National Spokesperson for Running Strong for American Indian Youth (www.indianyouth.org), and coauthor with Nicholas Sparks of *Lessons of a Lakota* (Hay House, Inc. 2005). He is the former American 10,000 meter and three-mile record holder, and former World Record Holder at six miles. Other accolades include: National Track and Field Hall of Fame (1976), US Olympic Hall of Fame (1984), National Distance Running Hall of Fame (1999), and Presidential Citizens Medal given by President Obama (2012).

PROLOGUE

I wanted to be a distance god.

There. I said it.

I would've broken out of the lead pack and surged away, thrown down some impossible late-race splits, devastated the elites as I stretched my lead—merciless, alone, almost floating. The field would've strung out and withered behind me as I burned and buried the best runners on the face of the planet.

I would've become immortal.

Was that too much to ask?

There's a theory in psychology that says we take on for ourselves a piece of every person we meet, even if we merely brush up against him or her in a fleeting, profound moment—even, I suppose, if he or she just runs past us or sits across from us in an overstuffed armchair.

I wanted to take on more of what the distance gods had.

Still do.

CHAPTER 1

ALSO-RAN

I t mattered that I wasn't a distance god. To me, I mean. It mattered that I was an also-ran, buried in the results an inch below the leaders in the races that mattered.

So I ran harder, longer.

Anything it took, bro. So what if at thirteen I got out of my parents' Oldsmobile and ran on the dirt shoulder of the highway to top off my week? What's the big deal if, ten years and tens of thousands of miles later, I lived on five-for-a-dollar Kraft macaroni and cheese so I could afford a plane ticket to Jacksonville, Florida, to take on some of the best distance runners in the world? It was worth all the suffering. Easily worth it.

The suffering didn't feel like suffering as long as it led to running faster. So the distance, the time, and the kills mattered. The rituals and the attitude mattered. The compulsiveness to rack up the miles mattered. OK, let me put it this way: *running* mattered.

Still, when I compared myself to the distance gods, I didn't measure up.

Yet.

That's what kept me going—the *yet* part. So I put in more miles and endured more.

I had to run. Like there's-a-saber-toothed-tiger-chasing-me had to run. I was desperate yet resigned because although I'd never tried to outrun a saber-toothed tiger, they looked really fast. But what could I do? I *couldn't* stop. Although I was slower than distance gods and saber-toothed tigers, distance running was the only thing I did well.

It was primal for me—in my genes—yet it was sublime and noble, even spiritual. It was so deep in my DNA, spirit, and identity that it wasn't fully within my control. You could say it was my destiny—I certainly did. Running to me wasn't merely putting one foot in front of the other; it was my life. It was who I was.

Running consumed me—sometimes like love, sometimes like cancer. Hopelessly committed to becoming a distance god, I was all in. The fallout of this quest to get faster—selfishness, poverty, strained relationships, injury—were dues I willingly paid for the coveted elite status.

American distance talent was historically deep in my day—the early eighties—so there was plenty of company, which reinforced my joining them on the roads. Muscling in on the extremely limited money would mean more time to train, travel to far-flung places, run in bigger and more important races, and eventually run at the front of the pack toward godliness. Until then I was just one more ectomorph dogging the young men who made a living at the thing I was passionate about.

The distance gods showed me how to be the best me—how to strive for excellence. I was competitive and envious when I perceived them as threatening my rise. But I was a teen, and then a young man, and from the perspective of middle age, I now see both the benefits and the nonsense of my behavior.

I remember them, though—the distance gods. There they were in high school, in college, on the roads, and in the military, daring me to keep up. I took that dare because I thought that I had to become a distance god to be completely me.

I worked the angles: Partial track and cross-country scholarships led to a full ride. There were shoe contracts, merchandise won and resold, $400 in an unmarked envelope in Tupelo, and a dubious road win in Albuquerque leading to a free trip to Lincoln, Nebraska. I networked with other runners for a ride and a couch to crash on for out-of-town races, and I hired a fanatical runner with a law degree as my agent. I even joined the military for the running perks.

In the end I was supposed to be a distance god, yet I always made my nut some other way. You can't say I didn't take my shot, though. You *cannot* say that.

The world of distance running was flat, so we *all* had a shot, which was seductive. Longer races allowed us nonelite athletes to compete against the best in the world. I measured myself against the distance gods, tried to beat them, and tried to break through to godliness. Before corrals and timing chips, we lined up and went for it, man—head-to-head against people you might've heard of. It was raw and fast. I didn't think about the multitudes behind me shuffling to the start after the gun fired. It was all about me, you see. It had to be. And, of course, about the distance gods ahead of me.

Maybe I blew it.

I overtrained, ran through injuries, and didn't mind my diet. Not smart. I guess Dad was right. "Boy, ya ain't the smartest," he liked to tell me, "but dadgummit, people *like* you. Now *that's* how you'll get ahead." I wasn't sure if I'd been insulted. My focus wasn't on smarts, but on *perseverance.* Wasn't that a *smart* plan? Likability meant nothing six miles into a 15K while hitting sweet splits close to my personal records (PRs) with oxygen debt creeping into my legs and lungs, a big-ass bridge looming, and the distance gods still pulling away.

There was no limit to the sacrifice. People quickly discovered I was all in. Sometimes really good runners backed off, not because I could outrun them, but because after running with me a few times, they learned the pain wouldn't stop. If my emotional pain wouldn't stop, then they had to feel some of that pain as well. If I had to race in a workout to gain their respect, so be it; plenty of my races were left in workouts. It wasn't worth it to them to keep hurting, but it was to me—I made that clear. In college they called me a "horse," which I took as a complement. Horses will froth up and run themselves to death. The difference between training hard and training smart got lost in my testosterone, youth, and need.

So the struggle was always worth it to me—every workout, every race—because I wanted them to look at me the way I looked at the distance gods.

So now you know.

Timmy Two-Mile was a wannabe distance god. There. I said it.

THE CHAMELEON COMPLEX

When I was a young man, I liked to think of myself as an undiscovered, wild-eyed distance ace. As I flamed toward fame, my imagined detractors would one day see me more clearly—with admiration and perhaps even contrition. You can get away with a lot if you're a distance god, and I counted on it.

I also thought of myself as a blue-collar runner. Most distance runners probably think of themselves as down-and-dirty hard workers. How could they be otherwise, considering the inherent effort required to run so far? I was no different; I loved to outwork and beat everybody I could. It was especially satisfying to beat guys I considered more talented. Of course when I lost to them, it just meant they were dealt a better genetic hand. Thus it was no shame on me—just biological dumb luck for them—and I renewed my effort, digging down deeper. I'd overcome genetics with effort. My running career was a marathon, after all, and only the finish and time mattered, not the early maneuvering, was how I had it figured. Talented runners became more common as I moved through the competitive strata: junior high to high school to college, and then out onto the wide-open roads. Finally there was my slow decline in the army and then my injury. Only in retrospect do I see that it was a predictable career arc, one I didn't think applied to me.

Once I became a distance god, I fantasized, I'd stay focused and grounded. I "cognitively rehearsed" how I would play it, which is psychobabble for thinking about it ahead of time. Also-rans would introduce themselves to me at postrace parties, and I'd humbly grant them an audience, letting them revel in my aura. Sure, I'd chat them up (oh, it's *no* imposition!), autograph their race bib, ask them what their PRs were, nod, smile, and make eye contact—not the least bit condescending. Although I could easily crush them—and we both knew it—I'd still show respect. We were all human beings, after all, and all distance runners. Eventually, though, I'd politely—*respectfully*—excuse myself. Perhaps I'd already promised to knock down a few brewskis with Alberto Salazar, a notoriously hard worker like me. So we'd bond over that, snickering at the guys who "need more rest." Maybe Bill Rodgers wanted me to log some late-night junk miles with him. Hey, Paul Cummings and I might do a little fishing early the next morning!

Even from the pinnacle, I would understand that we were all fortunate to be there, able to run faster than most, able to make a living at it. Sure, some of us were luckier than others because of those good genetics. But we—and by *we* I would mean us distance gods—also added hard work and a willingness to do whatever it took to throw ourselves into the subculture of zealous distance running, which by its very nature was grueling, was devoid of shortcuts, and suggested a solid disposition. It was certainly not for anyone afraid of a little wretchedness or sweat.

Before I'd excuse myself from the supplicant, I'd put my arm around his shoulder and squeeze. That's all he really wanted, after all—a little bit of recognition that even though he didn't run as fast, he busted his hump as well. He'd know I couldn't share max VO_2, slow-twitch fibers, or fanaticism. After all, it's every dog for himself out on the roads. Still, a side hug would go a long way—I'd know that—and it would perhaps even be something he'd tell his friends about over the years; maybe he'd even write it up in a memoir. That little bit of consideration would be nice of me—a bit of encouragement to an also-ran.

I'd at least do that much.

As a wannabe distance god, I considered my persona. I kept things interesting and offbeat, shocking and extreme. Leaps of impropriety weren't difficult for me then—back when I had nothing to lose. I wanted eye-watering edginess coupled with gasp-out-loud PRs. Despite mixed success at outrageousness and jaw-dropping times, I always had my thirst, which was plenty.

The dynamic of needing to become a distance god, plus the usual fear of death and being the sort of personality who spent a lot of time creating things to worry about, made me react strongly to boredom. I chose between boredom and struggle—and usually chose struggle—because in those silent spaces created by boredom, it was difficult to avoid my self-doubt, fear, and regrets. So my self-mythologizing served as a distraction. Maybe I moved to the front of a race that I had no business controlling. I framed that as having a big, hairy pair. At an Electric Light Orchestra concert, maybe I shouted my admiration for Jeff Lynne louder than the average fan, and then went home and played "Fire On High" backwards. "The music is reversible but time is not. Turn back! Turn back! Turn back! Turn back!" I framed that as youthful eccentricity, something I'd one day outgrow, just not while I was young. Or maybe I pissed in an elevator after a hard night out with the distance core, which I thought was wild and something the iconic American Olympian Steve Prefontaine might do. Perversion? Maybe. But as Voltaire said, "Once is philosophy, twice is perversion," and I'm pretty sure I didn't do that more than once. Once served the persona.

Usually, though, since I had an aptitude for language—which is a big reason I do talk therapy for a living today—I used words to strike sparks off my peers. My intent was not to bully, although I didn't mind a little one-upmanship. My intent was to better establish that pseudo-Prefontainesque persona. It also made things more interesting. If people pushed back with humor, then good—that wasn't boring. If they remarked how crazy I was, even better. We'd all have a grin. I wore *crazy* as a badge of honor so long as *crazy* meant *wild* or *fun*, not *psychopathological* or *unlikeable*. Just don't call me *boring*.

Of course not everyone had the same sense of humor. Good-old-boy New Mexican humor was my predilection, which careened into the scatological. Bodily functions and euphemistic names for intimate body parts were hilarious to me. A bull's scrotum made into a car wastebasket was a fashionable conversation piece. My "individuality" prompted rolled eyes and pursed lips by some of my more constricted, sexually anorexic, citified peers from Albuquerque, Lawrence, and Arlington. Young people cool with anonymity. Teens with better manners. Mature young adults. Boring was easy. I wanted to burn, baby. So I laughed at them and shifted to another distraction, another flash of entertainment. Still their judgment stung. Sunday mornings I awoke with a social hangover. Who had I offended? Who had offended me?

When someone took offense, I took great offense back. Why have such high standards of civility? I fancied myself a writer collecting life experiences, one of which was supposed to be wild-ass distance god. Besides, we hardly lived in a Victorian age, barely a decade from the peace protests, women's movements, Vietnam, and Woodstock. High school kids still ran quarters, halves, and miles, and at indoor college races, we still raced miles, two-miles, and three-miles. Disco receded to the background, and Elvis Costello pumped us up into frenzied kicks. Victorian my arse. Since we were all worm meat anyway, why not burn?

It was trite, but what better way to spend my youth than as a wild-ass distance god?

Perhaps a more parsimonious explanation would be undiagnosed attention deficit disorder. I didn't have it. (Have you seen how well Galen Rupp's been running? My *god!*) Well, maybe just a touch. Today someone like I was might ask for an ADD evaluation and perhaps medication. He might ask for something to level him out, a little something to keep the folks and teachers happy. I would not have asked though. I liked who I was for the most part, or at least I liked the role in which I tried to cast myself. But medication would be an option today—that's my point. That might not be such a good thing—to tamp down youthful spirit and suppress the learning curve. Besides, I don't like playing the role of Nurse Ratched.

Maybe I had the chameleon complex, changing my colors to whatever I thought I *should* be, oblivious to my authentic self.

Maybe I didn't have psychopathology at all but was only self-centered.

Maybe I was just young.

Possible psychiatric diagnosis aside, I wanted to spend my youth as a hybrid of Pre and Ken Kesey, the famed writer and leader of the Merry Pranksters. I wanted the attention and respect that distance gods and colorful authors were systematically deprived of but very much deserved. To me they were cooler than movie stars, rock legends, or thick-armed football heroes.

OK, full self-disclosure here: I still think that.

CHAPTER 3

STRIKING DISTANCE

Tear down, build up.

I pulled on the handrails to go *up* stairs and winced when I clomped *down*, my quads threatening to cramp.

I worked hard—you've gotta give me that much.

Hey, anything for the quest, right?

Yet they *still* pulled away from me—the distance gods. Every time. Every stinkin' time! Right from the gun. It wasn't like I ran with them for a few miles, got into oxygen debt, and faded. No. That's what distance gods did, not chase-pack wannabes. Distance gods won, faded late, or took it down to the wire. Guys like me? Bang! The distance gods were gone.

Studs. Such freaking studs.

Imagine how it was to be me—to hear my splits and know they didn't suck. Sometimes my splits were faster than my PRs just a year earlier in college, yet I remained invisible to the elites.

Wonderful. Just *marvelous.* (My snarky comments—that sideways anger—are something I'm trying to get a handle on after all these years. It's me playing the victim, and I don't do it when I'm being my best self. When I'm my best self, I'm more direct and assertive with no hidden agenda—less defensive, less sarcastic, less judgmental, and more accepting of the flaws and foibles

15

of others and myself. I'm nicer and quite frankly more *boring.* Boring like maturity, I hope—not boring like death.)

I didn't expect to break through and run with the elites so soon after college, but I wanted to get their attention or at least get within striking distance. I would do that at the US Olympic Trials in Buffalo, New York, in May 1984. Not fast enough in either the five-thousand or ten-thousand meters, I figured there was more room on the roads, and running a marathon in 2:19.04 seemed doable then—the way things seem doable when you're a somewhat delusional twenty-three-year-old male. If I didn't get a time in the teens, I wouldn't be close to the elites or go to the trials. I'd remain insignificant. That was intolerable. Oh, sure, I beat plenty of guys, but I figured they didn't want it as badly as I did; they weren't willing to stake everything. If I could get paid to run, I could focus on nothing but running, and the pieces would come together.

When I considered getting a real job and training around it, it felt like giving up—like death, like no longer raging against the dying of the light. I simply *had* to put everything into running, and poverty was not an obstacle—except when it was.

How else would I run like Alberto Salazar? Clearly I wasn't as talented as him, but I remember this one race you might have heard of: *the NCAA Cross-Country Championship!* (Sorry. Slipped into snarky mode there.) Anyway, you could say Salazar, Henry Rono, and I were briefly tied. Sure, they eventually pulled away from me—and by *eventually* I mean when the race started—but they crushed everyone that day, not just me. More hard work would compensate for our talent differences over time. One day I'd pull them down, I was sure—fairly sure, anyway.

Sometimes I got to win races too. When I led a race, I dug down deeper, stretched my lead, and put more seconds between the runner-up and me. Then I compared times. How badly had I humiliated him? Did he learn his lesson? Would he race for second place the next time we met? Suppose so-and-so had been in the race—how much more did I have in me? On my way to the front, everyone behind me should be awed and lose hope. The distance gods should fear my accession.

First, though, I needed to qualify for the US Olympic Marathon Trials.

The problem was I hadn't yet run a marathon.

What felt like destiny in my youth smacks of narcissism today. I've tested myself with standardized psychological assessments to ensure I'm on the right track now. Apparently I abused alcohol in my youthful, distance-running years (I'm *not* bragging, nor am I very contrite), had a dash of inflated self-esteem, expansiveness, and grandiosity, not unusual for a young man.

Yikes. All that time I thought I was just being interesting.

I retested myself focusing on what's true of me today, and I'm within the normal range on all scales. No psychopathology here, folks! You're welcome.

See, what I called *confidence* then rings of *cockiness* now. I'm not fully settled with it. The cockiness got smacked out of me over the years, but I'm not convinced that being brash and loathing to lose were bad for a runner striving for elite status. What's that conviction—that mettle—that made so many of us think we could run in front of all the others? Running was a common thing, after all, so I competed in a huge pool. A veritable crowd vied for the top spots, and were we not all worthy human beings with a right to draw breath, wear skin, and win races? We all deserved to win—at least we did from a politically correct revisionist perspective—but in some Orwellian spin, apparently some of us deserved it more than others, and by *some of us* I meant me, the guy who gave all. Was the shift from cockiness to confidence merely quibbling about the difference between young men and mature men? Was it wrong to dare for greatness or merely poor form to talk about it?

The highs of racing well, breaking records, setting PRs, and kicking butt are things I miss. They left me self-satisfied for days before fading. Traces of those memories surface today when I run. *Proud* might best capture it, although it's probably another thing I shouldn't even say.

There's still something cocky in me when I run. It's "Timmy Two-Mile" reasserting himself—this other part of me that lay dormant for a quarter century. *Timmy Two-Mile's on his way back!* I told myself when I had one of those runs where my arms swung easily; my chest, full of oxygen, heaved but didn't burn; my legs effortlessly turned over; I hit sweet splits deep into the distance; and I had to tell myself, *Hold something back, you ageless stud—save some juice for the race!*

Timmy Two-Mile was a skeletal youth with eight-pack abs and 7 percent body fat. He was often on the verge of blurting out something cheeky like, "This race is mine, hippie, so you might as well take off your racing flats unless you planted some kryptonite out there on the course." Said with a wry grin. It was a joke, of course, even if not everybody thought it was as clever as I did.

I know. I cringe to write it. At least now I know to scale it back. I didn't always know it though. I mean I didn't know it for sure. Yeah, I suspected it, but enough people smiled to keep me on stage. Most of my close friends knew not to take that part of me too seriously. Some of my close friends *did* take that part seriously, but I wouldn't know it until decades later when they struggled to reconcile who I *was* then and who I *am* today. All of them knew there was another part of me that would take them into the darkness if it meant finishing a step ahead. I took running extremely seriously, although I tried not to take myself too seriously. Often the difference got blurred.

Today I might say, *I'll just do my best for my age.* See? I've learned my lesson. Everyone who rolled his or her eyes then can take a chill pill now and unball his or her fists.

I resent the hypocrisy. Those who laughed the hardest then are the same people who gave in to their awakening addictions and have not lived beyond forgettable. They are also the most judgmental today. I could give them grace, and I should. Then again, I am chagrined and wish to defend myself. I know the right thing to say; it's their issue and not mine. Still it feels like betrayal.

They should've known my heart and not been seduced by the show. We were friends after all. Not that I'm portraying myself as a victim. I'm sort of mature now. There was enough flak and social wear that now I'm the one whose ears prick up over the braggadocio of a young man—which I let slip right on past me.

This is my penance, you see, and my growth. It's my way to show tolerance and make amends. This is my way to pay forward everyone who was ever tolerant with me.

Now I avoid friction. I do the best I can for my age, and I find that it lets me off the hook in a way that I'm not even looking for. It's kind to myself and more tolerable in the ears of others. Just between us, though, it doesn't satisfy the part of me that still wants to devastate the field, not just my age group.

Challenging the distance gods was an overwhelming task, so I was willing to flirt with hubris if it meant a bit more confidence. I knew I set myself up, and I assumed my good friends were aware of my vulnerability that lay just beneath the hard exterior of my competitive face. Prick the crust and there lay a squishy, soft core of low self-esteem. I must've had unrealistic expectations of others' depth of perception and willingness to grant *me* grace.

Why should I have such expectations? Because when I wasn't playing the larger-than-life role, I was tucked in some dark booth with a distance buddy talking over a pitcher of Bud and a red-and-white plastic cup full of salted peanuts. Humility was also my thing, and we discussed our pain and concerns, our lust and victories. Gray fifteen-milers gave us space to mull our losses, triumphs, and dreams. Emotional intimacy and profundity were strengths of mine, except I didn't know it then. Of course everyone connects with his buddies at this level, I assumed. Decades later I learned that the common denominator had been me and that some of my buddies haven't connected with another human being in such a deep way since then. Which is sad, of course, but that's another reason why I went into psychology and why I'm comfortable doing psychotherapy today. It was an aptitude, and it was the reason my bonds went deeper than endless miles and parties, communal living quarters, or countless highway hours spent traveling to the next race.

Misbehaving was purposeful; I knew how to act around someone's mother. My youth and my act would not last forever— I knew it even then—but I wanted to wring it for all I could. Assuming everyone knew it was my *shtick*, they were supposed to dig it too. If I came off arrogant at times, it was a *lovable* arrogance, right? It was consciously chosen, done mischievously and wryly, and just one facet of who I was. My youth, sense of mortality, yearning for individuality, and expected future running success justified my behavior, which of course needed an edgy persona to accompany it.

These days I do a lot less justifying, and I do have some regrets. The benefits of toning it down are obvious to me now that I have something to lose, now that I've been generally humbled. The benefits weren't obvious to me then, though, when toning it down looked like capitulating to the uptight moaners and critics.

I'm still afraid of death and boredom, but I don't distract myself at the expense and discomfort of others anymore. This makes my life less conflicted and stressful than it was during the lean years. There are no pursed lips when I walk into a room, no arms tightly crossed over bosoms unless it's a high school reunion or a college buddy's poisoned wife. But my wife liked my friends before she even met them. Loyalty means a lot to me.

If it mattered enough, I'd ask my ghosts, "Why're you bad-mouthing me, man?" and they'd answer, "But it's *true!*" And I'd say, "Yeah, but what about the bro code, dude? Besides, isn't there a statute of limitations?" I understand it's all they know of me—thirty-year-old data—so it's ignorance with a smattering of hypocritical self-righteous judgment, but still something in me expects unconditional positive regard from people with whom I've openly shared my life. Maybe I'm indignant because in my field you cannot diagnose someone without having first gotten to know them—or get to know who they are today. Maybe my fear of death makes me overvalue my life. I'm not saying that's wrong; I'm saying just the opposite.

Anyway, I'm more satisfied on the whole these days than when I lived to burn, to race, to work my way up. Life is not the struggle that it was, and I no longer get shattered the way I did.

Which is all good, right?

So I've toned it down. When I returned to running, and it occurred to me that I'd still like to win the Boston Marathon, I didn't take it seriously. That thought flitted right out the other side of my head. The point is that if I'm not careful, thoughts of having exceptionally high running skills still pop into my mind. It clearly borders on delusional, but it isn't because I don't truly believe it, and I certainly don't say it out loud. A dinner party where we sniff the cabernet and discuss the housing meltdown is not a good place to share it. My frontal lobe appears to be fully developed now and functioning normally. My judgment and impulse control seem to be much better, thank you very much. Even at twenty-three when I dreamed of winning Boston, or at least qualifying for the Olympic trials there, I had enough sense and experience from getting whipped by the distance gods that I knew I was much more likely to be struck by lightning than I was to win Boston.

Even as I neared my running-career peak, I already accepted I'd never be an Olympian or world-record holder. Before that realization, in college, my amateur status was important to the NCAA and me. After college it meant little to me except poverty. To give up my dream of being an Olympian and merely make a living as a runner was a huge compromise, a significant beginning of my letting the dream go. Once I got there, though, I was quite open to accept funding in any form. I didn't need to be an Olympian. I just wanted to stay out on the roads. By any means necessary, as they say. It was reasonable in a country that still valued amateurism in international competition during the Cold War, despite the obvious infractions by the rest of the world.

Here's how reasonable I am today: I will never win the Boston Marathon. That was true when I was twenty-three, and it's still true thirty years later. I won't even win my age group at Boston, let alone achieve fame and fortune as a runner. I will live in obscurity, grow old, and die—the exact *opposite* of Pre, who died approaching his peak with heavy metal across his chest, frozen at awesome. No, I can expect a gray decline and forced humility, which I can't even think about—at least not in quiet, dark moments when I awaken late at night, sometimes ruminating with regret, other times with fear.

Wonderful. Just marvelous.

CHAPTER 4

THE MARINE CORPS MARATHON AND OTHER EXPOSURES

The Marine Corps Marathon went nearby my house when I lived in Arlington, Virginia, so I jumped in as a bandit runner on a blustery November morning. I wanted company for another tough twenty-miler en route to Boston. It wasn't even like me to want running companions so much, which was probably why I got into trouble. Perhaps a buddy would've alerted me to the situation. Please don't rev up any catastrophic thoughts; it's not like I did something totally dicky like join the lead pack and cross the finish line. I already did that years earlier in a Kansas road race before the days of timing chips. I got sucked into racing when I hadn't entered, and when I should've peeled off so as not to spoil the results, I didn't. *I'm a competitor!* I thought. That was easier to live with than the truth, which was that I was excellent at being self-centered back then.

When I jumped into the Marine Corps Marathon, I wouldn't pull such antics. I'd done a couple of twenty-milers with my old college buddies Bruce Coldsmith and Kendall Smith and kept it at six-minute pace, but alone I struggled, so I joined the middle-of-the-pack joggers after the first mile and hoped the company and excitement of the race would pull me along. I was right.

I held my pace and enjoyed being a cheetah among cattle—someone on the verge of qualifying for the Olympic trials, someone who respected the sport too much to disrupt the official racers.

Here's where I got it wrong: it was colder and windier than I had estimated before leaving my house. No problem; once I got moving, I'd warm up. See, my default was to wear less so I could run faster. I hated feeling bulky and usually stripped off my sweats for intervals, maximum steady runs, and even for long slow-distance. I wouldn't get a tattoo because I didn't want the extra weight. OK, that's hyperbole. In truth I didn't get tattoos because they are permanent, and one thing I knew about for sure was the impermanence of the human condition. That's good if you want to become something but not so good if you're just holding on to the gains you've already made. Anyway, I liked to run light, so although I wore a sweatshirt, a beanie, and running gloves, I only had on a new pair of blue nylon shorts Brooks Shoes gave me. They were the fancy kind, "French cut," which we might call "freedom cut" today, not because of anger at the French, but for another reason I'll get to shortly. There were slits up each hip and a built-in brief that failed to keep my package either stable or warm.

When I changed direction, the wind made the flap on those shorts flip open, and I regretted foregoing my cock sock; sleet cut through to my crotch meat. It stung, but I figured it was temporary, just until I warmed up, which I didn't, and I went numb from my waist to my quads. Still I kept a decent pace as I ran serpentine between the thick age-group runners and enjoyed the crowd lining the course. It was fun to have an audience to appreciate my awesomeness.

Fourteen miles into the sleety Marine Corps Marathon, I whipped past the soft age-group runners despite my numb crotch due to those stinking French-cut nylon running shorts with the built-in briefs. It wasn't all misery, though, because as I cruised along, I pretended the Northern Virginia crowd cheered for me. They weren't as enthusiastic as the storied Oregon track crowds, but they were more supportive than I expected, maybe because they shivered on the sidewalk and clapped for warmth.

Eventually it became obvious they cheered for me, though, and whooped and pointed at my superbness as I zipped past.

They clearly appreciated the show, the slaughter I committed, a semipro among Joes. *I should wave*, I thought, yet I resisted, able by then to sometimes control my impulses, just beginning to understand that people prefer humility. So I only smiled as I dipped below six-minute pace and soaked in their adulation.

At fifteen miles I looked down at that French-cut flap. It had blown open again, and that built-in brief was jimmied aside. It wasn't my awesomeness the spectators cheered but the burlesque show I put on. Frostbit and shriveled, my penis had been exposed for God knows how many miles.

I still work alone for the most part; I'm a distance runner to the bone in that sense, whether I run or not. There is no team effort, no second man, let alone a fifth or seventh man—just my solo practice, of which I am first man, president, and sole stockholder. Tucked away in my office, I am still the solitary runner even in a crowd, putting in miles with few witnesses or accolades, a figurative speck trudging through the maddening deserts, anxious woodlands, and depressed farmers' fields of my clients' psyches. Apparently I have a personality that is compatible with both distance running and psychotherapy. I exploit this strength, which means there are fewer hassles, fewer unsolicited opinions, and fewer compromises I have to make. Autonomous, I am left alone to do the best I can in a career that is sometimes complicated. When I'm finished I lock my files and my office door then take off my figurative psychologist's hat. There are no cheers, pep talks, or high fives. I just put in the miles.

So I'm both prone and trained to overthink the nuances of behavior in others and myself—what's there, what's *not* there, sometimes to the point of obsession. I call it an aptitude, although others may call it neurosis—an imp in my gut.

The imp drove me over the miles, but I wasn't oblivious to my internal press and how it made me different. Some guys just ran. It was a *sport* to them. I am not smirking. Although I didn't understand them, I liked their attitude because it gave me an advantage. The guys who weren't devastated when they had a bad race eventually were not there anymore.

Me? A bad race pulled my bones out through my skin.

Showing up was a huge part of the battle; I figured that out early on, so I was there for the workouts and the races. Year after year I showed up to give some pain.

Now, though, I relieve pain. My clients wait for me in the lobby and pretend to read old issues of *People* as the crashing stocks scroll across the TV screen and the Black Eyed Peas sing "I Gotta Feeling" overhead. I receive my clients with a big, post-braces smile. This hides my anxiety and reassures them. After all they are more anxious than me, about to fillet themselves before a stranger. You can get away with a lot if you smile, even if you smile nervously. Not too much. Just enough. Both of us should be a bit anxious—me enough for preparedness, them enough to bare their neuroses. They're not there to chitchat. Everyone already knows it's hot in Scottsdale, Arizona, which is where my practice is located. We know traffic is bad. Road rage is worse in the summer. Still, we should talk about *their* problems, not *our* problems, and to already have a running start at their neuroticism is helpful.

My clients want to trust my professionalism, so I present to them a man groomed well enough to avoid excessive criticism. See? I pay attention to details, to include *their* story. I'm not so well groomed as to appear vain, obsessive, or materialistic. I buy my socks from Costco by the half-dozen. I wear clunky, black Ecco shoes to protect my abused feet and solid-color slacks and button-down shirts I bought at Nordstrom's the day after Christmas for half price. My hair is cut at Sports Clips rather than standing in front of my bathroom mirror like I did in the old days. I visit my dentist every six months. Clients are supposed to leap to the conclusion, "This man looks as if he sat in the front row in class. Perhaps he can understand me."

The front row was hardly my thing, but I have some other things going for me—like my smile, which means I'm warm, and my frown, which means I'm concerned. That's some of my body language, which I think about a lot. I sit five feet away from my clients, facing them, shoulders square, arms open, nothing between us literally and figuratively. Excellent eye contact and head nods are staples of mine. Sometimes I go, "Uh-huh" or "Hmm." Other times I have something insightful to say. It amazes me the things people don't see in themselves, but I'm not one to talk. Anyway, as a body-language bonus, I have a face that has never intimidated anyone, much to my chagrin as a youth, but a definite asset today. In short I'm a professional-looking, middle-aged white male who can be the screen upon which my clients project their frustrations. I can also be the granite of their recovery. Whatever works for them. They need to feel safe and know that I care. They need to feel understood.

Usually I do indeed understand them and can pinpoint their psychopathology in a jiffy. Sometimes it's not so clear, like when it's about barely buried, decades-old angst, baseless grudges, and unrequited dreams. Either way I let them know I understand, which can be helpful even before the more overt interventions begin. After they have filtered their story through me, I offer a treatment plan and away we go.

I'm one of those people who are educated beyond their intelligence, so when I don't fully understand certain clients, we just muddle through together. Endurance is an asset in both running and psychotherapy. When they refuse to change or get better because they're uncomfortable, scared, or there's secondary gain, and their friends and relatives drop off, I hang in there with them; I carry their pace for as long as they can keep it going. If I can't take their pain and stuckness, then how are they to endure it alone? No, I can take it. After I've proven to them that I can hang, then they begin to listen to me because I've listened to them. Sometimes we find we can't understand the limits of our talent, growing old, or premature death. Then it becomes more about acceptance, which can be the toughest thing of all yet the most helpful.

While on the clock, I present myself as more polished than when I strove for elite running status. Although I'd still love to be a distance god, I've accepted that I never will be. For me that's a big step. Somehow I feel better for the realization, probably by letting go of the angst of striving for it. That's a good thing, I suppose, except it leaves me feeling a bit empty.

In the meantime I'm humbled. Not by a single loss, but by a million tiny narcissistic wounds over half a century. My jagged, adolescent self has long been worn down into this man now on the cusp of old age whose heart you hold in your hands. I prefer to frame this as a cleansing confession preceding an emotional moving on.

Think growth, not defeat.

I look different today than when I used to burn, but at least I have not yet begun to shrink. I am still six one but am no longer 150 pounds of gristle and bone. There is more evidence of the easy life on me now, carried on my jowls and belly. My skinniness used to be extraordinary, but now there is nothing extraordinary about me. The slight paunch I carry is common for men my age and is something I've learned to shrug about, especially when my mileage is down. I am not outrageous, and I don't think it's funny to offend anymore. I choose my attire and demeanor more carefully these days. It helps my clients trust me.

My business card reads *Licensed Clinical Psychologist* and helps my clients make that leap to trust. It doesn't help them to know what happened in elevators after the bars closed or in the Marine Corps Marathon over three decades ago. They don't need to know that there are people who think I have changed as little as they have, our relationship stuck in the seventies and eighties. There's a truism in the health-care field that you shouldn't stay on staff where you do your training because you'll always be treated like an intern. So it is more helpful for my clients to pull up a positive stereotype about the profession and about mental-health-care providers. I'm as close to a blank slate as I can be, but there are constraints—some simply from my material manifestation—so I nurture whatever positive aspects of the stereotype I can.

So no family photos or personal effects are visible in my office. Other than its masculine decor, my office offers no profound insight into my soul. The colors are earth tone—nothing flashy or attention garnering. The picture frames, I am told by certain obsessive-compulsive clients, are sometimes crooked. They want to level them, but I don't let them. Let's call it an "exposure." They need to learn to tolerate nonperfectly hung frames on my office wall and generalize that to the crooked things in their lives. This is not a setup, not a planned exposure, but I'm able to wing it after so many years of having done talk therapy. Those frames outline matted diplomas and abstract art—no nudes or Rorschach blots. This isn't a movie; this is their real life. So I provide my clients a safe space. They can be vulnerable and unload.

In these ways I fit better into my clients' projection of non-judgmental helper, which I indeed try to be. I don't muddy things by sharing about the people who have disappointed me or the people whom I have disappointed. The angst I carry from not becoming a distance god I keep to myself. Besides, to share this would merely sound like a yammering hyena impotently circling a lion at its kill. It's not supposed to be about me or about running fast. It's about my clients, their problems, and how I can help. I'm a tool for their recovery. So I keep my personal history to myself, my desk uncluttered, and my walls professional but with a splash of élan via abstract art that is supposed to suggest that although I am now conservative, I am not yet dead. My files are secure behind three locks, which means that my clients' stories and apprehensions are safe.

It's also safe for me. Clients have verbally attacked me on occasion, which I like to call *transference* and not a normal reaction to a misstep by me. It's also safer that I have an unlisted home phone number and address. They can call the office. Although I am not ostentatious by Scottsdale standards, I do drive an eleven-year-old BMW four-door sedan with a Jayhawks license plate. It's a very safe car. I drive it home to my small family. We live in a gated community that would prove difficult access for disgruntled or enamored clients. So now everybody's safe.

When I'm in my role as psychologist, I like to think that I'm my "best self"—not a hyena at all. More humane. Compassionate. Thoughtful. Less sarcastic or likely to act out my own impulses and personal grievances. During a fifty-minute psychotherapy session, it's about the person on my couch. For most people that may not sound profound, but it's a big shift for me since I'm historically a self-centered and frustrated runner, which makes it sort of a big deal for *me* even when I'm there for *them.*

At twenty-three I could run ten miles in less time than it takes to run a psychotherapy session. Sometimes I run sessions a bit longer than fifty minutes. Although I understand it's a boundary issue, I may fudge it if a client is in crisis or to give them that little something extra—to let them know I value our relationship and that it's not all about the time or the money. Sometimes I slide my fee down for low-income clients. I always have a veteran or a vet's dependent on my caseload pro bono through the *Give an Hour* program that provides free mental health services to U.S. military personnel and their families who have been affected by the conflicts in Iraq and Afghanistan, and more recently terrorism at the Boston Marathon. It worked in running when I gave everything in a race—that little extra bit of spunk, that psychological lean. Often enough that was the difference between satisfaction and dismay. Since I do professional psychotherapy, I approach sessions like a race. I pace myself, but when the timing is right I don't hold back, and I make that extra effort. It could also be because sometimes I worry that I'm not worth what I'm paid. I think I got used to being poor. Right or wrong, there it is. It's another thing I'm working on.

It's always good to be self-aware, though. What are our strengths and deficits? When are we vulnerable and exposed, and how should we respond?

CHAPTER 5

PAUL CUMMINGS

Despite my best efforts to present myself as a cool pseudo-distance god, bizarre things kept happening to me. For example, after distance god Paul Cummings thoroughly spanked me at the 1983 Jacksonville River Run 15K, I sidled over to him at the post-race party. We should chat, I figured, because I met him in high school while on my recruiting trip to Brigham Young University. I wasn't Mormon, but I easily ignored that detail and focused on the running. Six years later I fancied myself a budding star worthy of a second brush with greatness. I reintroduced myself to Cummings.

He looked at me with this odd expression—as if I were an unregistered runner jumping into the race in front of him—and then looked down, totally denying my existence.

I slunk away and bid my time.

Now I have to ask: Paul Cummings? C'mon, I mean, *really?* He was an American Olympian, but it's not like my mom ever heard of him. So I might have overstated it when I said "brush with greatness" a moment ago. I had to point him out to her when he raced on *ABC's Wide World of Sports*. Squatting next to the TV, I turned down the volume then struggled to convey how fast he and those other distance gods were. I just couldn't impress my family enough with mere words. Perhaps at some point you had to have tried to run stride for stride with them.

So I pointed to the tiny runners on the screen and told brief anecdotes to my mother, father, big brother, and little sister. "This dude here with the porno-style mustache? Showed me around BYU. Told me not to step on the grass. Holds the American record in the fifteen hundred. He's a distance god. Paul Cummings."

Here's my big fat point: Cummings mattered. He regularly got his photo in *Track & Field News*. He warmed up somewhere else and then materialized right before the start at the front of the crowd; he grasped hands with other elites and forced a smile from a place of respect and a willingness to cream all who opposed him. He shook out his quads and hams and readied himself to rip us new a-holes. Later he'd hit the postrace party and then jet to the next paid appearance, the next big purse.

I wanted to be like Paul Cummings.

At twenty-three years old, however, my job was to trail Cummings and the other big-name runners.

And wait.

Who was out of shape? Who had miscalculated his taper? Who went out too hard? Who just ran through the race? Who fell off the back to be gobbled up by me?

Was I on the cusp of my dream when I beat an emerging distance god by the name of Matt Wilson? I'd trained with Matt on occasion when I lived in Virginia, and we had the same agent. Matt ran under fifty minutes for ten miles too, but he was no more a distance god than I until the Cherry Blossom Ten-Mile in 1983. Then he broke through and finished second to Greg Meyer, who broke the American record in that race just before he won Boston. Matt even beat Bill Rodgers who had won the race four times. Matt became the best pick for newest member in the elite club. That one bust-out race changed the way I looked at him. Of course the 2:12.57 marathon he ran the same year also helped.

So on the runners' bus at the Chicago Marathon, Matt got singled out by the race director for an appreciative round of applause. And who was the guy sitting on his hands next to Matt— the guy who got a lowly fifteenth at Cherry Blossom? I grinned, pulled my hands out from beneath my hams, and clapped maybe four or five times—enough to appear nonenvious but not enough to look like a brownnoser. Hey, I was happy for Matt. Really. He deserved the recognition and showed me how to be plucked out of also-ran obscurity. Still, would it have ruptured the race director's larynx to mention the guy literally rubbing shoulders next to Matt?

This of course made Matt a target for me. Although I feared him, I didn't want to give up too much. Matt wasn't yet a bona fide distance god by anyone's standards except mine, but he was getting the stench, so if I could knock him off...well, it didn't seem like such a bad strategy.

My day came at Asbury Park, New Jersey. It was incredibly windy, and I ran shielded within the chase pack. Just past five miles, there was Matt at the back of the lead pack—his shoulders held too high and his leg turnover slowing as he lost contact—the gap slowly widening between him and the distance gods bound for a payday. So I took on the wind for a minute until I pulled up into Matt's draft, checked out his leg lift, observed how he carried his arms, and noted how he breathed. Did I smell desperation? Did it seep out his pores and waft back to me like fear? Was it a bad day for Matt, or did he hold back to swat me aside on the kick? When he looked back, that was all I needed; I swung out and surged. Oh, I couldn't hold it. The point was to demoralize him, to make him *think* I could hold it, *think* that I was on my way to the front and that there was no use latching on and giving me trouble.

None of us ran fast that day because of the wind. OK, one guy did—New Zealand fifteen-hundred-meter Olympic bronze medalist and 1983 New York Marathon champion Rod Dixon. He won in a fast time despite the wind, which I guess is all part of being a distance god. For me it wasn't so much the time that day that was important but who I beat. Remember the old adage about not needing to run faster than the bear—you only needed to run faster than the *other* guy *also* chased by the bear. For me to beat studs like Matt Wilson was a step closer to the Paul Cummings of my day.

Hey, I had to do it. Even scavengers needed to feed. Besides, Matt had done it to me plenty of times, and I was certainly not above revenge.

I recorded the kill in my running log. His obituary, my irresistible rise.

Usually it wasn't someone as good as Matt who fell off the back. Rather it was someone obscure and overreaching like me—some cocky mother who sometimes got fourth or sixth or eleventh in a big race. *Track & Field News* would skip over that person's name in the results but manage to find space for an *important* runner who finished behind. It was too easy for sports editors and race directors to ignore me. That needed to come to a screeching halt.

Let's just say that when the Matt Wilsons faded, I was so there for the kill.

I never got a kill on Cummings, though—not even on one of his bad days. At the Jacksonville River Run—now called Gate River Run, the US National Championship 15K—I hit splits close to my PRs and then became roadkill going up that ballbuster of a bridge.

Crushed.

For my career trajectory, you see, I couldn't be satisfied with the stragglers—the hooves and the hide—for too long. Top runners needed to be beaten, even when they had a good day—by me, I mean. I needed a breakthrough race like Matt had had at Cherry Blossom—one that would qualify me for the trials and beyond. It would be the Boston Marathon. I planned to *so* go for it.

See, I wanted to be the hardcore hero who wouldn't back down, who took it to the wire every time and came back for more. Heart mattered, and I wanted heart like Dick Beardsley, the silver man who took Salazar down to the wire at Boston the previous year. Over the years I learned I wasn't the strongest, smartest, or the most talented, but with persistence and pushing it harder for longer than the other dude, it made a difference—maybe not next Saturday or even next year but someday.

It had to. It just had to.

Running in that space just behind the elites, I wasn't even a long shot at becoming an Olympian or a world-record holder; but I had a shot, just like everybody else who started the race. I wasn't even All American or a junior champion. For the record

I was a high school standout who got a partial ride to a Division I school, made All Conference eight times, and then went out on the roads—open class, bro. I was the guy who won the local road races, beating fields of thousands unless an elite showed up to slap me down. I rose to the point where it didn't matter how *many* people showed up to a race, only *who* showed up.

Over the years the crowd in front of me thinned.

Although it hurt to be so much slower than the distance gods, I loved racing them and measuring myself against them. It hurt worse to lose to someone I decided shouldn't beat me. That's when I forced a grin but tossed an internal tantrum. Oh, I sulked—I admit it. Sure I would drive ahead, but my gut clenched in frustration, disappointment, and fear. My temper got short and caused me to take off on a midnight eight-miler. For a few hours or a few days, depending on how important the race was, I was empty and dead inside—alone—because nobody seemed to care enough to understand how important my loss was to me. Yet another skinny man in a singlet—sometimes lots of them— thwarted my inevitable march to visibility. If it wasn't my goals being stymied by another runner, then it was the merciless clock.

Maybe I cared too much.

I *needed* to be good, and I defined *good* as anybody who beat me or clocked times faster than mine. Distance-god status was just as loosely defined. In my mind it not only included the obvious cast of characters—Sebastian Coe, Henry Rono, Bill Rodgers— but also pretty much anyone I thought I might never catch. It was relative to me, you see. I didn't think Rono thought about Paul Schultz—my college teammate who made the National Junior Cross-Country team. Rodgers probably didn't think about Brent Steiner—another college teammate who was a high school national cross-country champion and the fastest high school two-miler. But to me they were distance gods. I'll tell you about them later, but first I need to tell you more about Cummings.

Cummings broke the world record in the half marathon in 1983, the year he looked away from me. Because I met him on my recruiting trip, that was my excuse to approach him at the Jacksonville River Run postrace party. I wouldn't have done it otherwise. Really. I walked up to him against my own nature because I had already met him, and yes, he was also a world-class runner from the middle distances to the marathon. He was one of the most versatile American track-and-road racers in history and one of the top-twenty highest-paid runners worldwide. I wasn't a sycophant; I just wanted in his club, that's all. I didn't ask for a half hug. Eye contact would've been nice, though. I walked right up to him, shook his hand, reintroduced myself, and to jog his memory mentioned he had recruited me to BYU along with another kid named Petersen who was a 4:11 high school miler. "I was the guy who stepped on the grass and ordered iced tea at lunch," I said to jog his memory.

That was when he looked away.

Maybe his Mormonism compelled him to cast me out because that iced tea years before had opened a gateway to the plastic cup full of Stroh's I sipped. He didn't even try to convert me, and I was a fertile field.

So I walked away and plotted my revenge at the Boston Marathon. After that he would taste my wrath at the US Olympic Marathon Trials. I needed Cummings to know my name and fear it.

CHAPTER 6

HUBRIS

Did losing weight have to morph into some overblown affair culminating in a return to the Boston Marathon? When I returned to running after a quarter-century layoff, my seriousness directly correlated with my improved conditioning. The better my runs went, the louder the awakened Timmy Two-Mile reasserted himself inside my head. He yawned, put his arm around my shoulders, and whispered about me becoming some kind of running Lazarus, someone who would astound the running community by clocking young men's times in his fifties.

"You could quit your day job and get sponsors," Timmy Two-Mile murmured in my skull. "Screw the shoe companies. Go with the pharmaceuticals—Propecia, Viagra, Aleve."

The old feelings returned.

Back came the competitiveness and the compulsion. Shouldn't I be more mature the second time around and accept I will never be elite? Given another chance shouldn't I run smarter? Shouldn't I be elated to run at all, just to participate, and leave the competitiveness to the past? Instead I pounded out the miles again.

Since my career-ending injury as a twenty-five-year-old soldier, Garmin watches, chip timing, and Internet registration and results emerged. I began road racing before cheap cotton race shirts were expected, and now tech shirts were in. Serious runners trained with iPods and sunglasses, whereas in my day I didn't use my Walkman because *serious* runners, well, didn't. If someone misperceived me as a *jogger*, I would've been mortified. One time on a run through Arlington, I wore my Walkman—against my own best advice—taking the chance I wouldn't see anybody I knew. Then, of course, somebody I knew drove past. I was tongue-tied because the dude was all smiling and acting as if he just wanted to say hi and wasn't looking for weakness. I totally mind-read him: *Hmm, he wears a Walkman when he thinks nobody's looking*, he was thinking. *He's probably listening to* The Partridge Family. *Maybe I can whup him the next time....* So yeah, I was mortified, and after that my Walkman remained in my drawer, and white acid grew on the batteries.

The rise of the Internet gave me more ways to obsess during my comeback. I memorized the names and times of the fastest fifty-year-old males in Arizona when I should've been marketing, preparing for my next case, or reading a journal. The Arizona record in my age group for the road 10K was 32:28 held by Bill Rodgers. Yes, *that* Bill Rodgers.

"That sounds doable," Timmy Two-Mile said. "That's a tune-up race for you, stud."

I reminded myself that even at my peak—at, say, Cherry Blossom 1983—Rodgers ran past me like a spry grasshopper on his way up to the lead pack, and ultimately fifth place, as I lumbered far behind in my typical chase-pack position.

"Maybe the talent difference has leveled out with age," suggested Timmy Two-Mile.

"You had me at *doable*," I told myself.

So there it was again—my hubris hanging out. The problem was I always thought I was better than I ever really was. When people said I ran out of my ass, I thought I had finally run up to my potential.

To be good at the state level in my age group, I only needed to be as fast as a decent high school boy. I fluttered my lips at that. Had I declined so much over the years that now they patronized me with age-group wins? My running brain, frozen at twenty-five, still thought only the overall win *really* mattered. When did I become someone to be graded on a curve?

We'd see about that.

So denial kicked in as always. I'd be an outlier—not just the fastest in my age group. I'd beat the younger men. All I had to do was race at my old training pace, and I'd win most of the small local races, which I planned to use as tune-ups on my way back to Boston. My plan was doggone grounded of me; I patted myself on the back. I increased my mileage and added maximum-steady runs and fartlek training.

"It'll be a massacre," Timmy Two-Mile snickered.

Did the younger runners wonder why I shouldered to the front at the start? Why I wore *racing flats*? Was I serious? Look! Did I await the gun in starting position—one foot forward, the opposite arm matching—ready to push off and save that valuable second? Did I spread my elbows to protect my position? Really? I mean *really*?

I planned to be magnanimous. The young bucks would huff along all stooped over, and I'd ease up beside them. "Wuz up, little brother?" I'd smile—the hip, old ex-semipro—and glance down at my newfangled Garmin. "Six flat." I'd control my breathing as I ran away old school with plenty left in the tank.

Of course that didn't happen. At five and a half miles, some male anorexic jogged the opposite direction, shirtless, holding his racing flats, warming down after having easily won the race— arrogant pissant. He cheered for his girlfriend, who was some- where behind me.

Oh, was that my big kick? I passed a couple guys in their thir- ties, but was outkicked by the winner's girlfriend, who had the good sense to draft off of me. Think of that scene from *Breaking Away* when the bicyclist drafts behind a semitruck. The girlfriend was third-place female—maybe fourth. I suppose it shouldn't matter to me.

Maybe I shouldn't have watched my race later on home video. It *felt* like the old races from the eighties—elbows and assholes, balls to the wall. I should've left it at that, but no, I looked, and it wasn't like that at all. Did I *jog*? Why hadn't I lifted my knees?

Should I have worn a Walkman?

My motivation to become a distance god when I was young wasn't totally healthy. The fact was I wanted to be brownnosed more. That never happened to me enough.

Instead I had to strive for worthiness in bizarre ways—like joining the army. Imagine my disappointment when I discovered that getting brownnosed was just the opposite of what grunts experienced. Maybe officers got brownnosed, but I just got dogged out, and I hated life.

After my honorable discharge, I taught English and coached track at a rough high school in Albuquerque, New Mexico. Surely teenagers would brownnose a cool young teacher like me. Yet I got emotionally beat up daily by the shuffling adolescents with their baggy pants and their sneers. They didn't share my enthusiasm for *One Flew Over the Cuckoo's Nest* or *The Catcher in the Rye*. They didn't understand why it was so freaking cool to get the stink eye from Allen Ginsberg when I handed him my old copy of *Howl* to sign rather than buy the new edition he promoted. When a mob at a fistfight trampled the principal, I decided perhaps Manzano High School wasn't the place for me.

So I left Manzano and taught at a psychiatric hospital that needed an English teacher so the inpatient adolescents wouldn't fall behind in school. I used Pink Floyd and Metallica lyrics to insinuate poetry into their lives. Standing on my desk like Robin Williams, I recited Dylan Thomas as handfuls of teenage inpatients wept, seethed at incarcerated sobriety, and paced the back of the classroom in a poorly medicated manic phase.

Nobody brownnosed me there either, but I noticed the connection the psychologists made with the kids—it was deeper and more intense than what I could do as a teacher with groups of kids cycling through my classroom—so I again switched careers.

Guess what? Sometimes my clients lie to me. Sometimes the truth is withheld. Sometimes they get angry with me for telling them the truth. It feels disrespectful. I know it's unrealistic for people to feel about me the way I felt when in the presence of a distance god. Now I know wishing is one thing, needing is another.

So I tell my son, who's twelve years old, that respect is earned, even self-respect, and that someday, when he's a young man, he needs to spend significant time challenging himself, to work without a net, to learn what he's made of. He doesn't need to live The Runner's Life, and he doesn't even need to be a runner, but he does need a struggle and a passion—to give everything to a worthy quest. The struggle sets up something inside you that hardens like a concrete slab and lets you know for the rest of your life you'll somehow always be OK, that life won't wash you away. If he experiences hubris, I hope it's in pursuit of something worthy that is just out of his reach.

CHAPTER 7

THE RUNNER'S LIFE

I immersed myself in the quest. After college I moved to Arlington, Virginia, where my days began with a run along the bike path, through Fort Myer, and past the white-gloved soldiers in their blue-pressed uniforms and solemn, dogged-out faces. In my never-ending search for new routes, I crossed the Potomac and ran past the Washington Monument and deeper into DC. "Mayonnaise!" the locals shouted at me, and I waved and ran another half block to show I was not intimidated, that nothing would deter me. Then I took a hard left and jacked up my pace to subfive and scurried back to the capital, over the bridge to Georgetown, and down those steep gray stairs from *The Exorcist*.

Then I lifted free weights, showered, and drowned an entire chocolate cake in a bowl of milk, finishing it off with no problem. Nutrition wasn't part of my overall training plan because I powered through four thousand calories a day—mostly carbs—and figured I got what I needed somewhere in there. I trusted and abused my body as you would a 1965 Mustang with thin tread and thick oil that may need a jump start on cold mornings; but once it turns over, even a stock 289 small block runs pretty stinking fast. I rarely broke down, and when I did it wasn't for long. Nagging pain didn't stop me; I ran through it and usually got away with it. When I didn't I tested the leg hourly. A missed workout meant I deteriorated, wasted hard work, and fell further behind the distance gods. Soon, though, my mileage would be back up. Back then it seemed nothing lasted for long except my chase-pack status.

So I stuffed my work clothes into a backpack, ran to Miguel's Mexican Food Restaurant, and changed into my refried-beans-colored slacks, hard shoes, and embroidered pullover maria-chi shirt. The old adage that your first sweat doesn't stink was something I relied upon. I hope that wasn't another delusion. Anyway, six hours later I put back on my musty T-shirt and socks, those crappy French-cut shorts, stuffed my grease-reeking server clothes into my backpack, and ran home in the dark.

Still another shower and I became a hard, young warrior on King Street, shouldering into the bars of Old Town Alexandria to swill overpriced beer at sticky, thick-laminate tables and talk about Salazar and Beardsley with other skinny guys. Boston 1982: "The Duel in the Sun." They went for it, and neither backed down. They ground out 26.2 miles to the point of career suicide and sprinted at the end, and neither was ever quite the same afterward. I respected that. We all did. So we had a pitcher in honor of Big Al. We had another for Mr. Beardsley.

Ten hours later I picked up the C&O Canal in Georgetown and crunched along the dirt towpath as I banged out another twenty-miler. We talked intervals; fartlek; weekly mileage; whose couch we'd crash on for out-of-town races; how hammered we were the night before; cock socks and ski masks when it was cold enough to freeze our extremities and lungs; women, women run-ners, and women distance runners; the awesome trifecta of Steve Cram, Steve Ovett, and Seb Coe; and when to run our last long run or tune-up 10K before a serious marathon. We talked about our best races until the most levelheaded among us cracked, "Pace inflation!" and we slowed back down to six-minute pace.

While living The Runner's Life, I tested myself on week-ends. Tips paid for gas or airfare to races. Boston. Chicago. Philadelphia. Jacksonville. One time my agent, David Asaki, took all his guys down to Tupelo, Mississippi. Dave wanted his guys to run for Brooks, so I switched from KangaROOS, and then south we went where I got my strongest sniff of life on the roads. The race organizer picked us up in his van and took us to our hotel, and I felt very special, exactly the way I wanted to feel. The next day we swept the race; I placed fourth and won $400 cash, which was handed to me in a back room in a plain envelope. That was the moment my denial got penetrated, and I accepted that I would never be an Olympian. I had become semipro. So I lost my Olympic dream, but gained some validation that what I lived to do had value to someone other than me. I was pumped until I counted out Dave's cut. That left $340 to last me until Asbury Park, another race with prize money, where I won diddly-squat—but I beat Matt Wilson.

So I kept waiting tables.

Life on the roads for me wasn't like in school where the team took care of everything. It wasn't how I imagined it must be to be elite. Being me meant living in the middle. As a middle child, it meant striving to catch my older brother while also making sure I stayed ahead of my younger sister. As a runner in the middle, it meant I struggled to close the gap between the distance gods and me and stay ahead of the crowd trailing. Stalling out meant middle-runner anonymity and never being more than a waiter who ran sub-thirty-minute 10Ks.

So I needed a breakthrough race. I needed to get to the trials in the marathon and then run up to my potential—or out of my ass, depending on who's talking.

Overreaching for a guy like me? Perhaps. OK, yes, but I needed to stretch myself, right? Elites never got comfortable, so neither did I. They pushed up against the time, always pressing, leaning against the invisible barrier that separated PR from injury, a win from silver. I wanted directors to fly me to races and fetch me in fancy stretch limos, or at least in a van.

That sort of happened, except for the part about being flown in. The limo part happened, but it wasn't *my* limo; it was for Mark Nenow, this distance god who broke the American record for ten thousand meters. A group of us from Virginia happened to land in Florida for the Jacksonville River Run at the same time as him. We piled into his limo, and amid the smells of leather, stale cigarettes, and travel breath, I caught a delicious sniff of a possible future.

The next day Nenow lost to English Olympian Nick Rose. I rooted for Nenow—not that I was limo-biased. Me? The guy pressed against the limo door? I languished in the second pack, died going over the bridge, and struggled in anonymously. It was a dismal prognosis for the prospect of having limos sent specifically for me—an also-ran bohunk.

The depressive hangover only lasted a few days, though. Then denial kicked in as always, by far my strongest attribute. The pain, sense of failure, and self-animosity faded as I again convinced myself that I had only learned lessons to build upon, that my defeat was not a comment on my potential but on my training.

I would work harder. They would see.

The evening of the River Run was the notorious postrace party I'm always going on about. It was like a Hollywood wrap-up party, except the stars were kick-butt distance runners, and almost everyone wore blue jeans, running shoes, and short-sleeve Polo shirts. In an act of bravado, *not* brownnosing, I tried to chat up Paul Cummings.

Again, that wasn't even like me. I'm serious. I was a pseudoloner, which made long runs more convenient since I didn't always need a training partner. I battled my shyness to go up and talk to Cummings at all. I definitely wasn't a suck-up, though. Really. At my Scottsdale gym—which likes to be called a "club"— I saw Charles Barkley sweating on the Nordic Track, and I totally ignored his laboring behind. Another time as I climbed the stairs from the locker room, I saw some dude at the top wearing a lime-green jumpsuit. As I got closer, he got bigger, and I thought, *What the...?* It was Shaquille O'Neal, probably the only guy who could get away with an outfit like that. I didn't go up to him either. Or Steve Nash. Why? Because I'm not a groupie, a sycophant, a brownnose, a suck-up, or even much of a fan. I am *not* protesting too much. Now, if it were Matt Centrowitz Jr. or Bernard Lagat, all bets would be off. Just kidding. I haven't seen them in my gym yet.

Now that I think about it, it was indeed bravado that I approached Cummings. Yes, bravado—like pushing the pace when you know the guys you're with are faster than you. You do it because you're trying to move up to their level, maybe even put some scare into them. I saw myself as an emerging *peer*. If you had just joined a team, you'd introduce yourself to your new team-mates, right? That's pretty much all I did. It was premature as it turned out, but I was definitely not a *groupie* or anything. Imagine if I *had* become a distance god. Then there would be no wondering; approaching Cummings would've been part of an auspicious beginning, not a slow good-bye.

I ran against guys who even my mom had heard about: Alberto Salazar, Henry Rono, and Bill Rodgers. It was like taking on Tiger Woods in golf, playing basketball against Kobe Bryant, or swimming against Michael Phelps. It didn't mean any of them were going to talk to me, though. Even some emaciated Mormon my mom had never heard of denied my existence. He looked through me as if I were transparent and then at the linoleum floor.

So at the big postrace party, I slunk away from Cummings and concluded that until I won a meaningful race like the River Run, had a breakout race like Matt Wilson at Cherry Blossom, or straight-out beat runners like Cummings, I would remain invisible or at best a nuisance.

A part of me is glad I was ragged as a young man, but another part wishes I were slicker—that I knew better when to keep my cake hole shut. Like I told my son, Gentry, almost thirty years after I left Arlington, "People will like you better if you're humble. You don't have to learn the hard way like me." He's already humble, but I like to reinforce good behavior. We named him after his mother's maiden name. We were going to make his middle name the same as my father's, but Dad said it didn't mean a durn thing to him—he's not sentimental that way. So we made Gentry's middle name Timothy after me because it certainly means a lot to me. I only resisted at first to tone down any whiff of narcissism.

So I told Gentry, "You should do your talking on the track. I mean, if you become a runner."

"Oh, *really*, Dad?" Gentry said in a sarcastic tone because he shares half my genetics.

So I told him what I told my athletes twenty years ago when I was a high school coach long after my running career had hobbled to a stop: "Talk is cheap," which I learned from my own high school coach, Steve Silverberg.

Sometimes I talked like that because I had to endure yet another cocky teenage boy crowing over his big sub-five-minute win in the mile. I wanted to tell them they were acting like hyenas yowling around a lion's kill, but I didn't. See? I was mature about it—a role model if you will. I was in my early thirties by then, and I often reminded myself it was their turn now. I'd had my shot, and so I toned down the part of me that resented that ten consecutive 4:53 miles still put me two-and-a-half *minutes* behind Greg Meyer at Cherry Blossom.

Coach Silverberg used to say, "Never look back. The race is in front of you." That's where I learned it, and that's the clean version for Gentry. The real story is my high school coach was a badass wiry redhead whose face turned crimson when he hollered, "You got your dick rubbed in the dirt! The race is *front* of you! What were you thinking? I *told* you not to look back!" I didn't look back after that; I looked ahead—in races, anyway. I didn't look back in workouts either, which like I said I often raced as well—I admit it now. Back then a teammate might bend over, hands on knees, and gasp, "Dude…you're totally…racing!" and I'd huff, "Naw, man…that's only…eighty percent…bro."

It was racing. You wanna know something else? It helped not looking back; Coach Silverberg was right. It was aggressive, and sometimes new distance runners needed to be reminded to ignore their misery and go for it. When I became a coach, I hollered across the infield like Coach Silverberg. I told the boys to get kills, not to look back, and that the race was in front of them, but I left out the part about dicks getting rubbed in the dirt.

Desert Storm hit, and I cooled the aggressive language because it felt complicit in grooming the boys for combat and body bags, especially coaching at a low-income school. So I shifted to the part of me that took on Coach Bob Timmons of Kansas University. Timmie, who was inducted into the USA Track and Field Hall of Fame in 2011, was the kind of coach who sat for half an hour in the back of his pickup truck with me and puzzled over why I hadn't told anybody that Mom was ill but didn't seek medical care. Timmie believed in fair play, hard work, and winning.

He also stood on the infield and shouted at me to hit my splits, turn my legs over, stay within striking distance, maintain contact, and eventually move to the front.

So when I coached I shouted across the infield: "Don't look back—the race is in front of you! Maintain contact! Stay within striking distance!" I told the boys to look at the shoulder blades of the guy in front and hang on. When it was time to move, they needed to dig into that aggressive, cocky place in their gut and go go go, not look back, make the guys behind them invisible, and then get up on their toes and drive their arms as if their lives depended on it! I thought they should know that no matter how badly it hurt, it hurt less than sitting in the bleachers—a lesson they were still too young to understand. That was my job, though: to show them the door to The Runner's Life, step through it with them if they chose to—if they had the juevos and the desire— and to suggest to them, "Here's your opportunity—do you dare?"

They deserved to know the intangibles, that something inside that takes them beyond their limits and ahead of the guys who aren't serious. They needed to connect to their warrior selves, which needn't be out of control or brutal, but could serve them well if channeled properly. It was important that they trust their training, trust me, and trust themselves. They were, after all, the best the school offered—volunteers in a school plagued by non-participants—and none of them had trampled the principal.

A freshman with sore quads told me he felt like crap. "That feeling is *good*, not crap," I reframed for him. "Tomorrow you'll be stiff, but that'll feel *great*. It'll mean you're a little bit fitter, a little bit faster. While your remedial English buddies smoke doobies behind the 7-Eleven, eat Doritos, and check out how much weight Oprah packed back on, you're becoming a distance stud. Guess who I respect more?" If the freshman grinned, he was hooked. He'd stay out, and those sore quads would become nothing more than a piddling entrance fee gladly paid.

CHAPTER 8

BOSTON 1983

I won the Washington's Birthday Marathon in 2:26:22—a pedestrian time if you truly believe you're capable of running over ten minutes faster or if you're a distance god. It was fast enough to qualify for Boston, though, and easy enough to quickly recover at twenty-three years old. Back then you didn't have to qualify a year early, so a couple months later I was in Hopkinton as planned, where the weather was near-perfect: overcast and in the forties with a favoring tailwind. I was just behind the elites who bounced, rolled their shoulders, touched their toes, and sprinted from the starting line. This would be my day, I imagined, leading them all, the media swarming as I broke away and flabbergasted the running world. "Lightning strikes," I called it, in that something improbable happened to me. Matt Wilson was struck at Cherry Blossom the previous month. I got struck enough times at the high school and college levels to anticipate the moment when my preparation and unexpected developments would thrust me into the realization of my dreams.

The cannon boomed, and the elites ran away. I didn't go out with them to get into the photographs and on TV like some douche bag. Serious runners didn't play the fool. We didn't line up anyplace we hadn't earned, and we didn't fudge our PRs.

Fudging credentials was shameful, and even the insinuation of fudging credentials was cause to move the insinuator into arch-enemy status and hold a thirty-year grudge against him—for example, I mean.

I was almost apologetic about my PRs because they were weak compared to the distance gods; plus I knew I could run faster. A PR was a transient rush that gradually became not so thrilling, then mediocre, then embarrassingly slow, and then crappy; finally it provoked anger over having to live with it. I compared my PR to my not-yet-realized lifetime PR and then to what the elites ran, and I knew I was still too slow.

Serious runners go out at a pace that their training indicates they can hold. Still I had to press myself to move up, right? So I strung together 5:15 miles—not elite pace, but faster than Rosie Ruiz even off a train. In the worst-case scenario, I'd build up a time cushion before I flagged. Besides, figuring out splits on a fifteen-second basis was easier for a math-phobe like me. There was no way I could do that while my heart cruised at 160 beats a minute, so I had twenty-five splits written in red ink running from my left palm down the inside of my forearm.

Far ahead, Cummings, Meyer, and Benji Durden ran 49:11 for their ten-mile split. Such studs. (I'm shaking my head in awe right now.)

I should probably pull up rich memories about running through the various boroughs, but I don't recall much. Not because it was so long ago, but because I was in the zone, baby. Asphalt flowed past my eyes, and I looked ahead for my next kill. Sure, I had fleeting thoughts about my pace, how I felt, and who to latch onto and draft behind, but my body floated, my gait was smooth, and my head and shoulders hovered over my effortlessly churning legs. I *became* the race; my mind suspended—sort of depersonalized—with myself as a tiny navigator peering out the windows of my eyes but not connected to the efforts of the fleshy machine churning out a 2:15 pace past ten miles, past fifteen miles....

Then at eighteen miles doubt crept in. Was that a twinge in my Achilles? Did the spunk slip out of my thighs?

The pace started to feel fast.

I turned my thinking around: What about those killer twenty-milers you've done? You'll feel better soon. You can take the pain; it's temporary. Don't be such a wuss. Keep turning your legs over, hold the tempo, and loosen your shoulders.

I also reminded myself not to give in to Error, or mortal mind. That meant not to believe in distorted thoughts that would mess up my race, such as *I'm getting tired* or *I suck*. I was raised as a Christian Scientist—a religion chock-full of positive-thinking techniques but also with Jesus mojo to give it some kick. So controlling my thoughts was second nature. Although I had abandoned it three years earlier, I still automatically "knew the Truth" when I got into trouble. That meant reminding myself that reality is spiritual perfection—not imperfect matter, not a material body crashing on the Newton hills. In my head the words sounded like my own voice, but it was really an amalgam of my mom from Albuquerque, Coach Timmons from Kansas, and how I imagined Mary Baker Eddy from Boston—the discoverer and founder of Christian Science—must've sounded.

And then it got worse.

And the hills kept on coming.

Keep in mind that back then we thought Boston was a slow course. It was twenty-eight years before Geoffrey Mutai would point out our mistake with a 2:03.02. So I thought about the hills, my pace, and the fatigue that pulled me back into my body, and I eased up fifteen seconds a mile. With some cushion to play with, I could still lay down a 2:18 if I didn't fold completely. My break-through race could still be at the trials.

I needed to get back into the zone, and so I tried to claw back in there.

"Chariots of Fire" played from personal boom boxes along the way, which was totally inspiring if you were sitting in a lawn chair handing out orange slices. But my world crashed, so I was insulted. Oh, I get it: if I just had enough heart, I could hold the pace. *Really?* Yeah, I'd heard the anecdotes about heroes who kept going on nothing but heart. I toasted Salazar and Beardsley for God's sake, but, man, in the mortal world when I ran out of gas, then guess what—I was done. The fact was I couldn't *claw* back into the zone; I could only *slip* into it. It was desperation that made me start clawing. I needed energy, but I just trained for the distance and didn't take on fuel as I ran. At the time we didn't have GU and all these fancy-dandy interventions. There were oranges or bananas, sometimes Gatorade, and the guys mincing in back who thought they were so vanguard carried a Baggie of peanut butter. Not me, though. I didn't even take on water until after the first 10K and then only after sloshing out most of it before I learned to collapse the paper cup and manage slurps between gasps.

After twenty miles and the third time I'd heard the theme from "Rocky," I finally accepted that it wasn't my day, so I fell off my pace and jogged. The best I could do was to get some junk miles in to prepare for another shot in Chicago.

The whoop of the sirens that paced the leaders had long since faded, and I was in a quiet space for a while, except for the slap of runners' feet and encouragement from spectators. "Chariots of Fire" played again just before more sirens faintly sounded behind me; at first it was like a mosquito, but then it grew. Someone important gained on me.

Everything is longer in a marathon, even the folding part. In a mile it happens quickly; once you become aware of it, it has already overtaken you. In the marathon it's a slow melting down—drawn out and cruel. Unless you can live with a DNF (did not finish) in the results after your name or in your own running log, you have to finish. I couldn't. I never dropped out of a race even when I should have. Since Boston was a point-to-point course, and my ride was downtown, I shifted into survival shuffle just past Heartbreak Hill.

The roar and siren swelled behind me until it overtook me like a sonic boom. The press vehicles and police motorcycles surrounded me, and I was in a media bubble.

Joan Benoit trotted past.

OK, that sounded a little patronizing. She didn't "trot" past in cute girly-girl fashion. She *roared* past and then was gone. Joan freakin' Benoit, the first woman to ever beat me. I'm not saying that in a sexist manner. I'm saying that usually I knew who beat me, and before Boston it was always someone with a penis. This was the first time I'd ever been chicked.

Rather than compulsively compete as usual, I experienced another first: I walked in a race. It was the right thing to do, but still there was a veritable shame spiral.

Then the theme from "Rocky" came on again.

The Boston College students who lined the street screamed at me to run. They didn't shout for me to run 5:15 or 5:30 pace. It was enough for them if I jogged, as if I were an every-other-day, calorie-counting, Walkman-wearing slogger who struggled to the finish to receive his participant's medal.

The students looked like peers to me then, so I felt harassed and bullied. I jogged again.

They cheered.

Once out of sight of that section of crowd, I walked and marinated in my misery. Again I got "heckled," which was how it went to the finish—walking and jogging as a steady and growing stream of runners burned and buried me.

Benoit—two years older than me, ten inches shorter, and fifty pounds lighter—ran 2:22.43—not only a new world's record for the women's marathon, but it also elevated women's distance running to a new level. I don't particularly want to return to the sexist thing here, but you should know that it also meant that her marathon PR was way faster than mine—by almost four minutes—which is no big deal if you're some pot-bellied guy in his fifties, but if you're a twenty-three-year-old male who was sure he was on the cusp of receiving long-over-due distance-god recognition, it was a very big deal indeed. To be chicked, I mean.

Greg Meyer won in 2:09.00—history's tenth fastest and Boston's third fastest at the time. He's still the last American to win Boston. A month earlier at the Cherry Blossom Ten-Miler, he fell at the hairpin turn. Too far behind to see his spill, I saw him race back toward me on his way to an American record 46:13 with a possessed Matt Wilson chasing. It was both an honor and a humiliation to have measured myself against them.

There's a lesson there somewhere—something trite like always getting back up because that's what matters—except I didn't need the lesson. I fell down in cross-country but popped back up, so I would've gotten up too—I'm certain of it—just two-and-a-half minutes behind Meyer. Think how long that is. I don't think I can even hold my breath that long anymore.

No, the real lesson, I fear, has more to do with winning the genetic sweepstakes up front, adding an iron will on the back end, and tossing in ungodly mileage and some canniness. What I took away was that if your name was Greg Meyer, and it was 1983, you could fall and *still* flip the rest of us onto our backs and dominate us like an alpha male.

Then go to Boston and do it again.

I just tried not to think about it too much was all. I preferred to delude myself that someday it would be my turn.

Eighty-four runners broke 2:20 that day in Boston—still a record for a single marathon. Among them was Paul Cummings, who ran 2:16.05, thwarting my attempt at revenge. He qualified for the trials along with two hundred other runners. Far from qualifying for the trials, I did the survival shuffle and finished in 2:36-something. The seconds didn't matter; they just added to the disappointment.

That evening I called my dad in Albuquerque. He saw me on the national news. I was one of the guys in the background Benoit passed—the guy whose career gasped, the guy who was definitely *not* a distance god. Dad pointed out that millions of people saw a woman outrun me.

I said, "Great, Dad. That's just wonderful."

I wore this number in my "breakthrough race" as I attempted to get long-overdue revenge on Olympian Paul Cummings.

CHAPTER 9

PERSPECTIVE

Willliam James said, "Nothing is so fatiguing as the eternal hanging on of an uncompleted task." Chicago was to complete a task, but it was one of those races where the spunk just wasn't there from the start. A disaster at 2:56-something, I'd tell you the seconds, but I tossed out that data years ago during my I-have-to-move-past-running purge. Anyway, the Chicago crowd didn't participate like the Boston crowd had, so it was easy to survival-shuffle to the finish and prepare for a final push in Philadelphia.

Between Chicago and Philadelphia, I cranked out the miles. The distance-running zeitgeist was still about volume back then, and I felt like a wimp compared to the Australian and New Zealanders who put in 200-mile weeks, or even the Americans like Mark Nenow and Bill Rodgers who routinely put in 140-mile weeks. If I ran a bit farther and a little harder, perhaps I'd break through and get a limo—maybe even get introduced on the runners' bus. As a junior in college, I put in a single 120-mile week with intervals and broke down, losing half my cross-country season. Since my body couldn't handle elite mileage (*I* could handle it, but my *body* couldn't, you understand), I strung together weeks with more intensity. That meant 100-mile weeks with fartlek, tempo runs, and small local races.

Salazar raced Rono in a track 10K nine days before Big Al won Boston, so I ran a low-key 10K as my last maximum-steady work before tapering down, looking for an easy 31:00 or 32:00 and a confidence-boosting win. It was a good plan except a 3:55-miler from the University of Maryland named Per Kristoffersen took us out at subthirty pace. I knew he was good, but that gave me more motivation to take him down. So I sucked in behind when I should've backed off to save myself, but I couldn't force myself to let him go. On the contrary we seesawed the lead for five miles. You see, when guys moved out of their distance and into my specialty, I got a case of the ass over it. So sure, I latched on then pressed the pace, and by five-and-a-half miles—as we came around Haines Point in Washington, DC—I went around him in one final crushing surge to teach him to respect the distance.

He drafted…drafted…sniffed the finish, and slaughtered me in the final two hundred meters.

It was an effort I hadn't planned for, but at least it was a road PR, and I was wicked sharp for the Philadelphia Independence Marathon a week later.

I modified my goal to 2:19.04. How wise of me, I thought, to let go of hunting the Matt Wilson breakout race, run conservatively, and just qualify for the trials. But the fear and respect I developed for the marathon caused me to go out too slowly in Philadelphia—1:12 for the first half—and I cursed my stupidity. I had to run too big a negative split, especially considering that my half-marathon PR was only 1:06.01, which was also totally irritating because a mere two seconds faster would've allowed me a lifetime of saying "one oh five." Screw the seconds. I don't think it's just me who thinks this way—I just don't. Anyway, I ran a frantic second half in 1:08, finished tenth in 2:20.39—hardly a breakout race—and was still ninety-five seconds short of qualifying for the trials.

Stick a fork in me, as they say.

While competing for the All-Army Track Team a couple years later, I got injured and had to stop running. For a few years, I avoided anything to do with running. It just hurt too much to watch.

Eventually, though, I realized it wasn't healthy for someone like me to stay totally away from the thing I loved. My avoidance and heightened arousal around running reminders suggested emotional trauma. So I considered a sort of exposure therapy and approached running again as a high school coach.

The boys resisted their new coach—this guy who ran them at a level their previous coaches had not, who advised them how to properly obsess about distance running and how to engage The Runner's Life. When their times dropped, they complained less.

I didn't tell them I missed the trials because I was three seconds per mile too slow. I didn't slug a wall and grind out that the standard was later relaxed to 2:22.00 or that I took on nothing other than water during the race (and precious little at that). I left out those parts, and nobody ever noticed.

These days when someone finds out I ran seriously, they sometimes ask if I ran in the Olympics.

I chuckle as if it never entered my mind, then I say I wasn't even fast enough to get to the US Olympic Trials.

"The what?" they ask.

So it's difficult to keep things in perspective.

I have a buddy named Chuck Aragon who doesn't ground me in this matter. He feels he let everyone down because he only got fourth in the 1984 US Trials, missing the 1,500 Olympic team by *five-hundredths* of a second. He barely lost to Jim Spivey, Steve Scott, and Sydney Maree—three distance gods for whom I don't even need to cite accolades. All four—that includes Chuck—finished within a heartbeat of each other.

That is not hyperbole.

I said, "Dude! I was ninety-five seconds away from *getting* to the nineteen eighty-four trials, and you were six-tenths of a second from *winning* the trials! Man, you're a distance god. A little perspective, please. What I wouldn't have given...."

Chuck and I sometimes raced each other in high school—that's how I know him—and I even beat him once, which he claims not to remember. But I remember like 9/11. Although I was no match for him, I got more publicity because I lived in Albuquerque and he lived in Los Lunas. Then we both went off to college to live our dreams, but he got closer. He doesn't bring up our running past; it's always me who has to mention it. Maybe he thinks it hurts my feelings or that I'd be pissed, but that's not true. If you ran a 3:51.6-mile like he did, I certainly wouldn't hold a grudge against you for beating me, but neither would I lie down as you whipped me at my own distance. Chuck told me his road 10K PR was "twenty-nine flat or something." He wasn't exactly sure.

My 10K PR might as well be tattooed on my forehead—track *and* road.

Per Kristoffersen probably doesn't remember me; I'm just somewhere in the mix of his overall body count too.

Sydney Maree got third in those 1984 trials. He was a black South African suffering under apartheid, so he was excluded from Olympic competition. He became an American citizen shortly before the US trials. Afterward Maree came up injured, but he didn't report it in time for the alternate, Chuck, to take his spot. So the Americans only took two fifteen-hundred-meter runners to the Olympics in Los Angeles. Maree did time in a South African prison on a fraud conviction—unrelated to the anecdote I just told—and slept on the floor because of overcrowding. I don't believe in karma, but I do believe in behavioral patterns having consequences. Bad patterns usually lead to bad outcomes.

Chuck is an Olympian in my mind, if not technically. He was the first native New Mexican to break the four-minute mile, so in certain circles he's known as the New Mexican Roger Bannister. By *certain circles* I mean me. He's the only distance god I know well. Considering my running-career limitations, how was I supposed to get the inside scoop about life as an elite runner unless I asked him? Who else would I ask—Paul Cummings? So yeah, I asked Chuck about the trials. I wasn't being totally selfish; consider it pro bono exposure therapy. So I asked him about a rumor regarding a mattress with the Olympic rings on the tag.

"Did you really return that mattress to the store?" I asked.

"Yeah," he said, shrugging. "What's up with that?"

People don't usually ask for my opinion when I'm not sitting in my therapist's chair. Maybe they think they're curb-siding me and want to be respectful of my time. Maybe they don't want to hear what a rube like me has to say. I like them asking, though; it makes me feel important. So I said, "You're emotionally trauma-tized, dude." I don't think I projected my own stuff onto him, but still I added, "And you wanna know something? I get it, brother."

Really. I think I do. Just because my times were slower doesn't mean that I don't.

It's hard to keep running in perspective after I've trained so hard and wanted it so badly. Still I figure if I were to complain about missing the marathon trials by less time than I can hold my breath, I'd just sound like a hyena who had to settle for the hooves and hide. It would be impotent ranting in the ears of a true dis-tance god like Chuck—someone who went to the trials as a matter of course and almost made the Olympic team (and should've). Others' deception and bureaucracy—not Chuck's performance, talent, work, or desire—kept him out of the Olympics. Even his wife, Kathy, qualified for the US Marathon Trials three times and *isn't even sure if she qualified in the ten thousand.* How could she not know? I guess it's no big deal to her. She understands most peo-ple don't know the difference between a mile split and a banana split and don't care.

But I care, so I had to test Kathy. We were at the Stanford Invitational watching their daughters run. "So, Kathy," I said, "there's a rumor your 'thirty-two fifty-nine'," my fingers made snarky air quotes, "ten-thousand PR is really thirty-three flat."

"Oh no, I've got the splits," she set me straight. "It was thirty-two fifty-nine. I can prove it."

So she does care, and that's a relief because I care too, and that's yet another thing I don't think I'm wrong for caring about.

Twenty-eight years after I ran the Boston Marathon, I expected to qualify and race there again the same way the Aragons expected to race in the trials. When people say, "You ran *Boston?*" I see the same face I made when Chuck told me he ran the fifteen hundred at the trials a couple of times. So it's relative.

When I returned to Boston in 2011, some of the same dis-tance gods showed up again—like Joan Benoit. Paul Cummings wasn't there, though. It would've been cool if we raced again and we were these two old guys going head-to-head on the Newton Hills. He'd finally care who I was, and after I beat him on the kick, he'd elbow through the crowd to introduce himself to me and perhaps even apologize for any perceived slights circa 1983. I'd be all forgiving about it. No problem, bro. Just waiting for you to come around....

No, no. Better yet, we'd cross the finish line holding each other's hands up in a shared victory. That would resolve things nicely, don't you think? Humanizing him while rising me up? That's what I should be writing.

Instead Cummings wasn't there, and I was left grasping air, my only recourse to reminisce about the first time I met him in Provo in 1977. Henry Marsh—the American record holder in the steeplechase at the time—and Cummings showed me the campus and told me not to step on the grass. His lips tightened when I ordered iced tea instead of 7-Up like everybody else, but he still let me run on their awesome, blue track. Cummings walked with a lightness and reputation that the seventeen-year-old me envied and soaked in. I still can't grow a cool mustache like he sported, but I did everything to run as fast.

When I first raced him in Jacksonville in 1983, he reinforced his reputation by crushing me with impunity. I could even say that Cummings and the twenty-three-year-old me partied together that evening, and it would be as accurate as saying we raced each other, except only one of us was aware we had raced. When Cummings became aware that we were both at the party, he was less than impressed.

The last time I raced Cummings was in Boston at a time when we both figured we were fast enough to qualify for the US Olympic Trials in the marathon. Only one of us was. One of us had already qualified for the trials in the ten thousand; one of us was due back at Miguel's Restaurant to cover another shift.

I still want to talk to Paul Cummings, but not as a recruit or a suck-up—and perhaps never as a peer. But why not as a fellow devotee of distance running? That, of course, won't happen either since one of us had a running career that sputtered and fizzled out, never getting closer to the heavens than a distant sighting and a lingering whiff from those who had been there. The other soared about as high as a distance runner could soar, nearly touched the sun, and then tipped over in his fishing canoe and drowned.

CHAPTER 10

RABBITS SCREAM

My earliest memory is of sneaking into my parents' bedroom and sliding open the bottom drawer of my father's big dresser to the nest of things too valuable to throw away but not valuable enough to have a proper place: a coyote call whistle, lieutenant's bars, a scarlet high school letterman's award, a golden track trophy snapped off its marble base, and a slender folding knife (a bologna slicer from my father's slaughterhouse days). I pulled out the blade and placed the tip over my heart that was not yet strong and had not yet been broken. Would it hurt? What was it like to be dead?

At the thump of Dad's footfalls, I folded the knife and replaced it in the drawer. He filled the doorway and asked what I did. I shrugged and the matter was dropped.

In my field we put stock in earliest memories. People hold onto memories better when they're emotionally laden, and despite childhood amnesia, the first memory is meaningful because it's powerful enough to linger. It's a monolith of an emerging worldview.

So what does that say about me? Why *this* particular memory?

Maybe I was born for existential angst. When I was young, I liked to think it made me an intellectual rather than a neurotic. Maybe even as young as four years old, I merely acted out an environmental alienation I could not understand or articulate. Just maybe it's similar to that joke about a psychologist who shows Rorschach cards to a client, and the client sees sexual images in every inkblot. Finally the shrink asks, "Why do you think you keep seeing sexual images in these ink blots?" and the client retorts, "Hey, you're the one with the dirty pictures!"

Perhaps when Dad asked why I was in his junk drawer, I should've said, "Hey, you're the one with the knife!"

On the other hand, maybe I was just wired a little bit that way. Before I discovered running, I was an anxious, aimless boy. I was also a devout Christian Scientist. This created conflict between who I was and who I *should've* been. Today I might call this *musturbating*, a type of cognitive distortion. As a boy all I knew to do was pull my hair out strand by strand to decrease the tension. That was a little weird, and people started to notice, so I gave that up and switched to incessant blinking. That was way too obvious as well, so I tried stretching my lips by opening my mouth as wide as I could like a howler monkey. Still too bizarre. Besides, none of those things proved as satisfying as holding my breath while puffing out my cheeks.

So I had a touch of childhood obsessive-compulsive disorder (OCD), which felt like a press in my guts that wouldn't go away until I performed some ritual. I felt better for a few minutes, but the press would build again until I had to act out to decrease the tension. I drew in my breath and puffed out my cheeks.

It wasn't pretty, and it didn't go over well with my people. Keep in mind that my people were slaughterhouse foremen and rodeo queens, hunting guides and taxidermists—very high achievers in their New Mexican crowd—so the cheek-puffing thing was an indulgence not easily overlooked. My kin glanced at each other and nodded. They must've thought: *Mm-hmm. A* city *boy. That's halfa it right there. In a crazy religion. That's prob'bly the other half.*

See, I wasn't country enough for my cousins or sophisticated enough for the city. When my people saw lifeless gutted antelope they placed their hands on their hips and nodded, "Them there's good eatin'!" I just saw death and gore that I didn't want anywhere near my lips. So by ten years old, I had yet another reason to puff out my cheeks with my growing alienation.

It was a problem when I didn't climb back onto Shorty—the fifty-dollar nag that carried dead mule deer out of the Sangre de Cristo Mountains—after he scrapped me off by *purposefully* walking under a low tree limb. Even my female cousins had no problem busting ol' Shorty in the chops, hopping back up, and daring him to pull that crap on them again. Me? I didn't feel much like riding on the back of some large beast that had a mind of its own. Nor did I feel like sliding beneath greasy, old Fords and doing whatever it was a guy did under there. Fishing was monotonous. Hunting? *Bor-ing*! Sure, I made an effort to fit in. When forced yet again into combat boots and into the woods, I hustled to pound in the tent stakes, gathered mesquite for the fire, and smashed stinkbugs. Didn't I join my country cousins to knockout grasshoppers by flinging them to the ground?

My efforts to assimilate were thwarted the first and only time I carried a deer rifle. Dad, my brother Tom, and I hunkered beneath a piñon tree and watched the opposite mountainside for movement. I was secretly becoming myopic, so I not only couldn't see any movement, I couldn't see the other mountainside. Whether I squinted and shivered expectantly in the wilderness morning with Dad or fidgeted in church beside Mom on Sunday morning, I always passively waited for something to happen to me. Perhaps an unsuspecting buck would trot into the open and give me the opportunity to prove myself, or an omniscient being would manifest and remedy my flaws.

So I held my breath, puffed out my cheeks, and trudged behind Dad. Tom limped behind me because he had a lame foot and struggled to keep up. One time that foot caught on a root, and he stumbled, discharging his .30-30 into the leaves beside me. Dad relegated him to equipment guard back at camp, and I too was rendered empty-handed, the city boys grounded for everybody's safety. I feigned indignation, but really I was happy, free to chuck rocks at the intestines of the buck that had wandered by the campsite while we were gone. My aunt glanced up from her Louis L'Amour novel and without getting up from her folding chair shot the eight-point buck through the heart.

The truth was I didn't feel the need to have a hand in the killing any more than Tom did, although years later he expressed guilt that we were not the kind of sons with whom our father could hunt.

Dad snorted. He didn't need anyone. No sir. He kept his deer rifle well lubricated and zeroed in, a handkerchief in his back pocket, and his emotions to himself. He grew up hardscrabble in Roswell, New Mexico, in the forties, his own father dying of cancer when Dad was five years old. His mother then married a cowboy we called Daddy Bud, an old cuss who beat a black man to death after the man shouted at Daddy Bud's dog. That couldn't be true, I challenged once I had grown up. Turns out, no, it was not true; Daddy Bud had merely beaten the black man unconscious. Regardless, on his VA deathbed, Daddy Bud hallucinated that the ceiling beams were gallows and justice had finally caught up with him. When he died Dad stopped me outside my bedroom and mentioned, "That ol' shit Bud finally kicked it," then went to the armory where he was an officer in the New Mexico Army National Guard.

Wasn't I supposed to feel bad about Daddy Bud? I wondered. Obviously Dad didn't, so I just shrugged and went to school.

Dad, being the youngest in his large family, learned it was every dog for himself, which later became our family motto. He didn't orchestrate events or press connections. If we wanted to join him, fine. If not, he'd have a drink with us later, and we'd "swap lies." Anathema to Dad were any tokens of sentimentality or obligation, so gifts, cards, or expressions of love at Christmas, birthdays, or Father's Day were grudgingly accepted and not reciprocated. At eighteen I drew a portrait of him for his birthday, but he later said he was throwing it away unless I wanted it back. He figured he made an admirable, selfless effort to ask me at all since it would've been easier to wad up the portrait and toss it in the trash. It's in my closet today, overseeing my dry-cleaned slacks and early morning preparations, his unblinking face reminding me of my roots.

Intermittently throughout our lives, Dad reminded Tom, my sister Kat, and me, "I never wanted kids; that was your mom's thing. I just got horny one night." He always said it with his charming smile, though, and I convinced myself for as long as I needed to that he didn't mean it—until I hit middle age and could finally accept that he did.

Still, for a long time I thought I let Dad down too, not only because of my disinterest in hunting, but also because of my global apathy toward the more stereotypical pursuits of masculinity. One time my inexperienced shotgun blast crippled a cottontail, and it screamed. Hypothetically I knew rabbits could scream, but my imagination didn't adequately capture the atrocity. It was supposed to sound closer to the noise Dad made while we lay behind dunes and called in coyotes with his wounded cottontail predator call—*Ah-wahh! Ah-wahh!* We never shot a coyote—I never even saw one—but I felt warm to be included.

When I mortally wounded that cottontail, it screamed just like Dad's predator call. I froze. Yes, rabbits scream, and when this one did, I felt like the villain. Don't look at hunting from the rabbit's point of view—that's my advice. It was considered a character flaw at the time, all that cumbersome empathy, and it wasn't until thirty years later that I learned to make a living at it. There was no one back then to tell me: yes, there is horror in life; we didn't make the rules cruel, but it's OK to feel. You don't have to participate to be loved.

Dad stomped the wounded cottontail to death for me.

Dad was a good ol' boy in all the best ways, considered a pleasant man unless you were an animal. He saw it as merciful to pull out his bowie knife, place his enormous boot on an antelope's horn, and finish business. It wasn't Dad's fault that I looked the creature in the eye as it wheezed through the slash in its throat. Antelopes are runners, and even though I didn't yet know that I too was a runner, there was something in that beast that connected with me—like not running fast enough leading to a horrible death. I never blamed my father, though, but instead wondered what was wrong with me that I didn't enjoy it.

Afterward we ate what was killed: cottontails, antelope, mule deer, liver, hearts, whatever. Real men ate meat, and where I came from we often killed the animals ourselves. By "ourselves" I mean Dad. The gutted mule deer was skinned and cured, hanged by its neck, cellophane-eyed in the garage. Forced to go through our makeshift home meat-processing plant, I sensed horror. Think *Texas Chainsaw Massacre.* To make things worse, the beast stared accusingly, its dark parched tongue trapped between purple-and-black lips, its life snatched away in midstride. It haunted me, the accomplice in its murder. So that's what was for dinner—I couldn't avoid it—I cleaned my plate or I sat at the table until I did.

When I got braces, I manipulated Mom by saying meat hurt my sensitive teeth. She said, "But it's *tender*." I didn't tell her that it wasn't really about the meat being tough but about *me* being tender. Our compromise was hamburger. It helped if the flesh on my plate didn't look as if it protested its own murder during its final moments of terror.

Right around this time Dad showed me the Roswell slaughterhouse. He worked there before he joined the National Guard full time. We started at the vacuum-packed product at the end of the line, and the farther we went inside the enormous, metal building, the more the cows came back together. From bologna they became cuts, quarters, and then halves; then there were eviscerated and naked whole cows, upside down, staring and dribbling snot and fear. Finally we reached the kill floor where cows convulsed on concrete moments after a spike entered their brain.

So like I said, I wasn't thrilled about putting that mess into my mouth, vacuum-packed or not. Still, my touchy-feely crap had no place in the life I was born into.

The problem was these things had a way of coming out. When I held my breath and puffed my cheeks, my people wondered about me—that's all I'm saying.

CHAPTER 11

ZOZOBRA

My parents were the stars of their respective bloodlines. They waited until Mom graduated high school before getting married. Mom was seventeen and Dad nineteen—exceptional patience in postwar southern New Mexico. Soon came my brother, and they moved to the big city—Albuquerque. Two years later I came along and finally my sister five years after that. Mom raised kids as the women's movement gained traction and unsettled her, while Dad pursued the National Guard in an era of dissatisfaction with military misadventures.

So what were these young parents from Artesia and Roswell supposed to tell a kid who compulsively puffed out his cheeks in his subconscious attempt to manage anxiety? Dad insisted I cowboy-up and deal with the problem on my own, similar to how he had been raised, while Mom tried the techniques learned from her mother, who was a third-generation Christian Scientist.

"Do you *want* to look crazy?" Mom asked.

I shook my head.

"Do you want to see a *doctor*?" It was rhetorical, said by a fourth-generation Christian Scientist to a fifth-generation Christian Scientist, and she enunciated the word *doctor* the same way she would say *turd*.

"No."

"Do you wish to speak to a Christian Science practitioner?"

Again, no. Talking to the practitioner was like talking to the principal; either way I ended up wrong. So no, I did not want to talk to the practitioner. I'd find my own way.

Mom said, "Know the Truth." For good measure she added, "And just stop it."

I still felt the imp of anxiety in my gut, but I needed to better hide my compulsion. So although I still held my breath, I stopped the cheek-puffing part.

I was healed! It became a rare instance of Mom seeing my potential, I say even today when I play the victim. Mom would disagree, of course, and say it was the very fact that she saw my potential that she was strict. She foresaw me as a first reader in our church, kind of like a minister or priest. That, or as a Christian Science practitioner, kind of like a doctor or a psychologist except turbocharged by Jesus and a monopoly on the Truth.

I did indeed become a practitioner—just not the kind Mom envisioned. We'd disagree on some fundamental points, but since beneath my anger I adored her, I'd hasten to add that the religion at least well prepared me to feel comfortable practicing cognitive-behavioral psychotherapy.

Today I understand her strictness better but would add—based on years leading soldiers, students, athletes, and psychotherapy clients—that it's the *relationship* that is the most influential factor for change and guidance, and that's where she faltered. She certainly loved me and tried hard enough. I don't hold it against her much; she did what she knew; she emulated what had been modeled for her. As a father myself now, I can see that she knew what was best for me. Still, people don't care how much you know until they know how much you care, and as a boy I accused her of not caring. She did, but still I didn't let her off the hook. I withheld as much of myself as possible, stayed out of her glare when I could, and expressed myself passive-aggressively when I couldn't.

I probably could've benefited from some anger-management counseling or at least some communication-skills training. Since I didn't care to be the identified patient, and I didn't know about family therapy, how could I have suggested it? Besides, seeking help from health-care professionals was not allowed in our family. Since non-Christian Scientists were generally clueless about how people like us handled such matters, outside intervention had about as much chance of accessing my family of origin as I had to sprout skinny Ethiopian legs and win the Boston Marathon.

Although I thought of myself as someone with gumption, I didn't have enough of it to tell Mom the whole truth about the cheek-puffing "healing." The yearning hadn't gone away—just the symptomatic behavior. I'm torn about that now; she certainly didn't need more proof of her convictions.

Then I remind myself that I was the kid in that dynamic and let myself down off the cross.

Many years later I realized that when Mom told me to just stop puffing out my cheeks, it was my first lesson in treating obsessive-compulsive disorder, namely response prevention.

Eliminating the cheek puffs wasn't satisfying, though. I needed something more to really dig into the tension. Hair pulling, blinking, mouth stretching, and cheek puffing were out, so I timed how long I held my breath. Early efforts came in around a minute, timed using the one-Mississippi-two-Mississippi technique. Soon I used a ten-dollar Timex, and there it was: an official minute and a half. Early records, similar to running, were easily broken. My PR increased to a minute forty-five and then to two minutes—about the same time it took a fast high school boy to cover half a mile.

After I fainted in the bathroom during a record-breaking performance in the mirror, I only attempted records while seated. Now I indulged my compulsion longer, anywhere, anytime: as I watched *The Partridge Family* and ignored Mom and my brother's prediction that I'd end up simple because of it, while I spaced out during dummy arithmetic, or at Wednesday-night service while white-haired women in pearls and mature heels gave testimony about healing their breast cancer or someone's halitosis. Slumped in a green velvet church seat with my face turning red, I'd look over and—whoops!—Mom glared down at me.

When I got caught breathless, I'd shrug and explain that I *practiced*. This never alarmed anybody. I didn't *look* crazy if I didn't puff my cheeks, and that counted the most. Holding my breath seemed like a worthwhile endeavor, almost athletic, so no one questioned my sanity after that. *I* questioned it, but I was good at keeping my own confidentiality—or so I like to spin it.

Mom eventually got a wild hair and returned to school as an art-education major at the University of New Mexico. The *Hair* soundtrack played from the hi-fi cabinet as she presented herself in Jesus sandals, candy-striped bell-bottoms, a paint-stained smock, and a psychedelic bandana stark against her hair—dark as a Bible cover. "This is the dawning of the age of Aquarius..." came over the tinny speakers, and she did a brief go-go dance like Goldie Hawn. Come evening she returned with terra-cotta smears and smelled of pottery clay. All that, and she managed three kids and a marriage and taught Sunday school.

So I became a latchkey kid, which I mention not to describe neglect and curry long-overdue sympathy, but to better illustrate how easily solitary pursuits sat with me after I got over the initial fear of being alone and then began to like it.

Dad, similarly, had a time-heavy commitment as a full-time officer. Olive-drab and starched, he smelled of Sea Breeze and Brasso—crisp in his dress uniform with shiny captain's bars. He expected military order in his domestic life and prompt responses from his kids without complaint or tears.

The dichotomy between my parents escaped me at the time, but naturally I integrated both. The result was an interest in both freeing and controlling my mind and acceptance of both alternative lifestyles and rigid conformity.

Is it any wonder I'm conflicted?

By early April 1970, Walter Cronkite was reporting on Cambodia, Kent State, and National Guardsmen shooting students, but what mattered more in my world was that my breath-holding PR stood at a respectable two and a half minutes. At least it did until the morning Dad strode into the kitchen wearing his jungle fatigues and combat boots and told Mom not to go to class. Agitators occupied the UNM Student Union Building, the Hell's Angels and Black Panthers were in town, and the governor called out the New Mexico National Guard.

Dad didn't come home for three interminable days. Although he'd be fine because Christian Science protected him—a religion he wore as a marital convenience but did not practice (but *we* could still protect *him* through prayer)—I had visions of the city smoldering like Zozobra. Zozobra, or "Old Man Gloom," the giant marionette effigy annually burned in Santa Fe, moaned and waved his flaming arms but was ultimately reduced to ashes, ridding us of our worries.

While waiting for Dad to come home, I finally cracked three minutes holding my breath. My sense of accomplishment was tempered by how quickly Mom rushed to the phone when it rang late in the evenings.

When Dad eventually burst through the door dragging the scent of wool army blankets, canvas, and victory behind him, he may as well have been General Westmoreland. He regaled us with stories of campus combat, tear gas, and "hippies" who slapped the soldiers' bayonets and called them "fascist pigs." They naively assumed the bayonets were dull Korean-era issue when they were actually new and thus cut uppity hands to the bone. Maybe I snickered—which was mean, and I'm not proud of it—but I was definitely on the soldiers' side. Mom was too. Although she was into the whole psychedelic art scene, man, and even tie-dyed some T-shirts with peace signs, she also gift wrapped a sixty-ton battle tank for a class project. Already thirty, she hardly felt like the enemy. When students claimed to be victims of unprovoked attacks, she squeezed into the La-Z-Boy recliner tighter with Dad as they watched *Laugh In*. All was well. Look! There was Goldie Hawn in those go-go boots!

My family of origin did not seem paradoxical: tie-dyed T-shirts or olive-drab uniforms, teetotal or Happy Hour, Know the Truth or get an operation—all seemed perfectly normal to me. Mom stayed home from school so Dad could go to school with bayonets fixed? Made sense to me. Some students got stabbed? Listen, if you mess with someone who will stomp a screaming cottontail to death, don't be surprised if you get bloodied.

Meanwhile, the more I fed my compulsive breath-holding, the more it grew.

Unless something dramatically changed, it was not going to end well.

CHAPTER 12

SEPTEMBER 2, 1972

Listen, I didn't want to be *that* kid: sometimes the skinny, angry boy who didn't believe in doctors; other times the irritable, nearsighted underachiever.

The shy kid.

The sullen one.

People had to label me, I suppose, rely on some stereotype, figure out if I posed a threat to them, decide which of us would be dominant. After all I stood right there, usually off to a side, blatantly flesh and bone and opaque. What were they *supposed* to do if they didn't know me? I didn't blame them, except when I did.

See, being nobody hung in my gut like a bad race even before I became a runner. It felt like it was my fault, like I did something wrong. My thinly veiled secret, of course, was that I was defective. With nobody to talk to, it seemed as if everybody else was doing a better job dealing with the world.

So I drifted to the corners of the playground. Sometimes other boys were there first, but I didn't want to be in their group, see, because I labeled them too. They could make things worse for me because I was supposed to hang around other "perfect" children who were uncommonly beautiful and popular: the team captains and quarterbacks; the ones who climbed the gym rope in record time using only their arms. They didn't complain or hold grudges, and slights rolled off them.

Me? I carried grudges and five handkerchiefs—one for each pants pocket and one in my shirt pocket—to manage through allergy season since antihistamines were not allowed. I developed scabs on the corners of my mouth from vitamin deficiency because nutritional supplements were also off-limits. Even serious cuts received only a Band-Aid and an admonition to Know the Truth, never medicated or stitched. Perfect children didn't have buckteeth. They didn't squint.

I gave notes to my teachers, written by Mom, excusing me from the school eye exams. They unfolded the notes, tightened the corners of their mouths, and told me to go pound the blackboard erasers. My classmates filed out of the classroom as I retreated to the concrete school steps and raised a cloud of chalk dust.

The return of my peers marked the start of another year of stealth nearsightedness, pretending I needed a Kleenex as an excuse to walk closer to the blackboard, begging out of hide-and-seek. Another year of passivity lay before me because when you can't see anything, you tend to just sort of stand there.

In fourth grade I forgot to ask for a note from Mom the night before an eye exam. Not yet assertive enough to stand up to a teacher, I filed out with my classmates, feeling both like a traitor and like I finally belonged. A note from the school nurse went in the other direction. It was Mom's lips that tightened that time, and she glared at me over the official slip of paper.

When I got my first pair of glasses, I was astonished to see individual boulders on the Sandia Mountains and, in the opposite direction, volcanoes on the western horizon.

Still I refused to wear those glasses for the next three years.

By twelve years old, I figured out that if I bench-pressed three hundred pounds, all my problems would end. I hadn't seen anyone bench-press that much, but word on the street was that it was possible, and I imagined life was sweet for anyone that strong. So I needed thick, veiny arms that hung from my shoulders like sides of beef, intimidating as all get-out. Big, thick biceps and massive forearms. Real clubs. So I drank raw eggs and went out to our dirt backyard and pumped those cracked cement-filled plastic weights from Kmart that came with a hollow bar.

Tom benched all the weight we owned—which was impressive—but not three hundred pounds. He was a heavily muscled, 190-pound, fifteen-year-old intellectual who was socially and athletically awkward as well. He escaped his frustrations via power lifting and reading *The Hobbit*, Bertrand Russell, and the *World Book Encyclopedia*. He had a dollop of cerebral palsy, explaining that withered leg. Mom prayed for us both.

The misunderstanding about our religion was that we didn't *believe* in doctors. That wasn't true. We believed in doctors—there they were—but we also believed that they naively spread the belief that medical intervention was sometimes necessary. We knew better. We knew the Truth. To Know the Truth meant to understand our spiritual perfection, to not believe in the erroneous dreamlike material manifestation. With this understanding healing *always* occurred; it wasn't hit and miss like in other religions when people prayed to be healed. Oh, they were sincere, but they just didn't quite get it right like we did. But this certainty created an issue for me because clearly I failed miserably, and judging by the severity of Tom's limp, so did he.

Dad's patience eventually ran out. He took Tom for the operation that allowed him to be more ambulatory. Afterward, Mom refused to take Tom to physical therapy (PT), which she also saw as believing in Error, viewing his issues as no more real than a nightmare. So Dad took Tom to PT as well. Forty years later Tom thanked him for the heresy he had committed, even though for Mom it had been the deepest possible cut.

Afterward Tom not only walked but also ran. What Tom lacked in grace and coordination he made up for with tenacious indignity and his own anger, which he acted out against me with scant justification. Once, after some egregious act perpetrated against him by me, real or imagined, Dad held him back to the count of ten and then sicced him on me. Tom stalked me in his halting, limping manner. It was the scrape and slap of his footfalls that reminded me he was back there, ferociously determined. I, as terrified as I was determined, and only 105 scraggly pounds, stayed out of his reach for two miles. Getting tired I looked back hoping he had realized the futility of his chase and had given up. The resolve on his face unsettled me, and I ran into a cul-de-sac. He caught me and dragged me home by my hair. Although our shared genetics had not manifested in similar morphology, evidently there were other things we had in common. As a young adult, Tom completed a marathon.

I just wanted big arms like his.

See, before September 2, 1972, football, biceps, and maximum bench press were the currency of adolescent respect. My father played football in high school and had his warrior stories, which tended toward the *Huckleberry Finn* variety. Tom tried football, but his stories were more about survival than boyhood heroics.

Then there I stood, a twelve-year-old, stork-legged kid who didn't even like football, unpicked on the dirt playground. Maybe I should've yelled an undignified, "Pick me! Pick me!" except I couldn't force myself to grovel. Maybe I should've made eye contact with the popular boy who also got to be a team captain, like that was remotely fair. Instead I gazed at my shoelaces as each kid, increasingly tortured the longer we remained unpicked, finally moseyed over with relief to a team already filled with eye-rolling preadolescents. The captain should've known that if he picked me, I'd show fierce determination that rivaled that of a frustrated kid with a lame foot. Eventually I skidded my feet to the team that got "last pick," which everyone knew was no pick at all. Hey, I wasn't *totally* delusional. I didn't expect to be the quarterback or even touch the ball. Blocking wasn't really my thing either, but I wasn't the guy who was supposed to stay out of the way and not ruin things. Was that how they saw me? Was that *me?*

They had me wrong, you know. OK, yeah, I didn't wear short-sleeved shirts because of the soup bones that dangled from my shoulders. And yes, I bench-pressed significantly less than my body weight, which apparently needed commenting upon by the sweaty boys who loiter around bench presses. Success at sports that required strength, weight, coordination, or quickness eluded me. I was the kind of kid who was supposed to be an intellectual, right? Well, just suppose I wasn't? Then what? I had to learn to smoke and hang out at the Circle K?

I resisted their assessment of me. I just hadn't figured out yet how to connect to my peers. My gut told me that my peers were not the other boys who drifted to corners of the dirt playground.

How does a boy make sense of all that *before* he becomes a distance runner?

I was easily caught in tag since I couldn't see who was "it." My best guess was that I couldn't run the baseball diamond quickly either, although I needed to hit the ball first to know for sure. Before my adolescence I didn't show an aptitude for anything other than neuroticism. I couldn't even outrun a brawny kid with cerebral palsy.

So I lifted harder, longer, and heavier. I lifted when the bar was too hot to grasp and when my hands stuck to the frozen steel. Picture me arching my pelvis higher and higher as I bridged, straining to bench what my brother could curl. Still my arms did not grow large as sides of beef. Featherless wings come to mind.

Then on September 2, 1972, a lanky guy with a goofy cap won the Olympic 800 in one of the most inspiring runs of all time. Dave Wottle showed me that running was courageous. Something clicked inside me as profound as my adolescence, and with a supporting cast of Jim Ryun and Frank Shorter, my paradigm shifted.

What had I been thinking? My brother could have the weights and the three-hundred-pound bench quest. I ran two miles a day on the same route that Tom used to stalk me.

By March 1973 the decisive moment came in the eighth-grade 880 time trial when I kicked like Wottle and won. In less than two and a half minutes, I went from invisibility to there being six other junior-high boys who had no say over whether I was picked or not, who could not only *not* ignore me, but seemed eager to connect with me. For the first time in my life I felt unique in a good way.

If our earliest memories are so important, what effect might winning a first race have on an aimless, skinny boy?

Perhaps now you understand why I had to become a distance runner. Theory suggests that my anxiety served to keep unacceptable thoughts from my consciousness. Being a piece of crap at the center of the universe might be one of those thoughts. My anxiety facilitated me developing a not-good-enough schema, or mental filter through which I experienced the world. My fear of unworthiness caused me to withdraw even more, typical for people with anxiety.

I withdrew to my home, which at that young age was a microcosm of my world. The people in my home represented people everywhere. Critical comments, glares, and insistence on self-reliance were more confirmation of my unworthiness to be connected to others.

They say we're only as sick as our secrets. Well, since our religion was presented as the only acceptable way to think, which included perfectionism, a demand I could not meet, I felt defective, which was yet another source of shame and a major secret for me to bear.

On the outside there were my obvious imperfections: thick glasses, an overbite, pimples, soaked pockets as a result of unmedicated allergies, and a skeletal morphology. All this I interpreted as proof of my lack of value rather than the result of being an adolescent, facing unrealistic expectations, and having a lack of reasonable medical care.

And, of course, there's genetics.

The discrepancy between how I was *supposed* to be, how I *learned* to see myself, and who I *really* was, created an internal conflict I acted out in various ways to defend myself and keep others from recognizing my defectiveness. Successes led to temporary amelioration of my internal conflict; failures magnified my fear of being an especially defective human being. Perceived failure, real or imagined—subjectively it's all the same—had to be defended against by overachieving and braggadocio.

Competitive running served as a good tool to prove I had value, something to offer the world. At some level I *felt* that I had value, and a good race proved it. A poor race devastated me because it was confirmation of my feared low value rather than merely a temporary disappointment. With the vagaries of racing, my mood was very labile.

I wanted the label *distance god* to validate my self-worth. Failing to become a distance god didn't mean less-than-hoped-for success in the discrete domain of distance running, but failure as a human being.

So there's that.

CHAPTER 13

TIMMY TWO-MILE

The summer before ninth grade, I put on my gray PE shorts, yellow-mesh T-shirt, favorite pair of socks that went up to my knees, and leather white-and-red Asics Tigers; I called up my junior-high track buddy Bryan Nelson, and we ran. We estimated how far away something seemed and ran there and back twice a day. Sometimes it was to Manzano High School south of us or Eldorado High in the other direction. Maybe we went onto the clay roads in the vast East Mesa beneath the Sandia Mountains, years before tract homes took those routes from us.

By the end of the summer, I learned not only how it felt to run a hundred miles in seven days, but also how tightly we bonded when we went through the fire together. Bryan was always available to run because he was from a large family with no supervision. The phrase "running wild" fit Bryan, so I liked to say he taught us how to be teenagers. Throughout high school he drove too fast, had no curfew, and was the loudest kid on the jock wall when we hung out in front of the media center. All of this culminated in anguish for him, of course, since there was no dearth of teachers, coaches, parents, and paint-by-the numbers teenage peers happy to berate or shun him. I enjoyed his manic commitment to running; it matched mine and contained us both until he met his future wife and became a Jehovah's Witness. Then I ran on without him. It was running that kept Bryan together in the meantime, and he became another brother to me on those long runs and then on the high school cross-country and track teams. We stood in each other's weddings, and he named one of his sons after me. Bryan sets tile today, and over the years hired me as helper when I was between jobs. As hard as he worked as a thirteen-year-old preparing to run high school cross-country is how hard he works setting tile today. At thirteen we both just wanted to run like Dave Wottle.

"Talk is cheap," our new high school coach said. Coach Silverberg couldn't be sure of the numbers these spindly boys fresh out of eighth grade reported, but he suspended judgment since he liked the commitment. Besides, the truth would come out; there was no hiding in distance running.

The older runners scoffed, though, and rolled their towels into rattails and snapped at my nakedness in the showers. So the next day, when we ran across the mesa, I made them fall back with red faces and excuses.

My addiction took root.

My mother, always worried that I wouldn't amount to much, set that concern aside to fret over the weight I could ill afford to lose.

I ran anyway.

She threatened to make me stop.

I pouted.

She Knew the Truth about it.

I begged.

It worked.

I piled on more miles through the streets and across the high New Mexican mesa. It came easily, I admit it. Harder was accepting I was indeed a distance runner and not a freshman football player who clomped through the locker room in cleats, pads, and helmet, literally larger than life. Invincible. They had what I wanted.

Still I ran. It was all I had.

The running boom was young, so it was strange to see a half-naked kid running on the side of the road. Sometimes cars passed and Blue Swede blared out their windows. "Ooga-chaga, ooga-chaga...." That was me, hooked on a feeling. Sometimes insults came out those car windows, or beer cans clattered in the gutters. Screw it, man, I ran. I could run all day. Sometimes I did.

On trips down to Artesia, Mom read aloud *One Flew Over the Cuckoo's Nest* in our powerful Oldsmobile Delta 88. I interrupted her so I could run the last ten miles to Grandma's house.

She said no.

Nonrunners just didn't get it, so I cited the hellish workouts Coach Timmons put Ryun through. Of course I read *The Jim Ryun Story*. See? That's what the big boys did. Other kids tacked up Nixon "Sock it to me?" posters, while the Jim Ryun/Kip Keino Olympic poster overlooked my bed. In dummy math I plotted how much improvement I needed to join the elite schoolboy mile list of Ryun, Marty Liquori, and Jeff Danielson.

Mom acquiesced when my face set hard. At least I didn't act out my crazy compulsions anymore, huh? Still, she insisted on trailing behind me in the car on the shoulder of the highway, emergency lights flashing.

I don't remember much about the cross-country time trial except I couldn't sleep or really feel my body at all until after the race ended. I made varsity, though, and my buddy Bryan became the JV superstar, winning races, which I was a bit jealous about; I had to remind myself that varsity was better even though I ran fifth or sixth man and got my lunch handed to me badly all season.

What stands out almost forty years later is running naked through the mesa because streaking was a fad at the time, not a perversion, although we did it more than once. Bryan took it to the extreme and not only ran *miles* naked through the mesa but into town with his shorts over his head. I also remember Coach Silverberg running beside me during intervals. He told me to cut my stride. Even though blisters formed on my heels, I believed a runner's natural stride was a gift, and I ignored his advice. Eleven years later I would regret my poor teenage judgment.

Although I wasn't the fastest on the team, I was the fastest freshman, and people talked—not about my biceps and how badass I was, but about the freshman on the varsity cross-country team. In PE I got picked first until the other boys figured out that my growing reputation as a distance runner did not make me unsuck at the other sports.

I kept my age secret until the morning we climbed into a school van to go to an out-of-town meet, and Dad dropped off Dunkin' Donuts to celebrate my fourteenth birthday. It made the older boys more desperate, so during the race, while we led as a pack, the upperclassmen assigned finishing places for each of us with me fifth. Such shenanigans were part of cross-country, I assumed, and I didn't want to overstep my lowly status more than I already had simply by making the squad.

My biceps got even *thinner.*

Our cross-country banquet at The Royal Fork restaurant featured Mike Boit. A year earlier Boit won bronze behind Wottle in the Olympic 800. Today I wonder who in the crowded all-you-can-eat restaurant, other than the coach, understood how honored we were to have Boit with us.

It was my first banquet, and I won the most-mileage award because Bryan had been forced to take a two-week family vacation and couldn't run. That trophy is in my home office, up high and semidiscrete since I probably shouldn't care so much about such things. It suggests I haven't moved on with my life or done things to compare with *most mileage* as a freshman in high school. Yet the trophy survived the cleansing I undertook in my late twenties when I got rid of my medals, trophies, and ribbons. My stack of running T-shirts served as incentive for the high school boys I coached. I set up relays to get them through a tough set of quarters, and the winning duo won shirts. Jacksonville River Run 15K. BAA Marathon. Kansas Track and Field. BYU Track. The next day at practice, the boys wore my yellow-pitted shirts. My state-champion thirty-two-hundred-meter guy wore my old high school shirt, "Eldorado Track," but he added "Sucks" in black marker. I wasn't offended. See? Apparently I moved on. So I gave him my racing flats as well, the ones that took on Paul Cummings, Greg Meyer, and Joan Benoit. He busted out the seams the first time he wore them, and that was fine.

All gone.

My detailed running logs survived, though. They made it only as far as my army footlocker in the garage. Thirteen years of

The Runner's Life, of breathing, *bleeding* distance running. They stayed in that olive-drab footlocker for a couple extra years until I decided I hadn't obtained running closure because the logs beckoned to me like a telltale heart.

So I finally tossed them out too.

Almost every piece of tangible evidence of my dream was gone. Now it would be easier to settle down, make a normal living, and do something practical—something that didn't end up in newspapers, receive a trophy, or garner applause.

I accepted my disappearance from the running scene with all the dignity of a dictator squatting in a spider hole.

Except I cheated in my recovery. I kept my KU letter jacket, three rings, a watch, a few championship medals, an ironic athlete-of-the-year trophy from high school, news clippings, and a senior MVP trophy from college. They are displayed in my home office as well, in the corner, in a discrete cubbyhole where nobody looks, just beneath the most-mileage trophy placed too high to read the inscription. That's how humble I am now. The pseudo-Prefontaine persona is long gone, and I try not to lapse into the cocky killer attitude I thought necessary when competing. I don't say "kills" and "burn and bury" when I talk about running with my middle-aged nonrunning friends. I don't want them to look at me as if I'm a sociopath.

To read the inscription on the most-mileage trophy, I step up on the futon in my home office, balance on the wobbly wooden arm, lean over with my hands on the bookshelf, blow off the dust, and squint in the dim light. *Most Mileage 1973.* I don't do that often. Almost never. I look to the corner and just know.

Technically that was my second trophy. My first was a Soap Box Derby "heat winner" trophy even though I lost both my heats. They were just being nice to a twelve-year-old kid with a crappy go-cart. Dad was away at National Guard Summer Camp, so Mom helped me build the chassis using chicken wire and papier-mâché, the only medium she knew how to use. I, of course, was clueless. The car was way too light. Still, I was awarded a heat-winner trophy, which reeked of "last pick." I displayed it on the family fireplace mantel until Mom put it in my bedroom. Of course I interpreted that as a major maternal rejection.

Her next test came when the most-mileage trophy appeared on the mantel. *That* I truly earned, and it deserved to be there. It stayed a few days before it too was banished to my bedroom, which became yet another grudge to hold. The most-mileage trophy was no consolation prize. It survived my purge because it represented the first time I flat outworked everybody else and it paid off. It represented a new way of approaching the world. I would work harder but within my strengths. I'd never be a football player or have arms that swayed heavily with gristle and muscle. I'd never bench-press three hundred pounds. Yet it didn't seem so bad anymore.

Mike Boit clapped politely between bites of his dessert. I assumed recent Olympic medalists routinely attended high school cross-country banquets and didn't realize that Boit's coach at Eastern New Mexico University was Bill Silverberg, my coach's older brother. Bill ran for Kansas University and became a world-class distance runner. He went on to coach at ENMU and then the University of New Mexico, and he was instrumental in the early days of bringing Africans to America to run. That meant Boit attended his coach's little brother's high school cross-country banquet.

Becoming an Olympian was as straightforward as putting in the miles, I concluded that evening. I won a school letter and a most-mileage trophy, and Mike Boit autographed the back of my letter award. If jacking up the miles was all it took, hey, I was in. I mean here was this Boit fella, a guy with toothpick arms who probably sucked in football, in the Royal Fork Restaurant, just like me, going back for double desserts—just like me.

I became the scrawny freshman who wore his oversized letter jacket around school even when it was warm. It announced I was on my way to becoming a distance god.

Like Mike Boit.

Because I hadn't won a race since the junior-high time trial a year earlier, I asked Coach Silverberg if I could run freshman track. Lettering was cool, of course—it got me in the club—but I tired of watching Bryan win JV races while I got crushed by the older boys and was told what place I would finish.

Coach not only insisted I run varsity but also entered me into my first two-mile race. I wasn't thrilled. I dug three miles of rock-and-roll cross-country—the mud and blood, spikes, arroyos, and sand. It worked out great for me, but *eight laps* around the track? I was a half-miler, bro, like Wottle, Boit, and Ryun. A miler at most, like Dad, second in the 1954 New Mexico State mile. Long and boring wasn't what I imagined when I daydreamed about distance running, which was all the time.

In our first meet, I tucked in behind the leader, who was also my teammate, the school two-mile record holder and the orchestrator of my fifth-place finish in that cross-country meet. How do I pace that distance on the track? I sure didn't know, so I let him do the work for seven and a half laps and then came around him out of the last turn. Wasn't I *supposed* to kick in the last hundred yards? He swung wide, forced me out to the sixth lane, and dug his elbow into my ribs. Still I won, and he flipped me off at the finish line for my audacity. Had I messed up? Was I assigned second place but nobody told me—another brain fart for the freshman?

As much as my peers hated to run eight laps, I learned to relish it, and it loved me back. Forget rock and roll; this was symphony. Every lap was exactly the same, which was good and predictable, yet every lap was profoundly different as the field wore down. The idea was to keep the splits the same or faster, but most guys were intimidated, so they slowed down and saved themselves. It terrified them, but I embraced it, wanting to compose over two miles like a running Mozart. It was a structured, methodical, and organized container for my anxiety. When I broke the New Mexico age-group record for fourteen-year-olds, I became the distance.

I became Timmy Two-Mile.

My brother bench-pressed three hundred pounds that spring, so they wrote our last name on poster board and taped it on the weight-room wall along with the names of the other hulking weight hogs in the three-hundred club. It didn't remain up there long, though, because the drill-team sponsor decided she needed to protect her super-secret routines. So she took down the three-hundred-club roster, cut it into strips, and used those strips to block the rectangular windows in the gym doors.

When I entered the gym on my way to practice, I grasped the heavy door handle and paused—not for long, but long enough to feel the rush. At eye level, through the wire-mesh window, was the three-hundred-club poster with my last name on it.

Nobody was fooled. Still, for that moment, I had arms thick as beef halves.

Dad was the 1954 NM State runner-up in the mile.

CHAPTER 14

PRE

Monday mornings became kick-ass my sophomore year. The principal announced the results of the weekend's sporting events over the intercom, and since I was first-man cross-country now—a pseudoelite in a little pond—I grinned, flipped the hair out of my eyes, and unfolded my shoulders from around my chest. It wasn't my style to stand on my chair and turn as if on a music box, but I thought it *should* be. Pre probably did. Maybe the defending state champion Andy Martinez did. Rumor was he got paraded around Sky City Pueblo in the back of a pickup truck like a Native American code talker. A little bit of that would go a long way with me, and I knew what it would take. I wrote the answer on my hands, one inky letter for each knuckle:

T-A-K-E-S-T-A-T-E-!

The principal said my name, and the students turned around in their seats and scrunched up their faces.

What the…? *Him?*

Or so I imagined. But yes, me: the kid picked last who didn't like to hunt; the kid whom Shorty the nag scrapped off beneath a low tree limb; the kid who puffed out his cheeks. It felt like savory revenge even though none of those kids ever did anything to me. Maybe that was the problem; being unknown felt like a slight.

When people didn't talk to me, I assumed they disliked me, in which case they were added to my expanding ignore list.

See, my self-criticism had not abated. Were my glasses—which I wore by then because I was legally blind without corrective lenses—too thick? Was I stupid? At least running shifted my obsessions a bit from worrying what people thought about me to worrying what people thought about me *as a runner. That* I could do something about.

Running displaced holding my breath, like squeezing a balloon only to have it bulge out somewhere else. It was socially acceptable, rewarded even. Although I still fed the imp, my compulsive running was spun as a positive comment on my character.

I did not dissuade them.

Why was something that consumed me out of most people's awareness? How could they not know who Jim Ryun was? Hello? Earth to nonrunner! When Filbert Bayi ran 3:51 flat to break Ryun's mile record, shouldn't there have been a buzz around school? Everybody just clomped past in platform shoes as if nothing had happened.

At least my cross-country teammates understood. They knew distance running was the most fascinating of topics as well as the toughest and noblest of pursuits. Its awesomeness was not argued in my spindly crowd. My classmates knew how the football team did yet were clueless about my sport. Appalled, I vented to my buddies for whom the unfairness was clear and unequivocal.

When the cheerleaders left pep posters taped to my front door, or the *Albuquerque Journal* reported high school running results on Sunday, and when the principal announced over the intercom who won a race, the balance between football and cross-country, baseball and track, was more just.

Adults who bought into my paradigm helped justify my time commitment. Dad liked to shout at races, "Tee-um! Loosen your shoulders, boy!" My shoulders rose with my anxiety, so I shook out my arms to show him I'd heard, that we were a team, and I carried him with me. I held his attention for four or eight laps, sometimes as long as three miles.

Coach Silverberg had followed his big brother Bill to KU, trained under Bill Easton and Bob Timmons, and ran with

Ryun, which, of course, made him excellent by association. Coach not only understood but also expected a dedication that made total sense to me. His demands frightened off those who didn't view distance running as the highest aspiration for a teenage boy. Either you're on the bus or you're off the bus, as they say, which totally resonated with me and, I assumed, with Coach.

I was definitely on the bus.

Sophomore basketball fell between cross-country and track, but at my school, with an enrollment of thirty-five hundred, you already had to be good at a sport to make any team. I wasn't good. I shot the ball with two hands and wasn't sure about the rules. Immediately cut, I slunk away from tryouts along with my driveway-basketball buddy and running partner Bryan, who was also cut. I figured the humiliation was greater for me, though, because I already had three varsity letters.

So I considered wrestling. The fella who wrestled varsity at my weight was the state champion, and the guy who wrestled JV was also a badass. Getting twisted into humiliating knots and eating the sweaty mat was unbecoming for a runner of my growing stature, I figured, so I didn't even try out for the team. Looking back I wish I would've tried. Learning how to handle defeat with grace and learn from it—versus feeling crushed and seeking revenge—at fifteen years old would've been helpful in all domains across my lifespan.

Instead I did what I was good at, so with no winter sports to distract me, I put in a butt load of miles, ended up with a killer base, and immediately began winning races when track season rolled around. Specialization was again reinforced.

May 31, 1975, two weeks after the state track meet, I was bummed for only getting sixth in the two-mile. Andy Martinez, down from the molar of an outcropping called Sky City, ran a half lap ahead of me, war paint streaking his face. In a culture struggling to reconcile defeat, Andy was unbeaten. A dark-skinned, crow-haired, Native American kid, he ran far ahead of everyone, not just me, and then warmed down with his stoic teammates from Grants High School. He collected his gold, boarded his bus, and vanished without strutting or bluster.

That year Pre watched Andy run an indoor two-mile. He said Andy was further along than Pre himself had been at the same age. Pre probably didn't say anything about the ostrich-looking white boy fluttering far behind in that race. But Coach put his arm around my shoulder because I broke the Eldorado High School two-mile record. I wasn't used to males showing affection, and it certainly wasn't typical of Coach, so I didn't know whether to put my arm around his waist—like a *chick*—or what. Since I competed in a noncontact sport, I figured I had to be careful to distance myself from perceived femininity. Locker-room homophobia was endemic, so I let my arm dangle, trapped between our hips, and worried other boys might think I *liked it* liked it or, almost as bad, was a brownnoser.

Andy became four-time state cross-country champion, three-time mile champion, state record holder in the two-mile, and one of the premier high school distance runners in the nation in the mid-seventies, winning the AAU National High School Cross-Country Championship *twice*.

I sulked about my incredibly bad luck to have Andy in the same state at the same time in the same grade as me. A couple years younger than him, I lamented my youth. How fast would I be in two years? I was in it for the long run, and I could trail for a while. I would wait, pick people off, and move up. As I prepared to bike to the Royal Fork Restaurant where I now washed dishes, there on the coffee table lay the newspaper with the headline screaming through my self-pity that Pre was killed in an auto accident.

What was I supposed to do? Call in sick? Tear out my hair? When Daddy Bud died Dad just went to work. So I straddled my ten-speed and rode to the Royal Fork.

As a middle child, I always felt a bit pushed aside and forgotten, and so I learned to withdraw before I faced overt rejection. In later years I was never certain if I was really rejected or if my withdrawal caused my aloneness. Small talk was never my thing—it was a boring waste of time—so I kept busy in the dish room, where I didn't have to chat with the bus boys, cooks, or customers. Perhaps others mistook my solitary behavior for arrogance, and as I ran faster I convinced myself that perhaps I *was* arrogant. Arrogant felt less disabled than shy. Aloof? Even better. So OK, I *aloofly* tucked myself away in the dish room, alone but not lonely. I owned the dish room, bro. The grease, chicken bones, steam, and clatter were all mine. So what if I smelled like garbage and was the Templeton of the establishment? I was the best rat, stacking trays and plates and sorting silverware faster than anyone else. Complete control over my rodent kingdom was my thing, which was also how I liked my sports.

As I worked through the slimy, gray tubs it occurred to me that if Pre had been a Christian Scientist he'd still be alive. Not because he wouldn't have driven drunk (I knew many Christian Scientists who hypocritically imbibed, myself included, despite it being against the rules; my mother grounded me for a month for each infraction discovered), but because the car accident wouldn't have happened at all because he would've known the Truth about God's protection.

If it had happened anyway, well then, Pre could've been brought back to life.

Please don't be shocked. Remember that I was a young teen, and my Christian Science legacy went back to Mary Baker Eddy.

As a young girl, Mary Baker Eddy heard voices. She acknowledged them, and they went away. It turned out God called her name; it wasn't psychosis. She then healed animals and graduated to healing countless human ailments—from rheumatism to consumption, depression to overt madness. In 1879 she founded the Christian Science Church.

That's the story everybody heard, church members and non-members alike. Before the ubiquity of the Internet, however, you had to hang around long enough to overhear the hushed voices after the service and dig deeply enough at a Christian Science Reading Room—perhaps even have the potential to grow up to become a First Reader or a practitioner—to be privy to the full story.

Mrs. Eddy raised people from the dead.

She raised infants and little girls out of death, and when a man mangled in a wagon accident was carried into her living room and placed on a table, she prayed over his gruesome and lifeless body until he sat up and said, "Oh, I dreamed I was hurt, but I'm fine." She raised her husband from the dead on no fewer than three occasions.

Then there was Mrs. Eddy's trusted assistant, Calvin Frye.

Mrs. Eddy called for Calvin, and in his rush to the Great Mother, he tripped down the stairs, broke his neck, and died. Everyone freaked out except Mrs. Eddy of course.

"Calvin, get up," Mrs. Eddy said calmly.

And Calvin Frye got up.

On another occasion Calvin crumpled to his bedroom floor, dead again. The entourage again freaked out, but Mrs. Eddy went into Calvin's room and said, "Calvin, disappoint your enemies!"

Yet again Calvin rose.

Now remember this all happened *decades* before Pre died—not centuries, not millennia ago. It felt like very current, here-and-now stuff to me, not *wherefore art thou* kind of stuff. Mrs. Eddy never promoted herself as a deity or savior; instead she said Jesus showed us that we all have the power to heal—we just need enough faith and understanding. Great, except it left me frustrated that she could raise the dead, yet I couldn't even heal my myopia, let alone kick Andy's butt.

In my field if someone tells me, within the context of his or her religion, that a burning bush can talk, that his or her thoughts are heard outside his or her own skull by an omniscient being who grants his or her wishes, or that dead people can come back to life, I can't call it delusional. I'm tolerant and respectful of that person's religious worldview, and I cannot diagnose psychosis. After all more people believe in angels than do not, so it's "normal," the same way it was normal in Copernicus's time to know that the sun circled the earth. So I must consider the impact the person's religious worldview has on him or her. This isn't difficult for me to do, and I'd like the same consideration as you read on. To believe something with all your heart—to twist the facts to fit your theory and to continue believing despite the growing list of disconfirming evidence—is well known to me. It always fits—*always*—until it doesn't.

My job is to crawl into my clients' skin and peek out their eye-holes. Most people believe what their parents believed regardless of its absurdity in the face of science, and I was no exception. Once upon a time, I too believed that water was turned into wine, seas parted, and the dearly departed could be brought back to life if I understood that all matter was merely a manifestation of the *belief* in matter. Disease was the result in the belief of disease. Limitations—athletic and otherwise—were set by the limits of my faith.

Sometimes I still think about Andy, Pre, Calvin, and Mrs. Eddy.

When I shave, comb my hair, and generally attend to my appearance, trying to present myself with that clean-cut profes-sional look that feels like armor, I remember unbeatable Andy Martinez. Maybe I'll wear a tie striped like war paint. Although I'm in the box, I'm able to push the boundaries a bit, maybe even think outside of it. We're worried we're different in a bad way, so I reassure clients that the only "normal" person is someone you don't know well yet. Then their shoulders relax.

Sometimes I get into my car and think of Pre and that part of me that still wants to burn instead of rust. When my Beamer starts exactly as it's supposed to because I have a good job and keep my car maintained, I *really* like it.

When someone follows my car too closely, I might slow down to irritate the tailgater or I might speed up to make the prob-lem go away. It depends on whether I'm thinking of Pre or so-eager-to-please Calvin Frye. Not to sound like an old man, but the thought of road rage or being rear-ended on my way to work sounds like more trouble than it's worth.

When I sit across from clients, I sometimes think of Mary Baker Eddy, one of the earliest feminists, who presented herself as one who could enlighten with the Truth. She established The Mother Church in Boston, which became an international church at a time when women were too often either kept or trollops. She was the most influential role model for my mother along with her own mother, my grandmother, who family lore said had cured herself of breast cancer and other scary things. All three women were tremendous role models for me.

When I have a successful treatment outcome, I'm not paraded through the rez in the back of a pickup truck. I don't have wood-chip trails named after me. My clients do not rise from the dead. Sometimes the best I can do is dissuade them from following through on decisions that might result in ruining or losing their lives. I tend my own garden and suggest others tend theirs, as Voltaire recommended, one of the few things I still remember from my overwhelming freshman year in college. Often people get better and then no longer need me. In this way I disappoint my enemies.

My nemesis revealed himself that sophomore year of high school. A junior quarter-miler, he was talented enough to run varsity cross-country, a range which impressed Coach Silverberg. Coach, however, missed the attacks with gourds, rolled towels, and insults. He never saw my nemesis spread his arms wide and offer to take on the entire cross-country team in a fistfight. Perhaps you're thinking, a *cross-country* guy acting all tough? Yes. To make things worse, he was also a yell leader, so it was like being bullied by first-chair violin or a math tutor.

Even though I was an expert at ignoring hostile people, ignoring my nemesis failed, against theory, to extinguish his behavior but instead emboldened him. Since I was younger but had become quite visible, I was an especially juicy target.

Ironically he sometimes showed up at my front door to take me on a motorcycle ride. Unwilling to risk overtly rejecting him, I climbed on behind. He took me at macho speed into the foothills, caught air speeding out of the arroyos, and cackled as I pleaded with him to slow down. I also knew his girlfriend, and since her father despised my nemesis, I picked her up as if taking her on a date and then dropped her off at my nemesis's house. After their date he dropped her off in front of my house and honked, and I returned her home. What confused me was that despite these twisted gestures of friendship, come Monday afternoon he again strutted through the locker room with his arms spread wide, thumped his chest, and asked which of us wanted to take him on first.

My tactic was to humiliate him in races, which he didn't fully appreciate. He was expected to lose badly to me at three miles, so when he came within a minute, he was the first and most vociferous to extol his versatility and expected future rise to dominance. For me it was like fighting a little girl, an old man, or a dwarf because I couldn't truly win as long as he was categorized as a long sprinter. So I had to be more successful than him on the track where we did not go head-to-head. When the track banquet rolled around and I won the MVP award, I collected my hardware in an is-this-really-happening? daze. My nemesis was a close second for his 440 exploits and promised to kick my butt come next cross-country season because he thought his new-distance-runner spike of improvement would never level out.

I wasn't quick thinking, on my feet or otherwise. At the time I felt stupid, but now I know it's merely slower processing speed. Eventually I get there. That's why I like to say that I'm "educated beyond my intelligence"; it's pithy, suggests humbleness, and diverts attention to my true strength—perseverance. At fifteen, though, I resorted to a canned reply such as "suck it!" or just sort of stammered "OK," which is what I said that evening, hoping the trophy I cradled spoke my truth. If I had been more precocious, I might have replied, "You're obviously overcompensating for narcissistic wounds and low self-esteem. Clearly you're conflicted between being on the team and truly joining with us, or giving into your fear of vulnerability and risking rejection. Basically you're me times ten. However, you defend using attacks and taunts, pushing me away—someone you both respect and loathe—before I can reject you, and your overblown psychopathology would be laughably absurd if it weren't so cruel. If I didn't have to put up with you, I would feel pity. I'm sorry you've been mistreated and were sent messages of unworthiness, but to act out your pain and alienation against the team, who by definition are supposed to embrace and assist you, only defeats what you really need from us. I say this to you with care, from one wounded human being doing the best he can to another."

Then again I'd probably just pulverize him in cross-country.

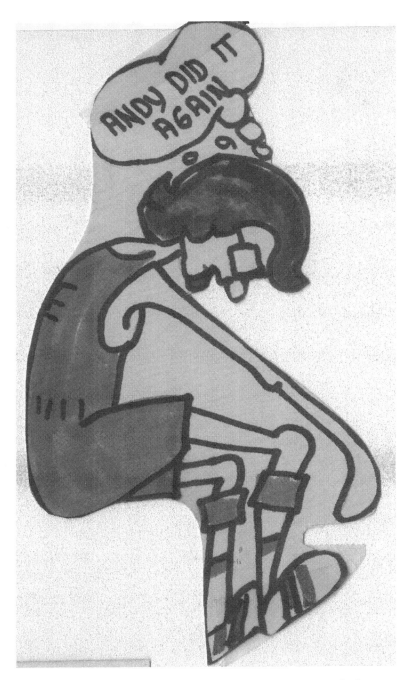

My artist mom made caricatures of each teammate at the banquet.
Unfortunately mine was accurate to include tube socks,
thick glasses, and losing to Andy.

CHAPTER 15

WAR PAINT

I modified my outward appearance my junior year to better match how I felt inside. Off came the braces and glasses, and I got hard contact lenses. Now nobody could tell I was nearsighted, so nobody would whisper about my weak-mindedness. I saw things better that year, like how the popular boys moved between groups and among individuals, how perkiness mattered, and how *pretending* to be confident convinced people I was confident.

I grew closer to my teammate Ralph Clark, whom I respected for his grit and popularity. If the workout were 8 by 440, I'd do a couple extra 440s before hitting the showers. Ralph, already in the shower, would ask where I'd been, shake his head, dry off, put his sweaty running stuff back on, and go out to the clay track to do two more 440s. It was a game we played, Ralph aping me on the runs, me mimicking him socially. He was a year ahead of me, extroverted, and wildly popular because he was so darn black-lab-like. So I learned social skills from Ralph: how to approach the other kids rather than stand off alone, act happy to see people, and suffer through small talk. My new chameleon color was more Ralph-like except with an edge he didn't have that I liked to spin as dignified rather than defended. My gig was to play the confident, crazy, extroverted track star, and sublimate the nerd whose only option was distance running.

Ralph became another brother, which was challenging at times because my biological brother Tom contented himself with only a couple close friends, which was easy to match. But when Ralph walked into a room, he became the focus. Relegated to the role of sidekick, I did not accept it gracefully since I was the "track star" (self-labeled) of our dyad.

When Ralph and I attended our ten-year high school reunion, we entered the party together, our names announced. There were cheers to Ralph's name, scattered shouts of "Raaalphieee!" and a surge of outstretched hands toward him. My name was met with relative indifference. Apparently nothing much had changed. I paid attention to such things, but to Ralph popularity just came naturally. He disappeared into the crowd, and although I made an initial effort to mingle, I soon ran out of energy and sought anyone willing to start an intimate conversation off in a corner somewhere, in my comfort zone, out of the tension and away from being "on."

In graduate school I tested myself with the MMPI-2, a personality assessment, and came up in the high-normal range on introversion. That fits for me. When I make a concerted social effort, afterward I need some time alone, as if catching my breath. Conversely after being alone for a while, I need to connect. When I was young, I would feel irritated or stressed when too social too long or sad and lonely when alone too long, and I didn't know why or what to do about it. Now I know, and rather than allow my mood to overtake me, I take a break or make a connection.

By the end of the evening of our tenth high school reunion, Ralph returned to me after he cut a slow swath through the adoring crowd. I knew he'd return and not just because I was his ride. He needed to go off into the crowd—that was one of the things I most admired about him—and I didn't try to change him just because we had bonded. He always returned to me, though, which sounds gay, but what I mean is he'd return to the guy who would stand in his wedding and he in mine, the guy Ralph would name his son after. All the glad-handers disappeared over the years. I, of course, was in it for the long run.

As a high school junior, if I didn't cross the vast mesa at the feet of the Sandia Mountains with Ralph or Bryan, then I was a solitary speck trudging over the clay roads. Sometimes dirt bikers buzzed past me, and sometimes I scrapped past teens having sex and keg parties in their pickup trucks. Six miles in the morning while the other boys slept, a ten-miler on Sundays when they rested, and a couple extra quarters postpractice after they warmed down put me further ahead. When I hit the showers, Bryan, Ralph, my nemesis, and the rest of our teammates already sang Led Zeppelin's "Immigrant Song" in the steam, taking advantage of the reverberating wet tile.

"Ahh-ahh-ahhhhhhh-ah!"

Ralph furrowed his dark brows. "Where've you been?"

"Just putting in a couple extra quarters." I had to grin. I had to.

Ralph left to get his running stuff back on.

"It don't matter," my nemesis said as he rolled his towel into a rattail and wet it in his shower spray to cause extra pain. "I'll still kick all your asses! C'mon," he spat, snapping that towel at me. "I'll take you all on!"

Ralph already knew why I was late; he didn't really need to ask. They all knew. I couldn't just *do* the workout but had to *lead* it and extend it, smashing them, my teammates, *my buddies*, because if that's what it took, well…they understood for the most part—they didn't make me choose. They'd squash me if they could; I knew that, respected that, and tried not to allow it. Late in the previous track season, Ralph and I went 1–2 in a two-mile, and Ralph just missed lettering. Was I selfish to snag the win and inadvertently prevent my buddy from lettering? I apologized to Ralph, who said, "I woulda been pissed if you had let me win." Ralph had an integrity that I also tried to emulate.

Sometimes on long runs, a neophyte whined for me to slow down, that we should all stay together. We were a *team*, after all.

Silly rabbit.

I looked over at Bryan and Ralph. They knew but didn't react because I got to lead by then. The new guy didn't understand that I couldn't show mercy. It wasn't personal, but who showed *me* mercy? Certainly not my nemesis. Certainly nobody on Saturday morning when the teams filed off buses looking for me. None of those guys slowed down for me. Those guys were predators, and they came for me specifically by then. They tried to hook my heel and pull me down from behind.

Either I'd be stomped like a screaming cottontail or be the one who stomped.

So I was ready when they stepped off their buses from far-flung places: Farmington, Gallup, and Las Lunas. I waited for them when they came off the rez or from Manzano where Mom taught art and years later I taught English and coached. They came to rumble, to thrust me back into invisibility and irrelevance.

Slow down, the new guy groused.

Maybe I pretended I didn't hear him; I did not wait on the weak. Maybe Bryan, Ralph, and I surged away so that the new guy learned the hard, inevitable lesson about the difference between JV and varsity. Maybe I said, "Just hang on a little bit longer; we're almost to the turnaround point," and then imperceptibly turned up the heat like a frog in a pot of water on a stove. There were other options besides me slowing down, right? The first that sprung to mind was he could keep up. He could tuck tail, turn around, and go back to school. Whatever. I wasn't heartless; I was offended. He wanted me to compromise my workout. How rude of him to ask me to be less prepared for the onslaught coming Saturday morning.

By outrunning my teammates and serving as cross-country and track captain, I had some power for the first time in my life. Listen, I knew I wasn't captain because of my compassion or verbal leadership skills, which were at best austere and less than diplomatic. No, my coaches unilaterally drafted me into the role because I ran in front, showed my teammates exactly what the coach expected, and then gave more. There were no cheers or pep talks. No slaps on the buttocks. Distance runners who did that were football wannabes, not latent distance gods. Coach detailed the workout; I pulled my sweats and then ripped off 8 by 440 with one-minute rest. Maybe I extended it a couple more on the sly. Maybe Ralph did too. My point is that in retrospect I understand my coaches' decisions better; you can do worse than have an athlete give 100 percent every day, year after year. When you send your team out on an eight-miler, it's good to know they'll do all eight miles the way you want them done; they won't find a boulder to sun upon for an hour, detour into an apartment complex to frolic in the pool, or stop off at someone's house to play foosball until it's time to run back to practice. That didn't happen on my watch—at least not with me. That was my integrity.

I wasn't a kid who sat in the bleachers in the colorful clusters of track boys and played grab-ass to pass time between events. I didn't lounge with my back against the aluminum bench, feet on the bench below, sweatshirt unzipped, sunning and fiddling with my spikes. Those guys were *participants*, not killers. They were "heat winners," not the guys I worried about.

Slow down? Naw, man. You don't slow down when you're bloodthirsty.

In my defense, who isn't brutal when you're fighting for survival? Once I let out a primal yell while challenged in the final hundred yards of a two-mile. It was a race against my most hated foe from a local high school. The backstory is months earlier we were locked in mortal combat in cross-country when he looked over at me and smirked. Twice. Smirking at me while I was in the middle of doing the thing that made me a worthwhile human being? Uh-uh. No, ma'am. So I said, "I'm not tired, are you?" He said, "Naw," and hit me with a couple elbows. I surged away and won.

Suck it!

Come springtime he wanted payback in the two-mile and had me beat until the last hundred yards. That's when that scream just popped out of me and I won at the tape. My spontaneous guttural display surprised me. In that moment it felt like a boot coming down, especially since had I lost it would've been my only loss to an Albuquerque two-miler in three years.

The next year Coach pulled us out of a track meet due to inclement weather. The race played out without me, and my most hated foe faced the star from Manzano High School. Elbows again swung, then they stopped midrace and started fist fighting! Clearly my opponents were bloodthirsty too.

So no, I didn't wait for the neophyte, and I didn't sit in the bleachers and play grab-ass. I psyched up alone in my 1965

Mustang with mag wheels and an acceleration pedal in the shape of a barefoot. "Funeral for a Friend/Love Lies Bleeding" rose to the crescendo and I beat the steering-wheel drum, ready for battle. I straddled the chipped railing, warmed up, put on my spikes, tight as cheetah claws, did my pickups, and stepped onto the track. There would be blood. Some perfectly pleasant boys were going to climb back into their bus sorely disappointed.

Today I specialize in treating people with obsessive-compulsive disorder. They are full of angst because after they shake hands they need to scrub with special soap in scalding water. It wasn't so bad the first few years when their compulsion merely kept them admirably clean and physically healthy. Of course it grew, as anxiety negatively reinforced does (such as when something *removed* provides a payoff, such as removing oneself from the filth of normal life results in less anxiety—yet reinforces their avoidance behavior, so it becomes more frequent, and they are increasingly isolated and unable to function normally. I could've illustrated via a rat leaping off an electrified grid, but I was being nice). Now their skin is raw and cracking. After we shake hands, I ask if they feel like they have to wash. They try to be agreeable and insist they are OK because I look clean and groomed. I'm a professional after all. It's the right thing for them to say, albeit a little white lie. Although I am indeed clean and groomed, nobody is clean and groomed enough to suit them. So I make it their first exposure, this shaking of hands, now having to sit for fifty minutes with a germ-infested right hand. The session ends and I open the door. They can either go right to the parking lot or left to the restroom to wash. Too often they go left. The prognosis is then more guarded, which I chart.

Sometimes they are afraid they hit someone with their car without knowing it, so they circle around to check, and now they're mostly driving in circles. That also doubles as a metaphor for their life. Other times they can't lock their house doors without jiggling the knob hundreds of times to make sure it's *really* locked. They imagine horrendous consequences. Then they jiggle the knob again.

Because danger lurks.

Unseen.

Insidious.

All the time.

Everywhere.

It's *possible.* So no matter how slight the risk, it's not worth it.

They jiggle the doorknob again.

It's a bummer for them, no question, even if the only true danger lies within themselves.

Still, they have to jiggle the knob one more time.

I tell them I understand. They don't know how well I understand, just that I get it. I say I think I can help, and stay professional, in my professional get-up and trappings. I don't share too much about myself, though. Remember, I'm opaque—a blank slate, tabula rasa. It's not about me, you see. It's about *them.*

Sometimes when a contamination-phobe comes in, I put a Tic Tac on my office floor and ask if they can eat it. They say no way. When I pop the tiny mint into my mouth, they are appalled. When they come in the following week, I say, "See? I'm still here, and I feel great!" If they're willing to accept the lesson, they begin to get better, and I can upgrade the prognosis.

It's a good intervention and not crazy—creative even. That pervasive rumor that psychologists are crazier than their clients sort of grates on me, maybe because it's sometimes true. It's not true about me—not anymore at least. But maybe it's another blind spot I have. Anyway, when I'm sometimes asked how I got interested in OCD I tell them I had a touch but outgrew it. It was *childhood* OCD, you see, and I'm clearly an adult now, so don't worry about me barking or anything. I don't tell them about my family of origin or how Christian Science complicated things for me. Nor do I tell them how running saved me. I just tell them that OCD is a disorder, not who they are. They heave a sigh, and we continue.

One Saturday I awoke and saw everything clearly. Literally. Distant objects were in focus without the aid of glasses or contacts. At long last my vision was healed! I would stand up at Wednesday evening service and give a testimony on how I prayed and cried myself to sleep for many years before *presto!*—at sixteen years old, I finally had perfect sight.

I planned to see how long it took Mom to notice I took half as long in the bathroom getting ready, swam with my eyes open, and rubbed my eyes during allergy season. When she would finally say something like, "Aren't you wearing your contacts?" I'd go, "Oh, I healed my eyes *ages* ago." "Why didn't you tell *me?*" she'd gasp, and I'd shrug. And when she wasn't looking, I might smile smugly—another point for the passive-aggressive boy.

I left my contacts at home, placed my glasses in the fuzzy bull's scrotum that doubled as a wastebasket, and drove to the track meet. What would this mean for my running? Surely it'd generalize in some wonderful way, allow me to transcend pain, and run without limits—perhaps even beat Andy Martinez.

As I warmed up for the mile, faces began to blur, and by the two-mile I could barely see well enough to stay in my lane. Of course I didn't get my thick wire-rim glasses out of the bull's scrotum—my ego couldn't handle going back to that place. So as I pulled away in the two-mile it helped to know that the green on my left was the grass infield, and the black to my right was the all-weather track, and I needed to stay on the edge between the two until I felt the finish string burn across my biceps and chest.

Imagine me peeling off my Adidas Spiders, green and black blobs down where I knew my feet must be, when the undisputed New Mexico high school distance god came out of the swirl of colors and asked for *my* autograph. Squinting to be sure it was indeed Andy who pressed his *1975 Track & Field Athletes of the Year* yearbook down at me, I couldn't have been more shocked and honored had it been Olympic champion Billy Mills leaning over me. I took the proffered pen and signed. Andy had been in the other meet run concurrent with ours, and he didn't seem as focused on keeping me behind him as I was on catching him. Was I so far beneath him it made no difference, like hanging out with a JV runner? In that moment I not only became Andy's peer but a fan. *God yes,* I still wanted to beat him, but I no longer resented his butt whuppings as much. Somehow they had shifted from cruel to merciful.

That's still the only autograph I ever gave.

Thanks for that, Andy.

It was my lack of faith that derailed me. By putting my glasses in the bull scrotum just in case the healing didn't hold, I showed a mustard seed of doubt. When nobody looked I put those glasses on and drove home, knowing that my faithlessness was all it took to give Error a fingerhold on my thoughts and kick the legs out from under what was otherwise a sterling effort.

I didn't consider that the hard contact lenses temporarily molded my eyes into their correct shape. That's my current theory anyway. At forty years old, I finally turned to secular science and got LASIK, putting my nagging nearsighted issue away.

Eventually Andy lost in the state two-mile to his own teammate and fellow Sky City resident, Gary Louis. Louis also took the title of AAU National High School Cross-Country Champion. Even though Andy won his fourth state cross-country title in a row, he wasn't the same. It was as if something broke inside of him after losing to Louis. Rumor was he turned to alcohol when his courage ran out, the war paint not enough any longer. Maybe it was the other way around, the alcohol came first, and as the addiction grew, the war paint could no longer compensate. Either way, Andy became beatable.

The track banquet at the end of my junior year saw my nemesis winning the MVP award for his quarter-mile prowess. It was my turn to be devastated. I won the award the previous year, so was I getting *worse?* I could not tolerate that thought. Still, he was a senior and deserved the award. He had taken us all on and won. We were even as far as I was concerned.

That summer I flew to Memphis for the National Junior Olympics and broke the New Mexico State two-mile record for sixteen-year-olds. I'd tell you my time, except I'm reading Alberto Salazar's memoir, and his five-thousand-meter time tied the world record for sixteen-year-olds along with Craig Virgin. He must've come through his two-mile *split* en route to five thousand meters (3.1 miles) much faster than my record time. And he was almost as fast as my five thousand PR set at twenty-two years old when I raced Olympian Bill McChesney in Eugene. Yet Salazar writes, "It certainly wasn't due to physical talent" that he ran as fast as he did so young. He doesn't believe he was more talented, just more determined, more obsessed. He sounds like all the rest of us who believe nothing was given to us, that everything we got we busted our tails for.

Well....

I began running in eighth grade with my buddy Bryan. He ran those high mileage weeks with me the summer before ninth grade. In high school my other buddy, Ralph, made sure he matched any extra intervals I tacked on. Yet I typically beat them both badly. They lost to me because I was more talented, which was my dumb luck.

Salazar beat me about as badly as I beat my buddies. I couldn't have trained any harder than I did without breaking down, and many times I did train to the point of diminishing returns. So Big Al, I understand you trained like a mad dog, but you also dripped with talent, more than the rest of us.

Accept it. We do. You made us accept it.

Anyway, for me it was better that I focused on the thrill of breaking weak records instead of comparing times. Of course I didn't know that when I was sixteen. Back then I thought my record-breaking performance was prelude to my participation in the real Olympics and smashing world records. As I flew home from Memphis I listened to America's "Daisy Jane" and was higher than the plane. Once I got home I ran up onto the mountain and looked out over the valley, west to the horizon, and thought that I was the fastest sixteen-year-old two-miler *ever*, for as far as I could see. It felt as if my dreams were within my reach. It was a great feeling. So great it was addictive.

Thirty years later I discovered that my two-mile time still stood as my high school record. It was my twenty-ninth high school reunion, and I attended with Renni, Bryan and his wife Lisa, and Ralph and his wife Vicki. I wandered off to mingle because I thought that I should since I was there hoping for some closure that tossing out my running stuff and coaching high school track hadn't given me. Wouldn't you know it; my old nemesis was there too, our class reunions having been combined. He didn't offer to kick my ass. If he had, I would've recognized him, but as it was, another quarter-miler from my year had to reintroduce us. I couldn't see my nemesis in the man in front of me.

Here's where I had a brain fart. My nemesis had a very common first and last name, and there was even another kid at our school with the same name, a rather pale, sweet, bookish type, nonathletic, and a bit squirrelly. That's who I thought stood before me; that's how the nonathletic guy would probably age. It was excellent heuristic thinking on my part, I silently complimented myself. Then it was clarified that this man before me was *the runner*, my *nemesis*, and he was offended at my confusion. I apologized like mad and tried to make up for it by calling him a state champion, the highest praise circa the mid seventies, to where we had apparently regressed. It was really quite big of me, I thought, to mention the greatest accomplishment of his life, since I did not care to assume better of him.

Clearly much had changed since the days when I anchored the medley relay and he screamed at me from the infield that I'd better win or he'd kick my ass. See, he ran the 440 leg of the relay, and when he came out of the turn, I was still pulling off my sweats. Have you ever noticed that it's when you're in a rush when all the wrong things happen? Well, my spikes kept catching on the inside of my orange cotton sweat pants as my nemesis bore down on the exchange zone. So I crowded into lane one as I yanked at those sweats with one hand, and waved to my onrushing nemesis with the other to steer him toward me. As you have probably figured out by now, having these brain farts was not uncommon for me. Just as common as my brain farts were my justifications for them. See, the three sprinters—220, 220, 440—warmed up together, while I, as the sole distance runner, prepared alone and lost track of the schedule of events. Thus when the time came to run the anchor leg I was still in full sweats. My nemesis glared at me over the baton like gun sights. Finally off came my sweat pants, I snatched the stick, and sprinted for two laps. My nemesis screeched from the infield that I'd better win, and he liberally mixed in epithets and seemed to have an awful lot to say for someone who was supposed to be out of breath, which was more distracting than motivating. So that was unfair to me, right? Shouldn't someone from my relay team have come up to me and said, "Dude, ya know our race is starting, like, *now?*" Indignant and panicked, I considered flipping off my nemesis as I ran past like when the school record holder had flipped me off when I beat him as a freshman in my first two-mile. Of course later that evening he was forced to call me and apologize. So no, I did not flip-off my nemesis at a track meet, during a race, in front of the athletes, parents, and coaches. That was good judgment and maturity; I patted myself on the back. I also considered stopping just before I crossed the finish, like the guy in *The Loneliness of the Long Distance Runner*. Although I wouldn't win, my nemesis wouldn't either, which would totally flick his nut. Of course I thought better of that as well, thinking it would unfairly cast me as the villain, and I'd be making calls to the entire relay team to apologize—the same guys who didn't alert me to the start of our race.

As I pulled away from the second-place team, I thought how lucky my nemesis was that I wasn't magical. If I were magical, I would make him inconsolably guilt-ridden over his mistreatment of me. This psychological torture (the latent psychologist thought) could only be ameliorated by me accepting his sobbing apology—a forgiveness I would be slow to grant, but eventually would. I know this makes me sound ugly. Please believe that I didn't typically let these thoughts out of my head. I only mention it now for the sake of authenticity and out of my belief that I wasn't the only teen with less than noble thoughts. Plus, of course, it was true that I wasn't prepared for my leg of the relay.

All I really did was win the race and conclude that should be enough to put the whole unfortunate incident to rest.

Apparently some people held grudges for a really long time, because at the reunion after I misidentified my nemesis and then tried to make up for it by calling him a state champion, he snipped, "I was *third* in state," a scab I inadvertently picked smarting anew. He stomped away in a huff, so upset he even forgot to kick my ass.

Apparently he was an adult now.

OK, this was asinine, but it still would've been one of my best snarky ploys had it been on purpose, had I been unhealthy enough to push his buttons after so many years. If my behavior had been premeditated, it would've been small of me—yet absolutely brilliant—to make such passive-aggressive comments.

I'm also an expert on uncovering pain, and I like to joke about it with Renni, who is an anesthesiologist and thus an expert at taking away pain. We are an ironic couple, I say, because sometimes I say things like that—she masks pain and I unmasked it. However, she and I both have vowed first to do no harm, so I don't use my skills to hurt others—not even an old high school nemesis.

It was a faux pas for me to confuse the two men—my nemesis with the squirrelly guy. Really. Before the reunion I had decided I wouldn't regress to my old aloofness, my silly defensiveness. I'd be grownup and mature, like I was in the medley relay, albeit a bit discombobulated, but mentally healthy for the most part. My narcissism was checked at the hotel door, and I was humble and considerate, *friendly* like Ralph in all interactions. I wanted my old classmates to know who I am *today*.

Maybe subconsciously I couldn't help myself.

That left the first quarter-miler—who by the way really was a state champion—and me alone, and I tried to gloss over the awkwardness by making nice with him. "The last time I saw you, you were selling used cars on Central Avenue," I said. Despite my well-meaning and accurate chitchat, I recognized my mistake by how he broke eye contact, twisted away a quarter turn, and looked out over the aging crowd. Apparently his job history was an issue for him.

I had one final gambit. I recalled that his father was my teacher in junior high, and I got suspended from school for fighting in *his* class. How funny was that? I didn't even put in the parts about how Dad picked me up from school and did not ask if I was OK, but only whether I had won or not, and I said I had, and he said, "Now you have to tell your mother," (sinister music in the background here). I served a shortened suspension because both the assistant principal, and the father of the kid who sat behind me who I walloped for pulling my hair even after I asked him nicely to stop, were Dad's underlings in the National Guard. The real punishment was overhearing my mother, a junior high teacher herself at the time, on the phone telling her friend what a rotten kid she had.

Today I still question how my loved ones may be badmouthing me behind my back.

Anyway, that other guy who really was a state champion quarter-miler? I thought it was quite an amusing anecdote to tell him about fighting in his father's classroom almost forty years ago. What else were we going to talk about? His state championship after he put in a big two years of hard work (during the track season, not year round)? Should we discuss how he was an all-state football player too, one of the coolest guys on campus, dated the hottest girls, and that it was exactly guys like him who drove the sixteen-year-old me to paroxysm?

That state champion quarter-miler said his father had recently died.

I expressed my sympathy for his loss the way I'm sure most of us do when chatting with a stranger and unintentionally uncovering an unpleasant fact. The difference was I had put on my Scottsdale psychologist hat by then, a comfortable fit for me and which usually opens up any new friend. Not to be nosy, but to be nice, compassionate. They could talk about it or drop it; it wasn't *my* discomfort preventing further exploration. People often share more intimately with me after they discover I'm a psychologist. They cannot get onto crowded elevators. Their spouse is a latent homosexual. Their kid sneaks out of the house. I've heard it all and much worse. Way, way worse. Believe me. But you see, I'm safe, and I'm supposed to know what I'm talking about.

The state champ only saw Timmy Two-Mile. He made a barking sob, and then he also turned his back to me and shuffled away.

So I stood there alone and speechless, wondering what I could've done differently. I remembered him as one of those larger-than-life freshmen football players who clomped past me in cleats and full pads while I struggled to reconcile varsity cross-country with freshman football. He wasn't as big or tough as I remembered. Today if we were to first meet in Scottsdale sans adolescent baggage, could we have joined and even had a healing interaction? That crazy stuff that happened at the Albuquerque reunion doesn't happen to me in my Scottsdale life, so what am I to conclude? If such ridiculousness can be so easily uncovered after decades, am I really so absurd to write this memoir?

In the midst of Andy's decline, Louis became my greatest obstacle to a state title, which was the most important piece left undone in the building of my teenage identity. It probably wasn't wise to place so much stock in a single race, though, especially since a couple years later *Sports Illustrated* printed that Louis was so far ahead of his competition that he didn't have to work for his laurels.

Beginning my three-year streak of city two-mile wins, 1975. Proof enough to me of my impending distance-god status.

CHAPTER 16

EMBRACE THE PAIN

My last high school race I was tucked behind the defending state two-mile champion, Gary Louis of Grants High. I had a strategy. Since drafting saved 7 percent of my energy even on a calm day, the question was whether Louis was more than 7 percent faster than me.

We hit the half-mile split on state record pace. To hang I stared at his shoulder blades, which were dark as sweaty leather and getting shiny as we rounded the track, relentlessly, cruelly dropping runners off the back until only he and I remained out front and pulling away. Tenacity and denial could be hurtful when paired, or helpful, depending. I had a tendency to hold on to things despite reaching the point of diminishing returns, and not becoming aware of it until the damage was done, but in this case I thought it best to hang on and ignore the burn that built in my legs.

Despite that, I so wanted to go around Louis, to shine before a packed stadium, to burn and bury him, the latest distance god to come down from Sky City Pueblo. I wanted to take my place alongside him as a state distance god, or at least pull him down to my mortal level. As a seventeen-year-old senior I wasn't known for my patience. At any moment I might unleash the adrenalin built up over the past four years, the years I spent backing up my

"Timmy Two-Mile" moniker, the years I'd spent preparing for *this* race.

Still, I could fake patience if it paid off.

Earlier, in the mile, a distance at which I was undefeated going into state, I faked patience. Then three of us came out of the final turn, I swung wide, got out-kicked, and ended up third, seven-tenths of a second away from a state title. The lesson was that strength, not quickness, was my thing, so trying to win in the last hundred yards was too risky.

Even so, I stayed behind Louis. I pretty much had to. We went through the mile split still on record pace and I hurt. Dude, I wasn't one of those wiry 125-pounders who bounced over the miles. Drafting was a luxury as my times improved and I either lead races or ran slower times. The newspaper listed the top Albuquerque track-and-field athletes, and I wanted to head both the mile and two-mile lists. I won the city distance trifecta of cross-country, mile, and two-mile, setting records, so yeah, I typically took it out hard, drew first blood, wore 'em down, pulled away well before the final lap, and ran state-leading times. It could not occur to my competitors from the city's nine high schools that they had a chance. When they got that into their heads they made it tougher on me. So I didn't play patty-cake, and I didn't play sit-and-kick.

Statewide, though, there were guys who weren't intimidated by me.

Louis was one of them, so now I clung to him in my signature event. He had finished half a second behind me in the mile, so I weighed three factors: my pride, don't leave the outcome to the kick, and Louis was beatable.

Still, as we went into the fifth and sixth laps the pace had me concerned. That was a switch because it was usually the other two-milers who were concerned. The pretenders let up to save themselves, and the contenders were psychologically low. After they heard the mile split they panicked. Why not? They were tired, yet still had a mile to go. So I didn't let up. On the contrary, I turned it up a notch, maybe even surged. I breathed softly, shook out my arms, looked strong and easy. Does he really feel *that* good, they asked themselves, or at least that's what they were supposed to ask themselves. So I pressed the pace, won the race before the string. When some guy latched on behind me looked back, I knew he hurt and thought about just holding his position. When he gave me that step, it was almost over. He found out how good it felt to slow down, to give in to the weakening. He'd give me another step, and then another, and slowly slip beneath my wake.

When I could no longer hear his breath, my own pain decreased. It just hurt less to win. By then I only had a couple laps to go, and I worked too hard to melt down with a half mile left. I'd hold on. No question. That point always came. And then I kicked. There was always something left. Always. That's what those extra miles were for, those additional quarters when everyone else had already hit the showers, the anger I no longer turned inward as depression but outward as fury at the end of a two-mile.

It was a devastating strategy. It crushed everyone all year. Nobody was willing to hurt that much.

Except for me.

And Louis.

I went into state having lost only once in the two-mile, and that was to Louis by a hundred-and-fifty yards one week earlier at District when I had a bad race. So there was a fourth factor I weighed in as well: Louis didn't think I could hang with him for two miles.

Now three-fourths through the race it was indeed all I could do to hang. I couldn't press the pace as usual. I just clung, baby. *Louis* pushed the pace. *He* tried to shake me out of *his* draft. *He* looked good. It was I who feared I couldn't take the pain, who might look back, might give him that step, and considered how state runner-up wasn't nearly as painful as trying to pull down a high school distance god.

I had three shots to become a state champion my senior year. The first was in cross, but I came down with the flu and created the senior runner's nightmare. What I feared most materialized because I believed that it could. The morning of state cross country I read from the *Science and Health,* the maroon-bound book bristling with tiny numbered metal markers, the onionskin pages marked with blue chalk.

I mumbled how crappy and depressed I felt.

"Don't you do it," Mom glared at me. "Don't give in to Error."

Mary Baker Eddy once commanded a dying girl, "Get up out of that bed!" and pulled the pillow out from beneath the girl's head. The girl got up completely healed, dressed, and went outside. Mom tried Mary Baker Eddyesque interventions, sternly telling me to "Disappoint your enemies!" and "Get up out of that bed!" while yanking at my pillow. I faked wellness a few times to get my freaking pillow back, but usually I was just indignant.

The medical neglect didn't seem abusive though. Just the opposite, I felt lucky. Although I didn't appreciate the suffering, I didn't think of it that way, but more as challenges due to my own erroneous thoughts. My specialness at knowing the Truth made all the tiny sacrifices worthwhile.

Mom's disregard for my discomfort and weakened condition before the state cross-country meet wasn't that she didn't care or was unaware of my suffering, but rather she didn't believe the *real* me, the *perfect* spiritual me, could suffer, and so she disregarded the lie, the material me that slumped over the kitchen table with the flu. She knew what running meant to me, but she couldn't show sympathy without believing what Error presented to her in a physical form.

Mom slid the Bible toward herself and we read *The Daily Lesson* aloud, which, in her mind, was the most wise and loving thing she could do.

I got sixth in state cross-country that day, not a good omen for a senior supposedly on the verge of distance-god status.

Six months later with five hundred yards left in the state two-mile, I couldn't wait any longer. I pulled out and surged. I passed Louis in front of the roaring homestretch crowd, the bell clanged, and I began a quarter-mile-long sprint.

Perhaps people paused in their conversations to observe the two-mile for a change. Perhaps they stopped by the railing on their way to the concessions stand and wondered, Why's he making his move so early? Did the quartets of quarter-milers practicing handoffs on the far side of the track, calling out, "Stick!" as they warmed up for the mile relay, stop a moment and declare, "Dang! Skinny white boy tryin' ta pull down Loui'? Naw, man! What?"

But now you see, right? Now you get why I couldn't wait for that neophyte on our long runs. My "most hated foe," my "nemesis," Andy Martinez, Gary Louis, and countless other skinny guys all busted their humps to keep me last pick. So you know what I had to do, don't you? I started my kick with a quarter mile to go. Watch.

I drove my arms around the curve. Despite what I said earlier about being a strength runner, I also had decent speed for a distance runner, which was why I sometimes ended up on relays. So I tapped into that and listened for Louis's footfalls to recede.

Let's be real; I ran in an event where parents, siblings, and teammates rolled their heads back and sighed, "Eight laps? Are you serious?" looked at their watches, took trips to the snack bar, the rest room, decided if it was worth waiting for the mile relay or to get a jump on traffic. They started long-winded conversations about the advantages of racing in Albuquerque if their kid was a sprinter, the racing disadvantages if he was a distance runner, and the benefits of training at altitude. Everybody despised the wind.

I came out of the turn going full out, bro. Three hundred yards to go and I still couldn't hear Louis. He slipped away, I imagined, as I sped alone down an empty backstretch. Did he glance back for third place? Did he concede that second wasn't so horrible, especially if he lost to an emerging distance god? After all someone had to be the first unseated by such rising stars as Billy Mills, Bill Rodgers, and Henry Rono.

Louis shot out of the turn, and by the time I recognized his gambit, he had three strides on me. I shifted down into my full-out sprint. As we entered the final turn I stopped him from stretching his lead, but he had me by ten yards.

If I closed the gap over the next two hundred yards I could get him on the lean. I would embrace the pain; of that there was no doubt.

Around the turn I reeled him in underwater slow.

Into the homestretch he still had me by six yards. And then five. Four....

The gap between Louis and me closed as slowly as a wound....

My obsessiveness and compulsiveness continued to serve me well after I left running, gave away my trophies, medals, and ribbons, tossed my running logs, and channeled it into studying. Obsession got me through graduate school. Afraid I'd get weeded out, I tried to learn *everything*, which was like getting a drink from a fire hose. I sat in the back row, away from the flame. In the end I was rewarded with a degree.

Now I go to work almost every day, and when I don't I still check my messages for any clients in crisis. Usually I don't have anyone on my caseload melting down so dramatically that they can't wait until I have time available in my office during normal business hours. I'm a small affair and mostly only see the walking worried. The floridly psychotic and dangerously addicted I turf to the big operations. Still I call my office to make sure. This is ethical, professional, and my fiduciary duty. I don't call it obsessive or compulsive. It keeps people feeling connected to me and the lawyers off my back.

I still worry too much about whether people like me or not. It's not unusual for me to pull up perceived slights from *thirty years ago* and feel aggrieved all over again. Sometimes it's people who disrespected me, other times it's people I disrespected and now regret it. No joke; thirty years. Thirty-five if you count high school, which I do. Forty years if you count junior high and that kid who got me suspended. It's time I got over it, but there's something inside of me that doesn't want to let go. It's unresolved, so I keep running loops in my mind searching for an acceptable answer, for justice as determined by me. In this way I empathize with my clients. I'm working on it the same as them. I know what it's like to have the old feelings connected to the thoughts return, just as hurtful, just as angry, all for no reason other than it is still unfinished business. I confess here. My imperfection would be truly laughable if let outside my own head. People would say I'm making up reasons to feel bad. They'd be right. It's better that it stays in my head at worst, that I let it go at best. Sometimes I tell

Renni, and when she validates my gripe my obsessing decreases. That said, all you see is a man in his fifties who appears to have few problems, unless you listen carefully, and then you discern he is failing to age with grace.

Now, when I perceive rejection, instead of impulsively going to anger and counterattacking, or crumpling into sadness, or running a fifteen-miler, I remind myself that I'm OK anyway, that not everybody is a good fit, that everything falls on a normal curve—some people love me, some people hate me, most people don't have a strong opinion one way or the other—that people make mistakes, especially young people, especially someone with a strong personality and something to prove. I forgive my detractors. More important, I forgive myself. I'm not exactly *better* better, but I am much better. Really. I think I'm mostly OK now.

I stood on the next-to-highest step on the podium as Louis shuffled past me to the top. "Nice goin', man," I said, which was how I talked when I tried to be cool. It was the first time I ever spoke to Louis, me being me, also because I learned long before not to expect sociability from the guys off the rez. He grunted and then squeezed my hand gently, guarded, like an obligation, as if I personally had committed genocide. His eyes never met mine. Instead he took his place at the top of the podium and cocked his head. The successful defense of his title and the breaking of Andy Martinez's state record were announced. Was he well within himself that last lap? Did he not work for his laurels? It's not like I saw his face as we approached the string. Was it scrunched up in agony? I like to think it was.

Louis beat me by 1.7 seconds, the time it took to draw in a deep breath and puff out my cheeks—also about as long as it took a cottontail to scream, although it seemed a whole lot longer when it was me waiting for the boot to come down.

An emerging distance god? That question was still unanswered as a seventeen-year-old high school senior. Me, Mom, Dad, Kat, and Tom, 1977.

CHAPTER 17

THE SAG WAGON

"**L**ock an' load, men!" Coach Timmons barked as he slid behind the steering wheel of the truck. "We've got four new tires and sunny weather! Hee! You *get* to run again today!"

In the face of yet another overwhelming workout, Timmie often held the enthusiasm for all of us. We clustered behind his rear bumper and waited to climb into the bed. Gnats stuck to my skin like pepper and collected in the corners of my eyes as I stepped into the truck. My quads felt the usual fatigue, so it'd feel good to sit, even if just for the time it took Timmie to drive us out of town. Since the good spots along the sides of the truck were already taken, I waded between the gauntlet of bare knees and plopped beneath the rear window. I was lucky; the last three guys had to stand.

"Hold on!" Timmie yelled. The truck lurched forward, and the guys standing clutched at our shoulders.

With my knees pulled to my chest and my arms around my shins, I was one of nineteen squeezed into the truck as it groaned out of the Memorial Stadium parking lot. My teammates joked with each other, and I envied their fellowship. They thought I was a shy freshman, but I saw myself as psyching up for the workout. On the bubble I ran fifth-to-seventh man, so my position on the team was tenuous. It was almost too much to bear as Timmie daily *x*'d out a square on a calendar in the locker room, counting down to the Big Eight Cross-Country Championship, proclaiming varsity runners must finish each interval of every workout in the top seven or risk losing their position.

So I approached workouts like a race.

My goal was to letter just as it had been four years earlier as a freshman in high school. This time, though, besides exceptionally talented older runners, I also faced overwhelming academics and homesickness. So I resisted the handful of guys on the wrong side of the bubble who had the same goal as me. They too sat stoic as paratroopers, looked down at their hands, and rested their foreheads on their knees. They knew it would hurt; it always did.

We crested a hill and were weightless for a moment. The standing guys sank into deep squats, their eyes wide.

"Yee-haw!" Timmie exclaimed in front. "It's a bee-yew-tiful day in God's country!"

Timmie often took us out onto the roads for softer surfaces and less traffic. Generations of University of Kansas distance runners ran on those roads before me: Glen Cunningham, Wes Santee, Billy Mills, Jim Ryun. Many All Americans, Olympians, and world-record holders. I wanted some of that, so I psyched myself up and prepared for the onrushing challenge.

A siren whooped as a squad car appeared. The cop eyed us, a truck bed full of emaciated young men. We must've looked like an Auschwitz work gang, except we were fit as all get out and starved-looking by design as we grinned beneath our shaggy hair. No one mouthed off even though we were in our teens and early twenties. We knew better than to embarrass Timmie. He was an unapologetic Christian conservative, which included respect for authority, our competition, and ourselves. Nobody wanted to disappoint Coach either, so we grinned at each other as the gum-chomping cop leaned on Timmie's window ledge. He said something about being overloaded, and there were chuckles from the cab.

A minute later the young cop went back to his squad car after Timmie let him off with a warning.

So you see I was far from the only new guy who bought into Timmie's program. The whole town bought into it—fifty thousand souls, twenty-five thousand when school was out of session. I felt especially committed, being alone, far from home, with something to prove. That wasn't a bad thing because it took away the option to slow down or quit. Not that I would have. I could go to school anywhere, but I went to Kansas to run. Anything that wasn't running was a mere detail to deal with to keep me running. So in my seventeen-year-old mind, if I didn't return home Christmas break wearing a KU letter jacket, I would have failed at the sole reason I went so far away to school. A knight on a quest doesn't stay in his village and wait for the dragon to attack. No, he goes out *after* the dragon, disappears for a while—say a semester or so—and then returns a man, the severed head of the monster on his pike. Being unreasonable when it came to running came easy for me. So yeah, I too bought into Timmie's program.

Many new runners showed up that fall of 1977, but midway through the season, some had already disappeared. That terrified me. They were good runners, literally track stars in high school or junior college. They had PRs faster than mine, so I rationalized that my times were done at altitude. In high school I trained on a dirt track that had tire ruts after it rained. But excuses meant nothing on race day. We all had excuses, but the guys who used them were the same guys who eventually disappeared. I no longer passed those guys on Jayhawk Boulevard between classes. They didn't show up sloppy and reeking at Joe's Doughnuts. Where were they? It was as if they died. Whatever happened to what's-his-face, you know, that miler from Shawnee Mission? Or it was some other dude, from some other place, with killer times who had balked, who questioned the work, who got injured and stayed injured, who was left home and then became yet another rising star who climbed into the back of the truck with us with the same high expectations but then disappeared. Somewhere. At some point. Nobody remembered when exactly.

It was honorable to sit in the truck week after week as others fell off. Eventually my tenure stretched into months and then years. I became a grizzled veteran who, for the most part, didn't feel much compassion for those who vanished. That was one more stud I didn't have to fend off any longer. I'm not saying I feel that way now that I sit at a desk, now that I cross my legs at the knees, but at the time, in the heat of battle, there didn't seem to be room for empathy.

The truck continued past the old homes once terrorized by Quantrill's Raiders, over the Kaw River, into north Lawrence, past the mills, and onto the farmers' roads. Oread Hill and the red-tiled roofs of the university receded as I rode backward in the truck.

Timmie slowed at an unmarked intersection where our dirt road bisected an identical road. It created a quadrant of brown-furrowed fields beneath which the winter wheat patiently waited to break through the dry clods. Timmie started to turn right; we shifted our weight and then he turned hard left, sending us crashing the other direction. We slammed our knees and elbows against the truck, and the guys who stood now squatted so low they used their armpits to clamp onto the sitting guys' knees.

"Everyone still in?" Timmie laughed, but he didn't wait for an answer. Instead he accelerated. It wasn't that Timmie didn't care how we were; it was that he understood why we were there, him included, and he didn't let details get in the way. Perhaps he wanted to take us on some rolling hills, changed his mind, and opted for flat and fast. Regardless, the point was he cared how I ran, which made him one of my favorite people. He cared for me from the moment we met.

The summer after my senior year in high school, a notorious coach for a local age-group team called the Supremes recruited me. If I wore his uniform in the National AAU Age-Group Championships to be held in Albuquerque, he promised to pay my way to the National Junior Olympics in Lincoln, Nebraska. Travel money was always an issue for me, so I agreed, and won the two-mile run for the Supremes. Then the coach neglected to send in my entry for the Junior Olympics (I was ninth the previous year, when I broke the state record for sixteen-year-olds). I was shocked that an adult would break his word and deprive me of one of the most important meets of my career. A couple betrayed Supremes runners and I drove to the regional meet in El Paso to beg our way into the qualifying races, but were refused. I watched the race from a grassy berm, and then burned off my frustration by wrestling the other athletes in the hotel room. We rolled off the bed and I broke my right hand.

The following week on my recruiting trip to KU, my hand was still painfully swollen. Of course I hadn't sought medical attention, and I couldn't mention the injury without making it more real. Since I couldn't offer my left hand without having to explain, I offered my swollen right. When Timmie came around his desk with his thick hand extended, I braced myself. I would not show weakness to this coaching god. He grasped my hand, his enthusiasm matched only by my pain. I didn't sink to my knees but hid behind a grille of gritted teeth. The mix of pleasure and pain would remain in our relationship over the next five years, filled with patriarchal kindness and physical agony. I never told him how much he meant to me, and now it's too late, which is something else I regret.

Thirty-five years after meeting Timmie, I told one of the guys who stood in the truck, Shaun Trenholm, about this regret. Trenholm was a freshman then as well, a 1:52(r) high school half-miler out of Chicago. I told him I wanted to thank Timmie face-to-face, to tell him how much he meant to me back when I had nothing except a dream. Trenholm said that Timmie couldn't even recall Jim Ryun, so I didn't stand a chance. I would not have a final moment with my beloved coach, at least not one he would register, so I wrote this book instead, which he will never read.

I wanted to thank Timmie for taking me around Lawrence before I knew the truck was infamous. Hardly a blue-chip recruit, I still thought very highly of myself to warrant so much of Timmie's time. Of course it wasn't about me but about Timmie's generosity and commitment. My true value was revealed just before we headed back to the airport. Although Timmie really wanted me to run for KU, they just didn't have any money, doggone it, Title IX and all. He suggested I walk on or go to Hutchinson Junior College. Perhaps KU would have something for me by my junior year when I could transfer in.

Humiliated, I returned to Albuquerque. Kansas had been my first pick. The quest had always been to go to KU on scholarship where Coach Silverberg and Jim Ryun once ran and Timmons still coached. I wasn't asking for a full ride—just a bit of validation.

Failing that, I'd pick another Division I out-of-state track college to win a school letter. New Mexico and New Mexico State made generous offers, but they were too close to home, and I *had* to go far away. I couldn't go on a quest and still live in my freaking childhood bedroom! A short drive was also unacceptable. West Point was in the mix, but they lost interest when I failed the eye exam. Junior colleges weren't on my radar at all. BYU offered books, one hundred dollars, and freshman English with Marie Osmond, sending a clear message that they thought I was worth something—at least a token scrap. So I sent in my deposit for a dorm room in Provo.

Mom was concerned. Although I had trained her by then not to get in the way of my running, she feared the Mormon influence.

It was all about the running, I assured her.

A couple days later, Timmie matched BYU's offer, replacing the Marie Osmond part with meeting Jim Ryun. That was all the excuse I needed. The next morning I boarded a Greyhound bus to Lawrence.

As the bus pulled from the curb, Mom cried in a way I'd only seen once before. She had said that she feared she hadn't been a good mother, being a teacher of other people's children and neglecting her own. I never felt neglected, I told her, because if she was going to boss me around, then I was fine with her being gone. That's when the tears came, which triggered me to rescue her. Even when I was angry with Mom and wanted to hurt her feelings, I only pushed her to the point of her softening, and then I would take back whatever I had said. So seeing her tears through the diesel smoke haunted me. Leaving home was about my quest, not her parenting, although they were related, I suppose; an athletic letter from KU would finally prove to us both that I was worthy of her unconditional love. At least that was my reasoning at seventeen.

Timmie pulled to the side of the road and was out of the cab before the pursuing dust cloud rolled over us.

"Everybody out! One mile."

I unfolded myself, slid over the side of the truck, and shuffled to the ditch. Impotent marijuana plants and bee-buzzing sunflowers grew wild next to the farmer's fields, so I piddled on them just for growing there all happy in the sunshine while I was about to enter hell.

Then we got on the jog, and the upperclassmen chatted about distance gods: Rick Wohlhuter, Tom Byers, Craig Virgin, and Jeff Wells. Although it was a good distraction, my tension built. Soon these unassuming, mustached, and bearded young men would crush and figuratively piss on me while in the throes of the scheduled workout.

Timmie followed us in the truck, and at a mile he crunched past and pulled over. He set an orange thermos on the tailgate and placed a stack of paper cups beside it.

"Hydrate, men," he said. "Stretch, then get on the line for your half."

He meant for us to run the pace we planned to go out in the first half mile of the Big Eight Cross-Country Championship, and he wanted it fast. He learned that the position runners held at eight hundred meters was generally how they placed, so we practiced going out hard, positioning ourselves well early in the race, and then holding that position.

We formed a line parallel to the driver's side mirror.

"Set," Timmie said, looking down at his stopwatch. It was the old kind with red and black hands that may have timed Ryun on these exact roads in this same workout, but scaled back a bit since Ryun wasn't real keen on cross-country.

"Go!"

My high school quarter- and half-mile speed proved mediocre now. The 880 and 1000-yard guys shredded me. Trenholm eased past, hoping to show Coach that although he struggled in cross-country, he would have something come indoor track. I could stomach Trenholm passing me since he was both a middle-distance guy and the first person to befriend me after I'd made my way to Kansas.

The bus ride to Lawrence itself wasn't without incident. A ten-year-old boy in the seat behind me put popcorn in my hair when he thought I was asleep. Halfway into the trip there was an hour layover in Oklahoma City, and being Sunday morning, downtown was as deserted of souls as a Hitler painting. As I searched for something to eat other than the vending machine food in the bus station, a man in his thirties in a faded green Skylark pulled beside me and offered me a lift. I didn't want to make small talk with someone I didn't know, so he whined about my coyness, but drove away. How friendly were Midwesterners I clucked to myself. When the man reappeared and offered to buy me a meal it began to feel creepy though. This was before Jeffery Dahmer, but still I balked more directly. Again he drove away agitated, and when he made turns around the block for a third pass, alarms finally went off, and I ran to a used car lot and hunkered between a couple of Chevy's. After the Skylark cruised past, I sprinted back to the bus station.

The little boy grinned at me with popcorn still in his teeth.

That evening Timmie picked me up in the truck at the downtown Lawrence bus station. He bought Kentucky Fried Chicken, took me home to meet his wife, Pat, an ex-KU cheerleader. He found me a room in Ellsworth dorm since the athletic dorm was already full, it being Country Club Week and close to the start of classes.

The first practice was the next day, an absolute killer, which I learned was foreshadowing. Exhausted, I shuffled back to the dorm. A muscular guy matched my stride. "A real ballbuster, huh?" he asked.

Indeed. We were both in Ellsworth, and when I revealed that in my rush to leave Albuquerque I had forgotten soap and tooth-paste, Trenholm gave me his extra, which was hard for me to accept, but I have never forgotten it.

Those of us who came from far-flung places believed in the program, and those who lived nearer already had it in their blood. Make no mistake, the KU track and cross-country program *was* Timmie, so to grumble about one meant to grumble about the other. Some of the disillusioned were guys who ran incredible high school and juco times but couldn't put it together at KU. Others were those who broke down and said we overtrained. Timmie searched for the next Jim Ryun, they sneered. The thing was, we all wanted to be the next Jim Ryun, we just didn't say it out loud; we showed up at KU and acted it out as closely as we could.

The disenchanted had a point, though; there was indeed a grueling screening process. Those screened out weren't off the hook, because they then had to look inside and determine what they lacked. Sometimes it was easier to blame Timmie. Although Timmie ran his program with heart, he assigned positions objectively by time and place. Jayhawk Track and Cross-Country would never be heartless as long as Timmie headed it, although it was always severe. Since I came from a high school program coached by a Timmie protégé, I recognized the workouts, albeit scaled-up times three. Besides, my perspective was the more the better, combined with a smattering of hero worship, so I double-knotted my shoes and got back on the line.

Bob Timmons coached at Kansas for twenty-three years. He won four NCAA championships, thirteen Big Eight Indoor Championships, fourteen Big Eight Outdoor Championships, and four cross-country conference titles. He coached seven Olympians, sixteen world-record holders, seventy-seven NCAA All-Americans, and twenty-four NCAA individual champions.

Did I mention he coached Jim Ryun?

So I threw myself into the breach. Eventually I became trauma bonded with Timmie and the other truck riders. I knew who hit it hard every morning and every afternoon, who finished the workout, who got into the truck before the workout ended, who busted it out on every run, and who made excuses. We all knew.

My trauma brothers and I ran to the point of exhaustion almost every day. That was the plan; Timmie wasn't cryptic about his method. Yet we did not collapse. Kansas runners didn't play that. We stayed on our feet, without the dramatics. Collapsing at the finish line, doing the rag doll, the floppy fish, calling for water, draping our arms over teammates' shoulders to be dragged out of the way, were not options. Uh-uh. Never. Those guys found other teams or wound down their running careers. Timmie, a marine during World War II who saw action in Okinawa and North China, had no tolerance for such histrionics, so neither did I. It fit my grimness. I stayed on my feet and walked it off. Anything less than fortitude was unacceptable. *Ever.*

"*Nobody* outworks us," Timmie announced, proud of his program's reputation as arguably the most demanding in the nation.

So when my legs barely held me and I had to dig deep I told myself, "Nobody outworks us!" When I took on the black-clad Colorado runners, lined up for NCAAs, or got paired against an Olympian in an Oregon duel, I reminded myself about the stifling Midwestern heat and brutal wind and cold we endured, and that nobody outworked us.

You see, although it's true that many athletes say they'd go through hell for their coach, Kansas distance runners *did* go through hell for Timmie. The only things missing were the flames, but we had the humidity.

The races were the easiest part of being a Kansas distance runner.

Before KU had computerized registration, we went to Allen Fieldhouse and roamed table-to-table and pulled cards for classes. Often by the time we reached the front of the line the class was already full. So I pulled out my King's X card, which was given to me by the Athletic Department, and was supposed to get me into closed classes so I could still make practice. The pasty-white, bearded graduate student took delight to inform me, "Closed means closed." The students in line looked way too satisfied as I walked away in the role of red-faced prima donna.

That wasn't how I saw it, though. With a full academic load and two workouts a day, I also missed Friday classes for meets, yet still had to keep my grades up to stay eligible. *The Partridge Family* hadn't made me simple; my GPA was low because of my workload. I certainly preferred to look at it that way anyway. I wasn't so much a dumb jock as a guy challenged to juggle bowling balls. Of course I was overwhelmed and looked for shortcuts everywhere except in running. Yet there was still the occasional professor who looked at my excuse slips as if I asked to get out of a grade-school eye exam.

I finished deep in the pack in that half-mile. That was a problem. The other varsity guys had already proven their worth. Even the only other freshman on varsity, my archenemy Paul Schultz, who was one of the top distance recruits in the nation that year, often ran first man on our team. Schultz hadn't finished in the top seven of that eight hundred either, and neither had some of the other varsity guys, so maybe I got a pass from Timmie. Schultz was the blue-chip future of our rebuilding team; I was the thankful kid they brought in at the last minute with leftover scraps. Schultz got second at the National Junior Olympic two-mile run in Lincoln; I washed dishes at the Royal Fork because my entry hadn't been sent in. Whether I was destined to be the spoiler to Schultz as savior star, or the uncelebrated dark horse who would one day unseat the leading man, Schultz was in my crosshairs (even though he was often so far ahead he was out of sight).

Trenholm walked along the drainage ditch, his fingers interlaced behind his head. Repeat miles were next, so his window to shine quickly closed. He nodded at me. We were in the flames together, and that warranted a nod. At that point he too thought I was a quiet guy. It wasn't until he visited me recently that we talked about the wilder personae that I cultivated over the next few years.

"I didn't think you cared what anybody thought," he said.

We were both fifty-two by then, and I was taken aback at how effectively I had concealed myself during college. So I confessed that much of it was an act, like a chameleon, to be whom I thought I *should* be as a young distance runner on the rise, to be Prefontainesque. Closer to the bone was my fear that something would keep me out of the truck when Timmie pulled away from Memorial Stadium. Whether I sat or stood in the bed, I needed to be included.

As the workout progressed, the truck functioned as a sag wagon. I feared my lack of talent or character would force me back into the truck before I completed the workout, a sign that my running career at KU faltered. My effort, however, would not be an obstacle.

Trenholm had the same fear. His greatest source of pride was his integrity, to include never getting pulled from a workout. When Timmie eventually did order him into the truck halfway through a cross-country workout, Trenholm felt shamed and imagined he was a burden to the team for taking up space in the truck.

Then he too disappeared.

I went to Timmie's office to persuade him to keep Trenholm. Behind his desk Timmie held up his hands helplessly. "I didn't ask him to leave the team," he said. "He quit."

"It's still one of my greatest regrets," Trenholm said almost thirty-five years later. We had both been coaches ourselves by that point, so I pointed out that it was just one bad day for an eight hundred guy doing an unreasonably heinous cross-country work-out in a notoriously demanding program. Trenholm shrugged. He had long ago forgiven himself for having a bad day, but could not forgive himself for quitting. "Coach told me, 'Shaun, sometimes wanting it badly just isn't enough.'"

Mom always made us look away from car wrecks. She didn't want our heads filled with horrible images, making them real for us. That's why I went into Timmie's office that day. Trenholm off the team was a car wreck. It terrified me that Trenholm could be broken, which meant I could be broken too.

"On the line," Timmie announced next to the sag wagon. "Ten times a mile between four fifty and four fifty-five, with five minutes rest. Let's go, men, daylight's burning!"

We knew how far a mile felt, and we knew we were below five minutes. We lived and died by seconds, so it mattered. Any one of us could hit a split within a second or two, yet the truck's tail-lights still did not brighten.

"It's long," sophomore star Kendall Smith grumbled.

"New tires," huffed Bruce Coldsmith, our first man when Schultz was less than awesome.

There were ten of us in the lead pack: seven varsity runners, two guys on the bubble, and Trenholm, who put it all out there instead of pacing himself, determined to flame out.

Finally the taillights brightened, and Timmie pulled over and hollered, "Five-oh-two!" as we pounded past. "No, no! Too slow! Five-oh-five! Five-oh-six! Why are you men dawdling? Five-oh-nine!" When everyone finished, Timmie moved between us as I bent over to recover. "These aren't champions' times, men!" he said. "Big Eight's just around the corner, you have to step it up!"

Timmie patted my back. "You gotta stay up with the leaders, Alba-cue-cue," he said lowly as if in confidence. "What's gonna

happen if we need your score? Being a freshman's no excuse."
He said it kindly, but was dead serious.

"'Kay, Coach."

"Get on the walk," Timmie said, then turned to Trenholm
doubled-over beside me. Timmie's eyes crinkled behind black
horn-rimmed glasses. "Hee! A *competitor.*"

Being called a competitor by Timmie was the highest praise.
He wanted competitors, regardless of how fast we ran. He wanted
toughness, and would coach the rest. Timmie was obsessive-compulsive about running, which was a good fit for me. He arrived
early at cross-country meets to walk the course, pick up twigs,
kick off pebbles, perhaps hunt down a rake if a particular spot
was too rough. He eventually built a course on his own Rim Rock
Farm and hosted the 1998 NCAA Cross-Country Championships,
and then deeded the whole outfit over to the university. So when
Bruce suggested the truck odometer might be off due to the new
oversize tires, it mattered to Timmie. Deep creases gashed his
forehead. "I'll adjust the times," he said, "You better believe I
will," and then spouted, "back on the line, men! Stay on pace,
stay together."

Then we began the second of ten repeat miles.

CHAPTER 18

CROW FLIGHT MARATHON

From the passenger seat of a dirty-white university van, Timmie wrestled an uncooperative Douglas County map as if he had just walked into a spiderweb. Finally, after some curse-free grumbling, he was semisatisfied with the lay of the crinkled paper in his lap and squinted down at the perfect circle his protractor had made the previous evening. At the center was a dot: his house on the west side of town. There were seven *x*'s on the perimeter of that circle, and each represented a start point, each twenty-six miles, 385 yards from his house *as the crow flies*, which we, however, had to traverse on foot. Running a mere marathon wasn't enough for Timmie, he made sure there were obstacles and uncertainty as well. Then he assigned three or four runners to a team, said no fair swimming, wading, or hitchhiking, and drove us out to our starts. If we navigated a perfectly straight course, without benefit of a map or compass, we'd run the minimum distance. That was unlikely due to topography, to include bare trees and a carpet of leaves obscuring ankle-twisting gopher holes, paint-peeling farmhouses and barns, barbed-wire fences, and clod-laden crops. Close to Thanksgiving, it was cold, gray, windy, and miserable—except for the companionship.

Crow Flight came after the Big Eight Cross-Country meet. It wasn't punishment for not qualifying for NCAAs, although it was a consequence. Mandatory, Timmie presented it as a race, but it was really a rite of passage. Some would say it was an annual hazing for distance guys, although a few track women, weight men, and jumpers volunteered. It begged, Are you committed? Will you give all? Are you with the program, with Timmie? Do you strive for greatness, or will you become another cautionary tale discussed on long runs?

Whereas the nondistance runners dressed with backpacks, canteens, almonds, bananas, and walking sticks, the distance guys dressed as if on a routine fifteen-miler. At most we wore sweats; we didn't even carry water in those days, back when we were invincible.

The eight-hundred-meter guys, who were not technically distance runners, were still expected to do Crow Flight. They wore hats with brims and carried Baggies of trail mix because they were, after all, almost sprinters, and there was an increasingly bigger difference between them and us. Many of them still had a residual distance-runner mentality, though, held over from their high school years. They were pressured to move up to the fifteen hundred as quarter-milers tested their success at the half. The quarter/half guys hated Crow Flight and talked their way out of it. The half/fifteen-hundred guys saw it as another way to prove they still had distance runners' hearts and testicles the size of shot puts.

Timmie picked starting points that had no parallel roads. He wanted to be sure we hit rivers so we couldn't make easy linear progress. Crow Flight ended up logging somewhere between thirty and forty miles, often depending on whether we guessed correctly where a river crossing existed. Was there a bridge on our left just around the oxbow bend? Perhaps to the right? Do you remember? The consequence for guessing wrong was additional miles of drudgery. Always the smooth surface of the roads attracted us, with the price of adding even more mileage. Still, the more mud collected on our customized pink-and-blue Nike Waffle Trainers, the more the roads beckoned.

With combat-like camaraderie and resignation, we took on Timmie's Crow Flight challenge. Once we navigated back to his home our reward was Mrs. Timmie's homemade chili, the promise of an end to a grueling cross-country season, and a T-shirt with a haggard-looking crow on front. One day I would grow too heavy for those shirts and use them as prizes after particularly good training efforts by the high school distance runners I coached. The boys had no idea what they had been given, but then neither had I back when Timmie mandated Crow Flight.

Crow Flight was Timmie, and those of us who survived one had a better shot at the other. That's why the weight men and jumpers joined in. They wore parkas and L.L. Bean boots, climbed out of the vans with "Hoorahs!" and the unstated message that even though they were bears among antelopes, they too had distance-runner hearts and were just as committed to Timmie.

Sure, I complained outside of Timmie's earshot. What if I turned an ankle? There were angry farmers with shotguns! We were tired after Conference! Was any of this *necessary?* Still, I was resigned and participated with dark humor. I had already learned that those of us who competed for Timmie showed up for Crow Flight, and did not show up in the results section of the sports page with *DNF* after our names. Timmie was crystal: Jayhawks came, ran, finished, and then came back for more. He never said we had to win, but we did have to *try to* win, and not "try" as in just doing our best, but try as in determining what was our best and then doing better than that. *That* was trying in Timmie's estimation. *That* was acting like a "competitor" by Timmie's reckoning, and Timmie's reckoning mattered. A lot.

So it wasn't only me who was dedicated, or just the distance runners, but everyone who called Timmie *coach.* When Timmie accepted a young man onto his team you became immersed. Soon it was like asking a fish, "What do you think about all this water?" and the fish replies, "Water? What water?" You just got used to it and it became normal. Crazy mileage. Crow Flight. Total engagement.

So I didn't ask to cut back the workout, climb into the truck before the workout was done, or get out of Crow Flight. I grumbled, taped up my shin splints and fallen arches, and told Coach I was good to go. Rest? Ha! Balance? Running for Timmie was not yoga. There *was* comparison, and there was judgment. Although our organized stretching routine had many yoga poses in it, Kansas runners who expected balance or minded their measure being taken didn't last. It was about becoming *unbalanced* to the point of near-breakdown, barely catching ourselves, and then surpassing what we thought were our puny limits.

The first team meeting began as a barbecue at Timmie's house, where he made us play volleyball in his backyard. As we segregated ourselves into our events Timmie rushed onto the court waving his arms. "No, no, no!" he shouted, and pushed a weight man to the other side of the net, dragged a sprinter to my side, and made me stand next to a jumper. "OK, then," he grinned, hands on hips, when the sides were mixed up enough to suit him. "Play some volleyball, men!"

After I missed a couple easy setups and a handful of opportunities to spike the ball, Kendall Smith out of Topeka West informed me, "Now I know why you're a distance runner." He had withheld any pleasantries up to that point as he crushed me in the workouts, so I saw his comment as making headway with him.

Afterward we ate chicken and corn on the cob, and then the team sat cross-legged on Timmie's shag carpet. Timmie paced the front of the room as he pumped us up for the upcoming cross-country, indoor, and outdoor seasons, reminding us that scholarships and accolades did not guarantee a spot on the team. He wound down with, "If you've won an individual state title, stand up."

Almost everybody stood. I, of course, remained on my thin, white, hairless behind. Yet I wasn't alone, but fidgeted between fellow freshmen Shaun Trenholm and Tim Schmidt. Schmidt was sometimes one of those guys who stood in the truck bed as Timmie carried us out onto the roads. He clamped his armpits on guys' knees out of fear of being tossed out of the truck while cresting a hill or taking a sharp turn. At particular risk being six foot four and 170 pounds, Schmidt was big for a distance runner. Timmie called him "Big 'un," which Schmidt twisted into sexual innuendo—always good for snorts from me. Timmie just grinned; he was clueless, I thought. Now that I look back, I think that although the nastiness was indeed over Timmie's head due to his personal wholesomeness, he was more aware than us that a friendly nickname was worth many torturous miles when our motivation ran low, if only to please our coach. He knew that even for staunch distance runners sometimes external motivation was necessary. Schmidt never took state either, even though he was a star out of Topeka Seaman. Both his and Trenholm's faces were as glum as mine as we sat while our peers stood. It was a wake-up slap. We had gone through the looking glass to a place where there was shame at not being a state champion.

Perhaps I made my move too late in the state mile.

Perhaps I made my move on Louis too soon in the state two-mile.

Although Kendall wouldn't sit by me, still he sat. That gave me heart. He never took state either—he was in fact a walk-on—yet he often ran up front with the freshman superstar Paul Schultz.

"Remain standing if you've won at least *two* individual state titles," Timmie said.

Some joined us on the carpet, but most still stood.

"At least three individual titles."

A few more sat.

"Four titles."

"Five."

Schultz from Omaha, Nebraska, still stood. He was also seventeen years old, but was nine days younger and lots faster than me, which irritated me from the moment we met. He was a devout Christian, graduated in the top 5 percent of his class, and very serious. I thought he judged me, fancied himself morally and intellectually superior, and saw me as no competition in running either. What was I to do other than project my own deficiencies onto him? Dude ran a 9:08.3 two-mile in his state championship, a meet record that remains unbroken to this day. Despite massive, muscular calves and thighs, his upper body was gaunt, so he looked like a centaur when he ran; a boy perched on top of a thoroughbred's legs. The Midwest stud had high school distance-god status, having been chosen to run on the US Cross-Country Team at the Junior World Championships, a very big deal and I knew it, so it motivated me over the years to pull him down and try to make him cry like Mary Decker. Again, my issue.

"Six titles."

Schultz finally sat down. Did I detect a half-smirk on his face? So yeah, I was intimidated.

Although Crow Flight was an extremely challenging run, all the long runs challenged me that year. Timmie often drove us ten or fifteen miles out of Lawrence and told us what pace we needed to carry back to town. We strung out within a couple miles, the eight-hundred-meter guys losing contact first, then the freshmen and walk-ons. I worried that if I fell off the back I couldn't find my way to town. Natives pointed out that *eastern* Kansas was hilly, easy to navigate, unlike the flatness of western Kansas. To me it was all flat, no mountain with which to get oriented. All the white farmhouses, clay roads, endless fences, cows and crows looked the same to me. The crop furrows evolved from dusty to muddy to sprouts of green to wheat that grew taller than us before being cut and bailed into huge rolls as the next cross-country season geared up. It all looked the same to me, whichever direction I ran. The distant tree lines and skies, blue and yellow, that gave way to heavy gray by conference, looked the same to me, especially since I focused upon the backs of the older runners to whom I desperately clung.

Timmie often appeared on the side of the road, leaning out of his truck window or standing by the side mirror, watch in hand, wearing his light-blue jeans and white, collared, short-sleeved dress shirt. I never knew when he'd show up, so it was another reason to keep up, expecting him anywhere. When I got a brief respite from obsessing about what Timmie thought of me, it seemed that a moment later he appeared, bemoaning my pace, shouting at me to "Maintain contact, Alba-cue-cue!" He already had a few guys in the back of the truck, *stragglers*, who not only had to sit as we ran past, but Timmie made them cheer us on.

Once I spied the red-tile roof of Fraser Hall in the distance, I could get to town on my own, then to campus, and finally back to the stadium. Timmie's truck would already be parked by the locker room. I'd stretch, lift, and walk over the hill back to the dorm.

A covered meal awaited me in the dorm's basement cafeteria. Maybe I ate alone, maybe Trenholm hunched over a row of glasses of whole milk because he lived on the eighth floor and was late for dinner as well. I couldn't linger, though, because I needed to sling on my backpack and hike up the hill to Watson Library. There I disappeared into the stacks, in a carrel, where I pulled out my thick textbooks and fell asleep. There was no way to resist the quiet smell of books, always so comforting, especially racked with fatigue and a longing for home. I would not give in though. I would not even go home for Thanksgiving because fall athletic letters had not yet been awarded. No, I would stay the course, pursue the quest, slay the dragon.

My face was in a puddle of drool when I awoke. The fruits of my lame scholastic effort while in high school left me as academically overwhelmed as the running crushed me physically. So I pored over the inscrutable books until the library closed, then hiked off the hill, past the night lights ringing Allen Fieldhouse hulking in the darkness, back to the five red-brick dorms spaced apart on the hill like a Kenyan's front teeth. I am not being racist; I'm just telling you what it looked like to me in 1977, at seventeen years old, back when I paid attention to such things, back when it wasn't the color of a man's skin or the content of his heart that counted, but how fast he could run.

When the elevator opened on the tenth-floor "penthouse," dormies tossed water balloons at me. It wasn't personal; it was just what they did instead of what I did. So I smiled and moved through them, the good sport, as "She's a brick...*house*..." by The Commodores echoed in the bay area. It wasn't that I disliked the dormies, it was that I didn't have time to get to know them, and I really just wanted to escape the day by that point, to hibernate for a few unconscious hours in my tiny cinderblock room, in my spring-squeaking twin bed that I yearned to let suck me in, to lay there motionless beneath my Jim Ryun/Kip Keino poster. So I cast down my eyes and headed down the hallway, the track guy who committed too late to score a room in the athletic dorm, who disappeared all day and every weekend, the golfer's roommate who didn't seem interested in partying, although the golfer seemed to have plenty of time.

My roommate was a generous and jovial nineteen-year-old Wichita kid who consistently hit three-hundred-yard drives and so had a full golf scholarship. He loaned me his shirts and his car—since I sold my Mustang to afford school—and was a good roommate except when he crashed drunkenly into our room past midnight after the beer bars closed, after two a.m. if he managed to sneak into a twenty-one club. The next morning he had one leg and one arm draped over his twin bed, sheets twisted and tangled, the room reeking of 3.2 beer.

Every morning I dressed in darkness, picked my way between scattered clothes, and went down the puke-smelling hallway to do my six-miler.

My roommate slept in a lot and flunked out by Christmas, so the next semester I was paired with a guy from Jordan who let his swarthy friends sleep on the throw rug between our beds. One time he tried to discuss the Israeli situation with me in his broken English. I managed to communicate that I didn't worry too much about any Israeli situation, but I did worry about being late for practice.

The one time I deviated from Timmie's program was as a fifth-year senior. It was off-season, early morning Saturday, and I decided I was powerful enough and hungover enough to skip the organized run.

Monday afternoon Timmie pulled me aside. Why did I miss Saturday's workout? I explained I did the run on my own at a reasonable hour and omitted the part about hanging out at the bars with Trenholm, Schmidt, Kendall, Bruce and half the cross-country squad until two a.m. Timmie rubbed the five-o'clock shadow on his jowls, glared up at me from his fire-hydrant frame, and said, "You're the *distance captain!* I know *you'll* do the work on your own, but I still expect you to be here and set the example for the other men."

"Hey, if they don't want it badly enough—" I stupidly began, because, really, at twenty-two I thought I had a good handle on what was needed. Why wouldn't we run alone?

"That's not the point," Timmie interrupted. "When I set a workout I expect you to show up on time and run it. You don't decide. You lead."

I acquiesced. Although there was something about the exchange that felt like a compliment, my gut tightened at the prospect of disappointing Timmie. Besides running three seasons a year for him, he also paid me to mow his lawn, stack stones into low rock walls on his farm, and clear brush on the emerging cross-country course. It killed me that he might think I wasn't as dedicated as he was.

The following Saturday he again held an off-season early morning workout. I was early and chipper.

"You rascal, Alba-cue-cue," he grinned.

I rode in the cab with Timmie and the other captain, Schultz, who tried to grow a mustache like Pre's. I grinned and rolled my eyes, my world back in balance.

I often think of that first year away from home and all the places I've lived: New Mexico, Kansas, Virginia, Vermont, California. Now I live in Scottsdale, Arizona, "the most livable city." Scottsdale was ranked number one in the nation in 1993 but is now ranked fourth, which is still darn high, probably higher than Lawrence or Albuquerque. I don't think people in Lawrence or Albuquerque care as much about that kind of stuff though. In Lawrence they care about the university, the basketball team, and Jayhawks. Albuquerque people care more about Hatch green chili, hot air balloons, and altitude training. In Scottsdale we run in the winter and stay inside in the summer. Skin cancer and cataracts are our things, unless you count golf resorts, luxury cars, and plastic surgery.

Scottsdale is a good place to live if you're a transplant like me. Transplants outnumber the natives, so I don't feel too weird, plus the natives seem more laid back, which has a calming effect. Sometimes it seems that people with money are a bit more on edge. With cell phones pressed to ears they turn left, almost hitting me even when I'm in a crosswalk with a green light and the little white man telling me to go. They give me the stink-eye as they roar past. It might be because they have the resources to rebound easily if something bad goes down, like a ticket, a wreck, or my mangled body, so they are willing to take risks with my life if the result is that they are just as fine as ever. It could also be that the same population that's motivated to generate lots of green crispy love is also aggressive while driving.

Here in Scottsdale we like to compare and compete with each other. We like to be number one, or fourth at worst, so long as it's not completely off the awards stand. We compete in road races and compare our children and cars. We deny it though. We say we are just trying to run up to our potential, age-adjusted. We say we are well preparing our children to compete against the Chinese. We say we only want a reliable car. Really we're afraid our neighbors and the other parents will see what inept and scared children we still are. It's there, just beneath the surface, and more difficult to gloss over than a parking-lot scratch on the Beamer. We are afraid our children, whom we love so well, will have a lower standard of living than ours.

Here in Scottsdale, where every child is diagnosed as "gifted"— or *misdiagnosed* as "not gifted"—we have plenty of compulsions and obsessions. We are afraid our mediocrity will be uncovered, and that our children will be average. So we overschedule them to prepare them to one day be CEOs, professional athletes, and doctors. I haven't met anyone yet who has said, "First Reader" or "Christian Science Practitioner," but as an apostate I probably hang around the wrong crowd.

My crowd sits at park picnic tables and is aghast at how the country has gone downhill in recent memory. We smile when we talk this way, but really we are worried that we will lose what we have, which feels worse than never having it at all. It feels the same as having crushed someone for years, and then they get that spike of improvement and out-kick me in some important race. I can better accept it if I still ran a PR, but mostly I can't accept it.

Sometimes parents ask me for a referral for their child. They ask me to keep it confidential, though, because they don't want ignorance and prejudice to edge them out of the platinum play-group. I say of course, and then I do. Keep it confidential. I don't ever see them myself because I wouldn't start with the blank slate. Maybe they've already tried to edge my son out of the playgroup and I'm still nursing a grudge. They don't know about hunting or Christian Science or even Timmy Two-Mile. They just see a middle-aged psychologist. I'm OK with that. We're just sitting at a picnic table and raising kids as best we know how.

Sometimes I still want to hold my breath, though. I don't. Now I know about response prevention. Think the opposite of Nike: just *don't* do it. Admittedly, I obsess over certain Scottsdale mothers who, in their zeal to parent perfectly and justify their exit from the workforce, spoil their lovelies, stomp on the fragile psyches of children not their own, hand down their dysfunction to another generation, and betray families they see only as objects. I have angst about mean girls who grew up to be PTO presidents and room mothers but haven't gotten nicer, only more powerful by adding minions of milquetoast husbands and cringing sons, daughters, and play-date companions. Now they drive minivans and SUVs and form grownup queen bee klatches to enable each other to spread poison about the principal, teachers, other parents who challenge them, and children whom they deem not worthy. Sometimes I call them on it and sometimes I do not. It never solves the problem because they just become more covert. They are way too hooked on their power and importance and do not wish to change, which is the same reason I don't treat addictions. At least my son knows he has backup, at least I showed up, which I call "reparenting myself," a concept that's also helpful in therapy.

So we strive to be perfect here in Scottsdale. Many of us set aside or hobble perfectly good careers to raise perfect children. The obsessiveness that once earned us an A+ in school now helps us squeeze out and raise perfect babies and inform each other through clenched teeth how simply *adorable* their hyperactive children are. We have play dates, and are relieved when it is not our child who threw the sand. It's nice that it's always the other child's fault. It's nice to have a choice which school to attend, which teacher to praise and slip a tip at winter break, which comes in around sixty-eight degrees. It's nice here in the desert, at a park, sitting at a picnic table. Although we are wary of Valley Fever, Mexican drug cartels, Mafia figures in the Witness Protection Program, and pedophiles masquerading as child-friendly adults, for the most part Scottsdale is a very livable city indeed, and we mostly only have to worry about germs.

So we cover the picnic tables with germ-defying paper table-cloths and sprinkle them with glittery stars, hearts, and springy-looking shiny things. It's not a birthday party; it's just another play date in Scottsdale, where the gated communities do not protect us from invisible things that fester and can infect a child just like that, *just that fast,* so quit bogarting the hand sanitizer.

Which all has the whiff of job security to me.

My freshman year in college we stretched on the grass as Jim Ryun sauntered up. It was as if that poster of him in the Mexico City Olympics, the one on my bedroom wall in Albuquerque that I carefully folded and rehung in my dorm room, pushed itself out from two-dimensionality, became 3-D, and said, "How you guys doin'?" Ryun told us a familiar story: a gawky, slight boy, nonathletic, wore horn-rimmed birth-control glasses, discovered distance running and Coach Timmons, and then everything turned around for him. He talked about other things, but I don't remember what now. Maybe he talked about being the fastest schoolboy miler, which he still was at the time. Maybe he talked about getting tripped in the Olympics. He probably talked about Jesus, that's a pretty sure bet. For some reason what I remember best was when he pointed to the whitish patches on his legs and said they made him feel self-conscious as a kid. I thought I knew everything about him, but I didn't know that he had vitiligo.

And then he left.

Years later Ryun paid for the entire track team to see *Chariots of Fire* at the theater, and then he briefly trained for a comeback. I'd like to say he trained *with me* for a comeback, but really we just did a few runs together. As we cruised down Mass Street he said he might be too old at thirty-five. I reassured him that he was not, as if I knew at twenty-two. See, I wanted to be instrumental in his comeback. I might have even picked up the pace a little bit too, you know, to help him press the envelope, help him round into shape, which I might even get a bit of credit for someday. Perhaps I imagined burning him off as well, I admit it, getting it done while I was a fifth-year senior and in killer shape, while he still worked to get his legs under him. I might earn bragging rights, perhaps even mention it now, thirty years later. Just as I

152

hit full stride past Quantrill's Saloon I glanced back—Ryun was gone, having silently peeled off and out of my life.

Let's face it: Ryun was no Marie Osmond. He was about a thousand times better, which meant BYU never had a serious chance against KU. No offense to Marie, I just think her mile PR must be much, much weaker than Ryun's.

Timmie peered over his desk down at us. It was before we left for the Big Eight cross-country meet, and we sat on his office floor before our last easy workout. "Men," he said as he pointed a stubby finger at us and raised his bushy eyebrows, "anything can happen in competition. That's why we run the race instead a just mailing in our times." The Colorado men and their stable of elite collegiate runners who ran sub-nine-minute two-miles in high school and were now NCAA All Americans didn't intimidate him. He itched for a rumble. I appreciated that about him, and felt like a little boy wanting to revel with him in the challenge, wanting so badly to please him, rushing to him when I did well, withdrawing when I didn't. "It's your chance to shine!" he said.

I shone all the way to a big fortieth-place finish, and my score was indeed needed, so it's no wonder the team only got seventh. The benefit of being on a team that was rebuilding was I got to participate even as a freshman.

We certainly didn't make NCAAs that year, so we all did Crow Flight, and by "we" I mean that Timmie also got out of the van. He and a couple of assistant coaches took turns squeezing between a barbed-wire fence. Timmie then trudged over the clods of a muddy field as he made his way back to Lawrence, a marathon as the crow flies.

Albuquerque twinkled on either side of the snaky black Rio Grande as I sped through Tijeras Canyon with *The Partridge Family* blaring, "Point meeee, in the direction of Al-buh-quer-queeee! I want to go hoooome...." It seemed an interminable time from the Greyhound bus and the Oklahoma City pervert to Christmas break. Proud to have gone out into the world, I was scared but determined, and now returned in my new red jacket with gold leather sleeves, a big blue *K* on the chest like the head of a dragon.

CHAPTER 19

FULL STRIDE

I lived in Lawrence the summer of 1978 to earn in-state residency to lower my tuition. The team got me a job at The Green Pepper tossing pizza, and I moved into Jayhawker Towers. There were seven of us distance runners sharing two apartments my sophomore year, which removed the last remaining barriers that separated running from everything else that passed as normal. So when school started I quit my pizza-tossing job and did morning runs with the cross-country captain, walked to class with the Andy Martinez of Kansas high school distance running, went to practice with guys who quoted *Track & Field News* like Bible scripture, and watched pirated HBO with the national junior college fifteen-hundred-meter champion. With my domestic life now fully integrated with running, compartmentalization wasn't necessary any longer.

I wallowed in running.

No longer the string bean in a household of football lovers, or the wispy apparition on the tenth-floor dorm, running now permeated every aspect of my life as thoroughly as religion.

I had hit full stride.

I cruised from Memorial Stadium, past Potter's Lake, and up onto the hill where I hurdled the neat hedges and dodged fat-bottomed farm girls on rusty ten-speeds. Along Jayhawk

Boulevard I wound between startled students clutching their backpacks, past yellow-stoned Hoch Auditorium, and then down off the other side of the hill and back to athletic housing, Jayhawker Towers, just across the road from Allen Fieldhouse. I stripped off my Nikes and socks, put my swollen feet into the cold pool, and endured anonymous hoots that came from the louvered windows of the basketball and football towers. I must have looked like a stork to a waterhole, but I added another piece to the kick-ass puzzle, so no apologies here. My new roommates joined me. They were high school track stars who became All-Big Eight and hopeful All Americans. They paid their dues and proved daily their willingness to pay an endless amount more.

Which meant we were all simpatico.

It wasn't unusual for us distance junkies to shoot our veins full of running. That was my gang, you see. Our crack house had running shorts that dried on the shower curtain rod, a wobbly breakfast table we rescued from the curb, the latest copy of *Track & Field News* curled next to a dirty cereal bowl, and a pervasive scent of sweat. From this base we cut down Division I athletes, put them in chalk, destroyed them on golf courses, cow pastures, and banked board tracks.

Back then we wore the famous Kansas Track shocking pink short-shorts and baby-blue singlet. The first time I put on pink I was naturally concerned that I looked foppish. Remember that as a distance runner I didn't have swaying meaty arms so I had to be careful not to do anything that could be perceived as effeminate. Although I didn't want to be hyper-defensive, I did strut a bit more so as not to risk girly-man accusations. So I puffed out my chest and acted like a stud who could pull off wearing tight pink shorts around hundreds of testosterone-driven athletes.

KU Track and Cross-Country had different shades of the school colors than the rest of the KU sports teams because once, in an important photo finish, a Kansas runner was not awarded the win because of his nondescript uniform. An indignant Coach Easton—Timmons's predecessor—shifted the uniform's colors to something nobody could ever mistake or ignore: shocking pink. Self-conscious at first, I learned that the other teams respected and desired the colors; I was often asked to trade uniforms, which was strictly forbidden.

I got a set of pink and blue to keep as a fifth-year senior after my last college race. A tornado touched down outside Wichita and TFA/USA Nationals was on the verge of being canceled. As the ten thousand approached, I lamented that my last race for KU would be a slow time. Then the hail and rain came in sideways and the track flooded.

Just great, I thought. That was sarcasm for *Why is nature always trying to jack me around?* I didn't even bother to Know the Truth—I was already way past all that by then, and never really thought it applied much to weather anyway. So I accepted that it would be all racing and no pacing.

Then minutes before the ten thousand, the eye of the storm came over us; it became still and red twilit, and conditions were near perfect other than the flooded curves. The tempo was killer, but I remembered how Timmie shouted, "Turn your legs over, Alba-cue-cue!" and Coach Silverberg used to shout, "Don't look back! The race is in front of you!" Even my mother's stern admonition came to mind, "Don't you do it. Don't give in to Error!"

Stan Vernon, 1980 Olympic Trials 10K qualifier, won, five seconds ahead of me. I sprinted in against a guy named Charlie Gray, getting fourth place, but also the school record. I thought that it was awesome that even those of us in the chase pack could sometimes exploit low-hanging fruit left by the distance gods.

Still, my name was skipped over in *Track & Field News,* but I kept the pink and blue track uniform for a few years until the sight of it and all the wonderfulness it represented became too painful to bear.

I'd frame that uniform and place it in my home office today, but it was another thing I threw away when I tossed out most of my running stuff—yet another regret. However, Trenholm was quick to say, "Ya know, if that's one of your worst regrets then you're doing pretty darn well." He's right. It's my nostalgia and sense of loss that makes me feel like he's wrong.

These days KU Track and Cross-Country are back to the traditional school colors—a nondescript blue with white lettering—and easily lost in the crowd. There was resistance to the change, but in the end the suits prevailed, uniformity in marketing the trademark won the day, so the shocking pink and baby blue was extinguished, the remnants folded into shadowboxes, or in my case, crammed into a box and placed onto a Goodwill truck. The scarcity of the uniform now just makes me feel the loss even more.

I wore the pink and blue my sophomore year when I finally beat Gary Louis in a preseason cross-country meet. He was a freshman at Haskell Indian Junior College, also in Lawrence, the same school Olympic ten-thousand-meter champion Billy Mills attended before transferring to KU. Louis was in decline; you could say he had issues. It's the human condition, I suppose. He'd soon drop out of school and join the Marines, but that sweet slice of revenge against Louis stood monolithic for me. I was a late bloomer, you see, immature, yes, and young for my grade, but I was blooming enough to finally run down Louis, and even got eleventh in conference cross-country, out-kicked for tenth and All Big Eight status by, of course, a Colorado guy.

We didn't qualify for NCAAs, so I did my second Crow Flight and then racked up the winter miles to prepare for indoors.

We were a tall distance squad, most of us over six foot, so our heads and left shoulders smacked the pillars inside lane one when we sprinted around the turns in Allen Fieldhouse. So we only raced in lane one, but worked-out in lane six, which saved our knees and the soles of our feet. I often finished off an afternoon of intervals by sprinting the field house stairs, up, up to the Wilt Chamberlain seats, two stairs at a time. Then I jogged over to the next aisle and down, jagged over and sprinted up again, doing a full circuit around Allen before I joined the other guys already stretched out on the shot put area beside the basketball court.

I paid as little attention as possible to the basketball players in the center of Allen and KU's athletic life. Their sneakers squeaked on the other side of the eight-foot-high curtain, pulled around their court like Dracula's cape, sort of secretive and evil because they sucked the attention from the indoor track team.

We shared the showers, though, and the basketball players strutted through, their chests in my face, built like statues and swingin' proud. As they passed they put their hands in my spray to see if there was still hot water, which was an affront to me, of course. So I told Schmidt that so-and-so had reached for my crank in the shower. He knew I was goofing, that the truth lay underneath, which was, why did everyone think basketball was so much more special than track? Just because they were in the paper every day with photographs even out of season? A revenue sport? Televised? What about us? What about the Big Eight Champion track team? What about how hard *we* worked? In Europe track was revered! Here basketball players could put their hands in my shower spray whenever they wanted, just like that? What gives?

Schmidt was sympathetic because the basketball players had once invited him to share their Gatorade—as if it were a big honor since apparently the drinking fountain was fine for track guys—only to reveal afterward that the current *Sports Illustrated* All American had urinated in it, *the same guy who had supposedly reached for my crank.* Such disrespect to my friend whom would one day have me serve as best man in his wedding! So he didn't mind me exaggerating about the motives of a basketball player. Schmidt encouraged me to lament that track was treated like the guy who puts the little blue cakes in the urinals. He liked to hear me whine that track was the ten thousand meters of the sports world. What was I to do since I was a ten-thousand-meter runner? I didn't rate a dollop of attention even compared to a pine-riding basketball player? They could check the water temperature in my spray, *almost touch my crank,* and somehow it was OK? So unjust, so wrong, especially since KU was a track school. *Track,* I tell you!

OK, now I get it. I saw myself competing against the basketball players for attention so my normal hypercompetitive attitude kicked in. Today, decades away from that perceived slight, I too get excited for KU basketball games beamed into Arizona, which is the great majority of them, especially if you have expanded cable, which I do just so I can watch them play. I now place a large Jayhawk flag in front of my house before every game, much to the chagrin of the Home Owners Association self-appointed enforcer. The enforcer strolls past, glares at my Jayhawk flag, at

Gentry's chalk drawings in the street, my unwashed car, and says that we should live on the west side, which he uses as a euphemism for white trash, minorities, and people who push HOA boundaries. However, my other neighbor two doors up, and the one behind my back wall, also display Jayhawk flags on game day. It's our little piss-ant Alamo out here in the desert, plus there's just something about power in numbers.

It took a long time for me to get to this point, though. I still haven't warmed up to KU football because they remind me when football stole the attention from our cross-country teams, when Transformer-sized players lollygagged across the outdoor track while we did intervals. Apparently *our* infield was *their* football field.

After indoor practice we showered and then braved windy ten-degree weather to cross the parking lot to the Towers. Schmidt—the rich kid who shunned fraternities for the company of distance runners. Bruce—our captain and star out of Alexandria, Virginia. Kendall—the backbone of KU distance. Although Kendall was All-Conference, he never ran out of his ass. He never let the team down either. Even when he and Schmidt had food poisoning at the Southern Illinois dual cross-country meet in Carbondale, both he and Schmidt ran the first half-mile so our opponents wouldn't be emboldened to see only five KU runners line up. (Had Schmidt scored he would've lettered, instead the lack of a letter gnaws at him over thirty years later.) Kendall rarely led practices or races, but he always showed up, and he always ground out the miles at a withering pace, forcing me to either submit to his unrelenting pressure, or put on my game face and pay the price to put him down, which felt a lot like racing. The next day he'd be back and I'd have to go through it again.

Kendall's tenacity was a big reason he stood in my wedding. I respected people who could run fast, who came back year after year, and embraced the pain.

I thought Kendall disliked me when I first showed up to KU. He was a sophomore and wore a bushy orange beard, which also very much impressed me. He did his best to ignore me, which I interpreted as his hard-earned right to superiority.

So I desperately wanted to move closer to him, to grind out the mileage the way he did, to be like him, except without the scowl. When he finally accepted that I wasn't going away we got comfortable in our roles, he the curmudgeon, me the brash interloper. We enjoyed the dynamic, my immaturity versus his intolerance masked as maturity. It wasn't boring, and I eventually won him over the way it's done when you spend innumerable hours stuck in a university van, in cheap hotel rooms, and going through the fire together on the roads and track.

Kendall was a smart guy and usually right if it was about trivial matters; there was, however, a slight disconnect when applying his intelligence to social facility. So Schmidt and I educated him on how to be young and silly. The more Kendall functioned as the social thermostat of our gang, the more we pushed boundaries and called him "The Old Man." It was all in good fun though; Kendall knew he was too socially constricted for a college kid, and we knew we were too wild for good taste. For me, Kendall Smith served as the parochial angel on one of my shoulders and Tim Schmidt the lovable devil on the other. Smith versus Schmidt. The dichotomy between the two could not have been more striking, the conservative Americanization of the former in dramatic contrast to the libido-driven raw original spelling of the latter. I stood between the two, in my usual spot in the middle, my arms around both their shoulders, comfortable with the irony. Remember, I was a middle child and I had a conservative, military "every dog for himself" father and a hyperreligious art-teacher mother, so the personality disparity between Kendall and Schmidt was not uncomfortable for me, only interesting. (Tim Schmidt used his surname, and I mine, to differentiate us.) Kendall was never too tired or inebriated to tamp me down, to let me know when I behaved like an ass, and when records I broke were soft. Schmidt just dug the ride, emitted his "Heee!" bray that was both irritating and hilarious, and tried to be more outrageous and clever than me, which he typically was, a dynamic we both dug. My spin was that we should all burn together while we were young.

My brothers and I crammed onto the elevator, and just as the door slid shut Schmidt smirked beneath his large, blue-tinted glasses. Kendall wrinkled his nose, pursed his lips, and groused, "No need," dismissing Schmidt with a wave. "Heee!" Schmidt brayed. "Just enjoy it, ladies." He grabbed Kendall's head and pushed it down toward his buttocks. They had their usual minor skirmish for five floors, then we spilled out into the brick hallway and strutted to 509-C and 510-C, we crashed into our shared apartments, and cranked up Electric Light Orchestra's new album on Schmidt's powerful stereo. It was loud enough for both apartments to feel as we put water on to boil for macaroni and cracked open Budweiser microphones.

"Night in the city, oh, oh, oh...."

Kendall appeared in our doorway. He was not amused. "Turn it down! Turn. It. *Down!*"

So naturally we turned it up, and I finally felt fully integrated into the "Phi Kappa Trakka" fraternity, even more so when I made All-Big Eight in the indoor two-mile.

So like I said, full stride, bro.

When it warmed up, we went outdoors, and I continued my effort in the steeplechase. I disliked the event because although I was exhausted after each race, I recovered very quickly, so I didn't think I had put it all out there. Still, it was how I fit on the team. It became another slight, though, because there were whispers among distance guys that the best runners took the coveted fifteen hundred and five thousand slots, and the fringe guys defaulted to the steeplechase and ten thousand. Come to think of it, it was Kendall who said that too, educating me, removing my self-delusion.

Anyway, the three-thousand-meter steeplechase was the closest to two miles outdoors I could get, so it became mine for a while. I dreaded the barriers, the water jump, the hurdling practice, and wasn't flexible or coordinated enough to be as good as I wanted to be. Schultz was also in the event, and would become Big Eight Champion and qualify for NCAAs the next year.

Steeplers did the heinous distance workout but over hurdles. Afterward Timmie spent extra time on technique with us because he was a hurdler as an athlete. He stood by a solid three-foot high wooden barrier and shouted, "Pull your trail leg through,

Alba-cue-cue! Now take that big step. That's it. *That's it!* OK, now go on to the next hurdle. Wait. Oh, no, no, no! That's not it. You're stutter stepping again. You should be able to alternate legs by now. Look. Now watch me," and Timmie popped his lead leg over the hurdle, stepped through and quickly pulled his trail leg around exactly the way he wanted it done. "See? OK, now. Go back and do it again. And no round-housing this time! I mean it. We'll stay here until it's dark. I know how to get the lights turned on."

So I did it again as the sun lowered and the chill of a Kansas spring evening descended.

I didn't go out for the steeplechase my junior year because I was injured, and Coach didn't say anything. I didn't run it my senior year either and again nobody said anything. That insulted me because I made All-Conference by the end of my sophomore year. Thirty years later I asked my friend Coach Joe Piane of Notre Dame if going barely subnine was any good, as if I couldn't make my mind up for myself, as if I didn't know. He said it was good, but something in me wanted to minimize it, to think he was just being nice. But something else inside me felt validated and was glad I asked.

Still I was happy to avoid the event my final years at KU, and decided I was a big boy now running the five thousand fresh, rather than doubling back after the steeple. You see it was easy to get lost on a team that boasted All Americans, national champions, world champions and world-record holders, some of whom today have their own Wikipedia page.

Even on as small a stage as the KU track team I found myself the best of the worst and the worst of the best. For example, a few years after college while in the military, I interviewed to be an army representative at the Boy Scout Jamboree in Virginia because I had been on the army track team. The lieutenant who did the interviews had, coincidentally, been on the KU team with me. He was loud and cocky, but he backed up his swagger, being the NCAA six-hundred-yard indoor champion. When they told him he'd be interviewing a fellow Jayhawk he didn't know who I was. Perhaps he'd remember me when he saw my face, he said.

So when I walked into the interview, preinsulted, saluting him was difficult. I reminded myself, salute the uniform, not the man. When I sat down across from him he had a familiar blank expression. I informed him why we should know each other, as well as about my so-called accomplishments. I refrained from chastising him for his failure to recognize me or learn Timmie's volleyball lesson.

He had clearly mellowed postcollege, had assumed more propriety as an officer. Me? A lowly spec-four, almost as pitiful as a private? I didn't want the responsibility of an officer, so I would have to salute. I knew better than to let my pride derail my goal of going to the Jamboree. The fact that he was an officer and I an enlisted man should not be an issue. Besides, they had asked if I wanted to go to Officers Candidate School when I signed up, asked again at Basic Training, and asked one final time as I ended my hitch, and each time I declined.

You're probably thinking: Subconsciously this guy was afraid of success. That's why he was an enlisted man with a degree instead of an officer. Taking the underachieving theme a step further, perhaps you're thinking, He *could've* run like Alberto Salazar, except he *held himself* back. He didn't become a distance god because he was *mentally* weak. A head case. He's another one of those guys who couldn't put it all together and then blamed others.

Let me reassure you that is not the case. I suspect you'll make your mind up for yourself, especially having read this far into my tome. Please be sure to note my anecdotes of effort and angst, my total dedication, before judging me lame.

Regarding the army I didn't want to be an officer because I wanted to experience being a down-and-dirty grunt. I didn't want responsibility over others, and becoming an officer required a six-year commitment. Two years was a good start, and if I didn't like it, get out. Otherwise I'd extend.

In the meantime the Boy Scout Jamboree was coming up, which would get me out of the inane duty that passed as a normal day in the Presidential Honor Guard. So I saluted the NCAA champion, didn't judge him on who he was in the past but who he was today, and was awarded the assignment. Not only did I appreciate his choice, but it forced me to consider that I had judged him superficially in the past, and should have afforded him the same courtesy of a full self-presentation as I would like given to me. Piggybacking on that, there were plenty of teammates I wasn't aware of, the walk-ons and freshmen in other events, and perhaps they think ill of me, as if I didn't learn the volleyball lesson either. Who knows? I just didn't appreciate it when it happened to me.

I had already suffered my career-ending injury by the time I lectured at the Boy Scout Jamboree, so there was extra time to lounge at the hotel pool with a sergeant named Mike Haywood. Mike was a former Oregon and Athletics West five-thousand-meter runner, and as I pimped him about life with the elites he revealed he was buddies with two-time Olympian Matt Centrowitz, which meant that soon the three of us sat in a Georgetown bar.

It's hard to find better guys than distance runners. Seriously. I miss that.

Today, decades later, when I watch Matt Centrowitz *Junior* on TV, I say to Renni—who's also really into track having competed for New Mexico and then became a grad assistant—"Did I ever tell you—"

"You had beers with his father in 1985? Yes. Every time you see this kid run."

"Seriously, though," I say, because I have this urge to continue, "I had a couple of pitchers with the four-time American five-thousand-meter champion and American record holder. I mean, there I was, sitting in a Georgetown bar, talking track with this guy who ran a *thirteen-twelve* five thousand! He was almost a *minute* faster than me!"

"Dad," Gentry says, not looking up from his iPad, "that's so twentieth century. Did they even keep records then?"

"No, it was an oral history passed down generation to generation around campfires. Of course they kept records," I say, even though I know he's ribbing me since he has my dry sense of humor. "But this kid wasn't even born until three years after I had beers with his dad. Now he's third in the world in the fifteen hundred!"

"So?"

"So? *I had beers with his dad!* I mean really, now that we're talking about it, it certainly begs that nasty little question about genetics. Take Chuck and Kathy Aragon. Is it really any surprise their girls are such awesome runners? My dad was state runner-up, and my mom didn't like to run. Imagine if Mom was an Olympian—"

"You can let it go now," Renni says, the person who knows me best.

Except I don't really want to let this go because I enjoy it so much. It's true I got lost on my own team, but it's also true that I had beers with an Olympian, and now I root for his son on TV.

Recently I roughhoused with Gentry in the pool in Mexico. His little buddy was with us, and they ganged up on me. Although Gentry's buddy was slender, he was thick-boned and heavy compared to Gentry. I groaned to toss the kid away from me, and then grabbed Gentry, his wrists long, thin, and light like mine, his ribs showing lumpy around his back to his spine. Gentry doesn't have an interest in football or any other contact sport. He's a straight A student even though I tell him he doesn't have to be perfect. Getting a B every now and then might do him well. He's a gentle, polite, creative boy with no interest in fishing or hunting or even shooting the .22 pistol my dad passed down to him as an heirloom.

Gentry is, however, tenacious. He's unrelenting when he wants to be, especially when he thinks his pride is on the line. Even after I tossed him away countless times in the pool, he kept coming back at me saying, "Bring it on, old man!" even though I had him by 120 pounds. He wore me down. So I called a truce because he wouldn't give up even when it made sense to do so. Nope. A truce wouldn't do; he demanded a complete surrender, which I gave.

When I imagine Gentry beginning one-hundred-mile weeks in a year or so, I don't want that for him. I tell him he doesn't have to be a distance runner. It's part of a sport that's only glamorous every four years and easy to get lost in. Basketball players will put their hands in your shower spray uncomfortably close to your penis. I tell him he really just needs to find his own place, his passion, whatever that is. It's OK at twelve to not know. I sure didn't.

His face has no miles on it, and I want to protect him from that. A part of me doesn't want him to suffer through all the miles should he decide to become a distance runner.

Another part of me can't think of anything better for him.

Being consumed and lost on the team was a whole lot better than not being on the team at all, so I'm not complaining. Perhaps it allowed me more freedom to move between events, like from the steeplechase to the five-thousand/ten-thousand double. Being further from Timmie's focus perhaps allowed me to exercise my right to party. I was, after all, almost the son of minister, and felt entitled to all the wildness the stereotype implied.

I mention the "minister" part because around that time Mom was asked to be Second Reader in our church in Albuquerque. It was an honor she declined for reasons that weren't clear to me at the time. Regarding the "wildness" part, as I grew confident away from home, I asserted my on-air persona and acted out as loud and rowdy and full of testosterone as I could.

On weekends we went to Quantrill's Saloon on Mass Street. We crammed ourselves into a roughhewn booth, sticky with stale beer, and bounced quarters into each other's plastic cups. We chugged whether we won or not and discussed how seriously cool it would be if William S. Burroughs—a Lawrence resident—sauntered in and joined us.

We sang with the Stones. "I'll never be yo' beast of bur-den...."

Maybe we teased some thick-tongued bar girl who challenged the table to a chugging contest. Maybe Kendall—our best chugger—barely beat her, and as a good-natured loser, the bar girl said, "Let's kiss." He said, "Let's not," which earned him an indignant slap across his furry face and an uproar of delight from us for such high-quality free entertainment, turbocharged because Kendall was the last guy you'd expect to get slapped by a girl. Schmidt and me? Sure! But Kendall? No way. Never.

Personally I think we were *all* at full stride at the time—at or approaching our athletic peak. Unfortunately a couple of us were at our life peak as well, but wouldn't know it for another thirty years.

Who came out without his wallet? Schmidt again, ironically the most privileged of the group. He always paid us back, though, and was always up for a good time, perhaps the most fun guy on the team, sometimes at his own expense; he didn't care so long as there were giggles. Another round? A pitcher of beer was glass then, seventy ounces, and only cost four dollars, a single buck on dollar-pitcher night. Having run twice that day, and weighing just a bit more than a large greyhound, it didn't take much to ramp me up. Still I complained about the expense, back when ten dollars lasted all Friday night.

And yes, I'm aware that I sound like an old man now.

By ten thirty we sat on the tabletop and chanted, "Free beer! Free beer!" The bartender brought over a pitcher from a blown keg, half beer, half foam, which didn't teach us a lesson in propriety.

By eleven forty-five the lights came up and last call announced, so we ordered a final round and then chugged more because it was wasteful to leave beer on the table. Soon we pulled our coats on over our gray *KU Track* sweatshirts and braved the dark cold, our shoulders high, hands thrust into our jeans pockets as we shuffled to our cars, an indestructible Dodge Dart, a Mad Mercury, sometimes Schmidt's red Trans Am, which T-boned a police car that winter while racing up the icy Towers parking lot ramp, which we thought was funny, so very *Animal House,* and yes, there were toga parties. No, Kendall did not wear a toga.

We powered around the corner and up the street to Joe's Bakery, the doughnuts still hot and wet from grease. I often ate a dozen in a single sitting; not that I'm bragging, but they were that good, even better than a microwave burrito from 7-Eleven. Hey, you had to eat something after the bars closed, everyone knew that, so the box of doughnuts steamed from the hole-in-the-wall bakery to the car, and were mostly devoured by the time we got back to Towers.

I suppose I should say something here about alcohol abuse and drinking and driving and how wrong it was. It was a different time, and we were lucky. When the Trans Am hit the cop, no alcohol was onboard. Still, I'll be a total hypocrite when Gentry starts to drive: you know, zero tolerance and all, especially here in Maricopa County where Sheriff Joe will toss you into Tent City with the murderers and illegal immigrants for *any* level of alcohol in your system. I merely report here what happened thirty-three years ago. The truth was the drinking age was eighteen for 3.2 beer, so although the laws didn't encourage drinking, they certainly facilitated it. There were plenty of hurt feelings, psychedelic yawns, and hangovers, but no DWIs or accidents, and I never missed a workout or a class because of the wildness. Perhaps it stunted my potential, I'll never know, but I doubt it. Most of the best distance runners—and distance gods—that I knew enjoyed their beer. For many of us it was as much a part of the distance-running culture as fartlek and stretching. I certainly don't recommend alcohol abuse to anybody, but highly recommend the camaraderie to everybody.

Anyway, back to the early spring of 1979. Wouldn't you know it—I forgot to pee on the car tire, and here I was now on an elevator. So yeah, I urinated in the elevator. I don't recommend that either. That was wrong, I knew it at the time, but in my paradigm it was just a little bit more wrong than peeing in a pool, and perhaps fine if I got away with it, which I did, until now. Besides, people make mistakes, especially teenagers 850 miles from home, young for their grade, inebriated, and who are a part of something bigger than themselves, like a school, a team, a gang of Division I athletes, like seven roommates who burned together through those long, vigorous, college years.

Back in our toasty apartments we turned on HBO. Kendall jiggled the wires on the board to clear up the picture and see if *First Love* was on again. Susan Dey from *The Partridge Family* was naked, man, *Lori Partridge was nude*—at least topless—which took us to three in the morning when we finally had to shut it all down because Timmie scheduled a 7:00 a.m. workout. It seemed like a conspiracy, as if he knew what we were up to. What was it about old people liking to get up early?

When morning came we were back on the track, though, and did the workout fast and felt fine because we were young and living the dream. We said we worked hard and played hard and seriously, somehow it all got done, the miles, the partying, the academics, everything else, pretty much in that order, and we did it well and we did it as a family.

The only part of my life that I did not share with my buddies was my religion.

When I was ten years old, I caught a horny toad and put it in a small cage. I soon grew bored and placed the cage on a windowsill in the shade, then went to play with the neighbors. A couple hours later I returned to discover the shade had disappeared, and the horny toad was baked. I prayed for that horny toad, but soon buried it in the backyard along with the sparrows I also failed to pray back to health. Alone in the sweet smell of the lilac tree, I softly sang "O' Gentle Presence" as Mom's silhouette was outlined on the backdoor screen. She was right. I did enjoy *Gilligan's Island, The Partridge Family,* and *The Brady Bunch.* Fractions mystified me, and I hadn't predicted the summer sun easing across the sky and removing the shade, which, of course, made me a horny-toad murderer.

In Sunday school I wondered why I was such a moron. The Sunday school in Albuquerque was large from the flush years of the fifties, as was the church itself, a cavernous structure. Both could hold many times the congregation that showed up on Sunday mornings. As the Sunday school population dwindled, so did the church congregation, whose hair was increasingly cotton and metallic gray. We sprinkled ourselves throughout the auditorium for Wednesday evening testimonial service, like spreading peas around a plate. There I would give no inspiring testimony of having raised a horny toad from the dead.

The shadow of extinction was cast even longer when we went down to visit my maternal grandparents in Artesia, New Mexico. The local church was a small, narrow room with folding chairs, perhaps better suited for an Alcoholics Anonymous meeting. Family lore was that my grandmother prayed away her breast cancer there, and because of that, and a lifetime of piety, she was the dignified First Reader of the little church. The Second Reader, the only Christian Science practitioner left in southern New Mexico, was Grandma's best friend, and they often read to each other in an empty church.

Me? I prayed for perfect eyes and less stupidity.

Over the years, since obviously I couldn't do Christian Science perfectly, I poured myself into doing running better, the story you are mostly familiar with now. What I haven't related yet is that by the end of my senior year in high school, I won my high school's Athlete of the Year award. It reeked of irony. Nominally I was a better athlete than the three-sport letterman who caught touchdown passes, dunked the basketball, and hit home runs. My dominance in city distance running through high school, and city records in the mile and two-mile, forced the coaches to choose me over better overall athletes.

It's a lesson I learned well, and it applies today. There are many people smarter than me, and many of them do psychotherapy. I have many bright and educated clients, but I do what I do over and over, year after year; I gain experience in an area in which I have an aptitude, and I improve. Now I'm only about as intimidated by someone presenting with panic disorder with suicidal ideation as I am with a marathon. A challenge, sure, but we'll get through it, and nobody's going to die.

Anyway, I didn't place that Athlete of the Year trophy on the fireplace mantel; I didn't tell my family about the award at all. Being a parent myself today, I better understand how it must've hurt Mom to learn about my award through a family friend with a daughter my age. At seventeen I didn't know why I committed such a massively passive-aggressive ploy. Of course *now* I understand that I wanted my mother to accept me just the way I was, terribly flawed but wanting to be lovable. She didn't have to gush over me, to look at me as if I was a distance god, but if she had I would've made an effort to act humble. When she didn't, or when I accidentally slaughtered a horny toad, I did my usual thing, which was withdraw, to the point where even when I orchestrated a victory I withheld from her out of spite. She had to take the bad with the good, and failing that, she'd get a double shot of nada.

Twenty-five years later while in graduate school, I was required to take my turn on Fernando, which is what I called my therapist's leather couch—this decreased my tension and sense of brokenness at having to be in therapy. I told her about winning Athlete of the Year, and my therapist validated me. Then I felt safe enough to express my concern that I wasn't intelligent enough to get through the doctoral clinical psychology program, and I illustrated my point with the horny toad story.

My therapist offered a simple yet profound intervention: "You were just a little boy," she said. "You didn't know."

Something we might all say, right? Timing is important in life but especially in psychotherapy, and her timing was impeccable. It seemed to remove the obstacle that blocked a flood of alternative thoughts. She was right I *was* a little boy. I *didn't* know. I didn't do it on purpose. I wasn't stupid, I was ten. It was an accident, not malicious. So I forgave myself. I didn't have to be perfect at ten years old. And even though I was older and an ex-teacher, I didn't have to be a perfect graduate student either.

It was a true healing.

So when I noticed a run in my therapist's stocking, rather than be disappointed that a psychologist would be so careless in her grooming—or concluding that she couldn't be a very good psychologist if she let such details get past her—I realized that I too could be imperfect. I could perhaps have unpolished shoes yet still be a competent psychologist and help people the way my therapist helped me despite the run in her stocking.

I should polish my shoes more often, sure, but I do occasionally wear a tie. A tie clasp keeps it tight against my chest. It's a tiny silver piece that Mom made for Dad while she taught art at Manzano High School, ten years before me. It keeps her with me, even as I do the thing of which she would not approve, my concerned mother whose own mother had been hard on her, so she was hard on herself, and so was hard on me.

However, sometimes I use a horny-toad tie clasp that Renni gave me. It mostly reminds me that I don't have to be perfect, but it also reminds me about things slowly going extinct, such as horny toads, certain religions, perhaps even obsolete cognitive schemas.

*Paul Schultz on the ground, Tim Schmidt on my right,
Kendall Smith sans beard on my left, Coach Timmons, Jeff Hayes,
Brent "Swaney" Swanson, and David Bauer, 1978.*

CHAPTER 20

LIGHTING STRIKES

The summer before my junior year, I built ripraps, which are rock flood-control dams in the Southwest. Out in the mesa where I often ran, a dump truck unloaded its broken concrete chunks gathered from city road construction sites. I carried the fifty-to-one-hundred-pound chunks up the side of the dirt berms, a heavy, hot task, especially in June in New Mexico. The easy part was placing wire over the concrete chunks, so I talked with my fellow workers who were kind enough to speak English when I was near, and they raved about what a sweet job we had. Me? I'd feel sorry for a mule doing the work. Then it was back to carrying the chunks up the berms like a mule. I went through a pair of leather gloves every few days, and despite my exhaustion, I had to get my run in afterward. Although I didn't like to think of myself as weak or a quitter, after three weeks I turned in my hardhat.

Next I took a job at a six-screen theater where I tore tickets, picked gum out of the carpet, and loitered at the back of the auditorium and wondered why all those people *paid* to see *Meatballs*. When I wasn't cleaning up matinee puke, I was out on the roads putting it to the age-group runners. I toyed with them by that point, the grown men who had methodically demolished me when I started racing on the roads as a high school boy, collecting ribbons for my bedroom wall.

They had aged; I had improved.

So by the time I showed up in Lawrence for my junior year, I was in great shape, back with guys who thought six-minute miles were "conversation pace," not race splits. I won the cross-country time trial, and then led the team in the first meet, which to me were clear signs that I was on my way to becoming a distance god. So eager was I to remain in front, I put in more miles than even Timmie scheduled, 120 miles including intervals, and discovered my training limit. I broke down, and by the time I semirecovered it was conference time.

My parents drove to Stillwater, Oklahoma, to watch me suck. Before and after the race, Mom went off by herself and then returned a few minutes later. She was smiling sadly, I thought at the time, but I know in retrospect that the tiny wrinkles around her mouth and eyes were just a bit deeper. She wouldn't extrapolate what was wrong beyond "female problems," a catchall phrase that meant I should leave it alone.

When I began to rebound, the team qualified for NCAA Cross-Country in Bethlehem, Pennsylvania. There was no NCAA age limit in 1979, and the quality of the field was perhaps the best of all time. Henry Rono of Washington State held four world records: steeplechase, three thousand, five thousand, and ten thousand meters. The Kenyan Olympic team practically participated, along with a slew of other studs. In the Oregon box were Salazar and all the other Oregon heroes. There were the Colorado guys and mighty UTEP. Villanova had Marty Liquori offering them support. I thought Ryun should be with us. How intimidating would that be?

Of course I considered going out hard, hoping to hang on—maybe get in some pictures—but instead I ran my own race. There was a moment, however, immediately after the gun fired, that we were *all* tied. If I had it in me I could've won. We were all given that chance, which I love about distance running, all excuses swiped away. Then, of course, the race played out, and Rono beat Salazar. Sure I got whipped like a walk-on, but everyone got whipped except Rono, and there was no apology necessary when losing to Rono in his prime. I ended up a big 124th place, which helped the team get 22nd.

Those are not typos.

However, I did beat a Colorado guy by the name of Mark Scrutton, a fact I mention here only because it will grow in significance later. I crow about these things when I can, which is of course a personality flaw, but it can be an endearing trait if we've already bonded and you keep an open mind.

In the meantime we returned to Lawrence after Thanksgiving, and Timmie *still* made us do Crow Flight, which totally blew my Crow-Flight-as-a-consequence-for-not-qualifying-for-NCAAs theory.

After my career-ending injury, my discharge from the army, graduate school in Creative Writing, marriage, and teaching and coaching at Manzano High School, I taught in a psychiatric hospital for a couple years. A fourteen-year-old girl was in there after her stepfather raped her. For weeks she seethed silently at the back of my English class. Then one day we did experiential work and walked up the La Luz, a trail that snaked six miles up the Sandia Mountains. I chaperoned her up the switchbacks, and as the dyads of patients and staff spread out, she and I eventually hiked alone in the wilderness.

"You're not going to leave me are you?" she asked.

I reassured her. Getting up the mountain was no big whoop to me; I had run up it many times, even raced up it a couple times. The first time I too was fourteen years old. I had just told Bryan Nelson it'd be a cold day in Hell if he ever beat me at any distance, and then he beat me up the La Luz. The second time I was twenty years old and finished behind Al Waqui, the Walatowa Pueblo Native American who had multiple wins up the La Luz Trail, Empire State Building, and Pike's Peak, setting records in each. I worked at Rio Grande Metals at the time, and a nine-inch diameter steel bar fell off a rack and broke my big toe days before the race. I still ran, and Bryan drove around the mountain to pick me up. His face brightened to see me "win," when really I was so far behind Waqui it only appeared I had won. Still I realized Bryan was one of my staunchest supporters all along, not a threat. He then convinced Rio Grande Metals's owner to buy steel-toed boots for all the warehouse men. Everyone should have a friend like Bryan. So over a decade later—I must've been older than thirty by then—as I walked up the trail with the angry female inpatient I reassured her again that I'd stay with her, no matter what, my student, at her pace, no problem.

Later, as she tired, she asked again, "So…you're not gonna leave me?"

I told her that unless there was kryptonite on that mountain…well, you know. That satisfied her until she gasped as we neared the top of the 10,678 foot peak, "You're *really* not gonna leave me?"

I would not, and she made it up the mountain.

The next day she stayed after class. She had a photo book, and she opened it upon my desk to present each photograph to me as a treasure, turning the pages with only the tip of her finger so as not to smudge the photos of elusive unicorns in their natural habitat of bucolic waterfalls and peacock-infested woodlands. She trusted me with the special book of her idealized world free of predators and people who left her.

What was I to do? I showed great interest, of course, but since I was in the role of teacher, I had to say, "These are truly beautiful photographs, and although these horses are real, someone has attached fake horns onto their foreheads. Unicorns are mythical creatures. I'm sorry."

She was silent as tears welled up. I wanted to console her, to not be the old man taking away her fantasy, but in teacher training we learned never to touch female students, to always remain above suspicion of anything inappropriate. Teaching in a psych hospital made that boundary doubly important. So I didn't hug her or touch her in any way after I took away her comfortable delusion.

The psych tech came and took her back to the unit a bit saner.

I wasn't supposed to be in the 1980 Big Eight Indoor Two-Mile. Our team was so strong that even though I was All-Conference and ranked, I wasn't ranked high enough to warrant a spot on the traveling team. A wannabe distance god could be bitter in such a situation, so you can probably guess that I was beyond bitter, but truly mortified. I was pissed at Timmie. Although I assumed the assistant coaches lobbied for their own athletes, Timmie was the *head* coach, *my* coach, and should give me the nod, even against statistical evidence in favor of another athlete. We had a good *relationship*, which I wanted to leverage.

Still no.

Then a triple jumper got hurt in practice, and I was on the bus.

Now back to Mark Scrutton of Colorado. He was the heavy favorite. The Junior National Champion from England, he dominated Big Eight distance running (except at NCAA cross county months earlier, when he obviously had a horrific race). Early in the two-mile he was boxed in, not controlling the pace the way you'd expect. I hung in the back of the lead pack through the mile, in the zone, pulled along, not feeling the pace. That wasn't bad for a guy like me, to hang with the big dogs, but Scrutton grew frustrated since he should've been stringing us naughty puppies out by then. Finally he ran inside the orange cones, busted loose, moved to the front, broke the race open, and began dropping us. With 220 yards to go I was in fourth place and felt good. I sprinted around a Kansas State guy on the turn, and then around an Oklahoma guy on the backstretch. I closed on Scrutton...and the race ended. Runner-up was excellent, I thought. Being the big silver man to Scrutton was like runner-up to Al Waqui up the La Luz Trail, pretty much a pseudowin, which was how us also-rans sometimes liked to look at it. I could never beat Scrutton when he had a good day; everybody knew that, unless you consider what happened next.

An official told me to go to the topmost step on the awards stand, that Scrutton was disqualified for running inside the cones. I was the Big Eight Indoor Two-Mile Champion.

A miracle? Not exactly. Christian Scientists didn't believe in miracles. Sure, I prayed for that to happen, or to be more precise, for me to outright whip everyone and prove how wrong Timmie and the assistant coaches were to threaten to leave me home. So no, not a miracle. You put the right ingredients together and you obtained the expected, scientific, replicable outcome, even if it was all done only in your mind. Secular people called it the intersection when preparation met opportunity; when hard work met good timing. Others called it running out of my ass again. I called it finally running up to my potential, Knowing the Truth, and being prepared when lightning strikes.

So I stepped to the top of the awards stand having finally won "state." Now I'd stand while the others sat, perhaps not when Timmie asked for state champions exactly, but if he ever asked for conference champs I'd humbly rise, a shit-eating grin on my face that would be misinterpreted as humility.

Kendall grounded me by saying I'd always have to add an asterisk, *Big Eight Two-Mile Champion**, to point out that Scrutton really crossed the finish line first.

Trenholm vehemently opposed that advice, saying, "Scrutton was DQ'd, man. You won. Everyone plays by the same rules. You're the Big Eight champ, bro—no asterisk."

I went to the Colorado camp and held out my hand to Scrutton. "That's not how I wanted to win it, Mark," I said. He took my hand and nodded. Clearly his devastation was inversely correlated to my elation. Still I wasn't going to disrespect him by trying to make it better for him. I wanted to beat him and I did, and if I had another opportunity I'd beat him again. Still, I wanted him to know that when I stepped on the track my heart was pure; I looked for a clean fight and a clear win. If the suits wanted to jack around with Scrutton, well, they could slap-fight it out between them.

I just ran, bro.

Scrutton wouldn't make that mistake again. He won almost everything after that, to include the NCAA cross-country championship in 1982, and he went on after college to be highly ranked in the world on the roads.

After indoors I came up injured and was left home for the first time in my running career. People liked to say we over trained, peaked for indoors, and were fried for the more important outdoor season, more important because the Olympics are outdoors. I ignored them. Even though the Scruttons of the running world were supposed to greedily win all the big races, I considered it a good strategy for me to peak while the distance gods coasted; it had gotten a guy in the chase pack an individual conference championship.

Big Eight Two-Mile Champion*, 1980.

Hobbling with an iliotibial band problem, I stayed in our spooky old mansion across from the train station that we rented that year. We had left our two apartments in Jayhawker Towers in favor of the mansion. It was built in 1888 by the personal physician of Maximilian of Mexico, the emperor who reigned from 1864 to 1867 before his capture and execution by firing squad. Dr. A. G. Abdelal was also captured, but eventually released to settle in Lawrence and build a house that five distance runners inhabited almost a hundred years later. It was our pseudofraternity house and mostly awesome except on winter nights when it got so cold glasses of water froze on the bed stand. Still, we were in it together, and that's what counted, except when I was left home. I Knew the Truth, but still lost most of the outdoor season. I sat on the grand landing and called home feeling sorry for myself. It was tragic that I couldn't run for the first time since winning the eighth grade time trial. What could possibly be worse? Mom understood, said my Big Eight two-mile win inspired her, she was sure I'd soon be running and she'd be better from her mystery ailment well before I got home for summer.

Dad met me at the door and his face told me everything that had been kept from me while away at school. The house had an unfamiliar smell that hospice workers and oncologists are well acquainted with. I went into my parents' bedroom, and Dad slipped out the opposite direction like a lifeguard trained to dive deep when a drowning person fights too hard and pulls him down with them.

Mom lay in the stale bed. "I didn't...want you to...see me this...way," she said as if running intervals. Her lungs filled with the runoff from the thing that ate her from the inside out as she lay there in her pink nightie, her left arm and hand horribly swollen. Through the opening of her nightie she was discolored, like an eggplant or the downside of a cadaver. She saw my eyes and pulled the nightie together with her good hand, then squeezed her eyes shut and turned her face away from me as pain washed over her. High-pitched whispers eked out as she prayed, and I knelt beside her bed and witnessed as she sank a little bit deeper into agony.

After the wave passed, she pointed to a can of Pepsi on the nightstand. It was within arm's reach, but on her left side, the arm that no longer worked. A bent straw stuck out of the can, so I held it to her dry lips. She sipped between gasps as I stroked her hair. She always wore her hair to her shoulders, brown and curled at the ends like *That Girl*, but now it was scalp-short and smelled like a pelt. Staying clean became a miserable, monumental task, so Dad cut her hair and bathed her when he could when he was home.

Dad was not home much in those hectic days while dealing with the residue from the New Mexico State Penitentiary riots. Three months earlier in February 1980, Zozobra visited Santa Fe. It was one of the most violent prison riots in US history. Thirty-three inmates died, guards were taken hostage, and the state police and National Guard seized control. So Grandma came up from Artesia to care for Mom, care for my little sister Kat, and to Know the Truth while Zozobra visited us as well.

Mom let the straw slip from her mouth. "I'm...drowning," she gasped.

"Disappoint your enemies," I said. I did not yank the pillow out from beneath her head. I'm not sure if that's a regret or not.

Instead I thought how everything preceding this would be dated as *before* Mom was healed of breast cancer or *after*. I hated that I even thought the word, gave it a name and more power. There it was, though, *breast cancer*, and all the challenges before it, two decades worth, had essentially been time trials for me. *This* was the culmination of all *that*. The OCD. The sternness. The Bible and the *Daily Lesson*. Sunday school. Church. Testimonies. Notes to school. The press to be better than I was, to rise to expectations, to realize my potential. The races to prove I had more to give. That lightening can strike like in the Big Eight Two-Mile. Even my injury was God's plan, because not qualifying for NCAAs outdoors allowed me to return home two weeks sooner to where I was most needed, home to save my mother.

Mom's eyes grew wet as she reached up with her good hand and put it on my face. "They keep...leaving me," she said.

She meant the Christian Science practitioners. A parade of them grew frustrated, and one by one removed themselves from her case to allow the clearer thoughts of another to try. There had been three.

Then there were none.

Then I came home so there was only me.

Mom's eyes shifted between despair and hope that somehow I could take the Error out of her thinking like taking caffeine out of soda. After all I was the fifth generation, the generation when we finally figured it all out. So I had strong lineage, perhaps stronger than the three professional practitioners who preceded me. So it was I who was chosen to run the anchor leg of metaphysical healers, the Carl Lewis of Christian Scientists. Sure, I had been someplace else, off in my own distance runners' world, and now showed up late, figuratively yanking off my sweats as I reached for the baton, Error screaming it was going to kick all of our asses, but a win could still come out of this.

Think of it another way: as my teammates surrounded the track, they clapped and chanted my name because the team needed those last few points in the five thousand so the mile relay could sew up the win—a complete healing.

Think of it any way you need to, but the point is the pressure was on me; everyone else had already done what they could.

Hey, anything can happen in competition, right, that's why we ran the race instead of just mailing in our times. Clearly we had prepared. We didn't need a miracle; we just needed lighting to strike again.

Here.

Now.

Over the ensuing two weeks, I threw myself into healing Mom. Sometimes she moved from the bed to the gold felt couch in the living room and clutched a throw pillow. We prayed and read the *Daily Lesson*. I tried to inspire her with the words she had given me over the past twenty years, and sometimes she opened her eyes wide, "Yes, yes, that's right," she said. Other times, in her psychosis from pain, lack of sleep, and lack of oxygen, she talked to people not in the room. I asked who she talked to, hoping she'd say Mary Baker Eddy or Jesus or God or anybody who could help, but instead she seemed to awaken, and replied, "Oh, nobody," and returned to her tragedy. When she finally cried, "It's just words now!" as I sat beside her with nothing more to give except more words, it felt like running against distance gods, watching them pull away no matter what I did.

Every day, every hour, I anticipated she would raise her eyebrows and say, "Why, it was all merely a bad dream." She'd pop out of bed, kick over the wheelchair Dad had rented, and trot off to church to give a testimony.

Sometimes I still ran, though. I couldn't help myself. Besides, it cleared my thoughts from what had become a moaning thing on the other side of the door. I ran up the La Luz Trail and stopped at the stream for a drink. Guilt dogged me, remembering Mom ask, "You're not going...to leave me too...are you?" and I replied, "No, Mom, I'm just going on a quick run." So I returned home to the place she could not escape, laid on the floor beside her, prayed for her to sleep, to know the Truth, to awaken from her nightmare, to get a break from the torture. Her breathing became shallower, her eyes more desperate and pleading, the pain longer as she was less able to control it using only her mind. When brief sleep finally came, it was the best part of a long string of ugly days.

On June 1, 1980, Dad sat on the foot of my bed. "Your mom's gone," he said. "Do you want to see her?"

No. I didn't view Mom's emaciated shell; I would not look at Error. Although disillusionment can come in an instant, I couldn't turn a lifetime of indoctrination off like clicking a stop-watch. So they picked up the forty-one-year-old body without me as a witness, albeit, my imagination immediately moved into the empty space: an unmarked station wagon from the coroner's office, a gurney with black wheels that wobbled on driveway gravel, a stained sheet, lumps where my mother's face must be, her feet, her breasts.

My first instinct was to grieve alone, so I ran up onto the mountain again, pumping my arms, bounding boulder to boulder, and finally stood spread eagle and yelled down to the smoggy valley, "Why?" I felt silly to be so melodramatic, but I didn't know how to grieve. Sure, there had been dogs, sparrows, a horny toad, all of which I grieved alone. Except for what I'd seen in movies, the sadness I experienced the previous couple of decades was trivial compared to the all-encompassing devastation concurrent with the melting down of my worldview. I couldn't distract myself even with runs into exhaustion; even with a dramatic shout off a moun-tainside as if I were in a bad movie with bad writing and I provided the trite dialogue. I regretted it even before the word came out, still self-conscious even in the nadir of my life. Apparently I didn't lose that, I was more self-aware, raw and naked, and watched myself behave like somebody wracked with grief.

My religion had answers. I knew that—religions always do—but Mom would stay dead; by then I was sure about that as well. So I squatted on that quartz boulder and stared over the brown city and out to the volcanoes on the horizon. Years earlier I had squatted there after I broke state age-group records, a series of apexes thanks to distance running, feeling a glimmer of what it must feel like to be a distance god.

This time it felt like the opposite of that.

I didn't wonder if I could raise Mom like Mary Baker Eddy would. Not by then, five years after Pre died. No, I wondered why Mom couldn't have had one last freaking sip of that Pepsi. Would it kill anyone if she had just one last sip?

The alone thing was unsatisfying that day; I needed a con-nection, to share my grief with someone who was wretched from the loss of Mom as well. When I hugged Dad, his arms came up between us and he turned, hid his face, his vulnerability too much for him to bear. My brother Tom was just as opaque, left after the memorial service, and returned to Oklahoma City where he now lived. My grandfather came up from Artesia, the man from whom I take my middle name, and he sobbed at the loss of his only daughter. Grandma told him to stop it, to pull it together, and then they too went home, no longer needed, no longer an inspiration.

That left Kat. She and I were most similar in the family: average academically, too concerned about what others thought of us, tuned in to pop culture and to being a kid. I pulled her into my devastation, but she resisted me as well. She needed to shut down, so she joined her drill-team girlfriends who gave her the gift of distraction. "It hurts too much to talk about," she told me when I pressed her, the stock answer I'd hear many times as a psychologist sitting with other suffering people. She wouldn't deal with her grief until years later when it rose from its insidious dark place and forced her to look.

So with the bathroom door locked, I stood before the mirror and watched tears run down my face. How odd, I thought—tears on this twenty-year-old face after I had promised myself I would not do that again.

The last time I cried was in seventh grade. A bully in PE literally kicked my butt after I missed a basketball layup, so I got huffy, and he got huffier and challenged, "At the bus stop"—probably the four scariest words to a junior-high boy. So I agonized all day, got off the bus, and waited for him. I needed closure regardless of the outcome because sitting with the dread was even worse. He clomped down the tread-plate steps and sneered; this skinny boy with glasses and braces gonna to do what? The bus pulled away with Bryan's face pressed against the glass. I told nobody about the impending match in case things didn't go well for me.

We went into the mesa followed by a dozen squealing boys, and without preamble the bully tried to kick my testicles a couple times. I had scars on my inner thighs for years afterward. He unbalanced himself on his third kick, which allowed my wind milling arms to overwhelm him until he curled into a ball and declared, "I give!"

I kept myself together until I got into my bedroom where I sank to my knees and sobbed as quietly as I could. Eventually I went into the bathroom to clean myself up, my twelve-year-old face wet in the mirror. *What a weakling*, I thought, *a coward*, mimicking my brother's labels for me, misinterpreting my emotions as signs of weakness and cowardice. If Gentry came to me today with the same situation I'd tell him that there are many kinds of strength. Big, thick arms are only one, but determination is another. I'd tell him that he was courageous to stand up to a bully whom he feared, to wait at the bottom of the bus steps when taking flight was the safest physical—but worst emotional—option. I'd tell him that doing the deed despite your fear is courage; without the fear there would be no need for courage. There was no one to discuss these things with, though, and I thought I could trust my own thoughts, so I hid myself out of shame, and resolved to be stronger. At dinner that evening I reported nothing extraordinary.

Eight years later after Mom had been wheeled away, I again watched myself cry alone in the mirror and felt weak and cowardly.

So we screened out friends and relatives. We were "fine," they were told. We came from self-reliant southern New Mexican cowboy stock with a heaping helping of Christian Science. We truly believed we were fine; none of us knew any different.

Others weren't so fine, though. Their shock and anger percolated up through their grief. They didn't know Mom had been ill. Sure, she didn't return phone calls, but that didn't mean she had *cancer*. Surely she would've told them!

They couldn't hear that Mom was ashamed too, believing she had brought the cancer on herself by believing in Error. She didn't want to give it power by talking about it or naming it, not even to Dad or her practitioners, who knew as well but would not utter the word either. Mom and the practitioners said "erroneous thinking" and "mortal mind" but never "breast cancer." As she declined she berated herself more vehemently for her weak-mindedness and fear.

As early as the Big Eight cross-country championships in Stillwater, Oklahoma, Dad had offered to take her to a doctor, just as he had for my brother's lame foot many years before. As I covered ten thousand meters through a cow pasture, Mom struggled with the temptation. She had to accept Dad's offer of medical intervention or soon lose it as an option. By the time I ran to a disappointing fifteenth place finish due to overtraining, Mom had decided to stay the metaphysical course.

Seven months later she died a martyr.

They say they cremated her and scattered her ashes over the Sandia Mountains. At least that's what happened if you can trust the mortician. I imagined a sallow-faced fellow dressed in black, perhaps wearing a frayed top hat, one bony hand flopped over the other, probably ogling my mother's nude and purple body before she entered the blaze. It didn't occur to me to participate in the process, or that we could take possession of her ashes. That too would be buying into the lie of material and temporal existence. Besides, the ashes were merely the last vestiges of her betrayal. She simply vanished that day, leaving a cancer-scented impression on the mattress and a can of Pepsi on the bedside, a bent straw still sticking out the top.

For the next few months, I pressed my face into that throw pillow on the gold velvet couch and smelled Mom's cancer and pain. Despite it being awful, it still somehow attracted me. Even the scent of her putridity was a bit of *her.* Gradually it faded, though, and no matter how hard I pressed that pillow to my face I could not bring her back in any satisfying way and only smothered myself.

Thirty-two years later I called the mortuary and made sure Mom didn't sit unclaimed up high on some dusty shelf in a cardboard box. They assured me she did not. I chose to believe that the mortician really did burn her up and scatter her on the windy mountain. Was it the mortician who did the actual deed, or some flunky? You know, the guy in a white undershirt with a belly that lopped over his blue jeans? The guy who regrouted the floor when it started to look shabby, changed the oil in the hearse sometimes, and every now and then took the white rape van around the backside of the mountain and tossed out some more ashes. Did the boxes pile up? Three? Four? Did the boss say, "Stack 'em all up an' we'll make it in one trip?" Did it matter? Surely it was somebody just having another day, somebody who poured out human remains as casually as chalking lanes onto a clay track. Do you think he at least wondered whom it had been, this former person reduced to ashes in a cardboard box? Did he wonder if she was homeless, unloved, and died in an Albuquerque alleyway? Was her name at least scribbled in permanent marker on the box flap?

She was born Ariel Isabel McGeachy, but I knew her as Mom. Others knew her as Terri Tays. She never knew any of her children's spouses, any of her grandchildren or great-grandchildren. She was wife to a career soldier, the mother of three, and a Sunday school teacher. Although she was raised to be a Christian Science homemaker like her mother, she embraced the women's movement and returned to school during turmoil and wearing psychedelic garb. She became a high school art teacher, but on the side she scavenged pieces of decrepit wood from old water troughs and abandoned homesteads to make frames for her paintings of broken-down windmills. Her brush was her lance, the *Science and Health* her shield. She was still in transition to whatever she was becoming when she was forced to choose between an idealized spiritual world over a carnal survival.

She's probably blown all the way to Boston by now, to the finish line on Boylston Street, or perhaps even a little bit further to the Mother Church.

Terri Tays, 1979 Manzano High School faculty yearbook photo.

CHAPTER 21

BURN AND BURY

I called Coach Timmons and redshirted my senior year. I'd stay home to help with my little sister, not that I had a clue how to help a fifteen-year-old girl who just lost her mother. Of course I'd return to KU in a year. Just because Mom died didn't mean I didn't still burn to be a distance god. So, yes, I'd train like an Australian. With Mom gone I ran all I wanted; there was nobody left to set limits.

Kat was torn between following the course laid out by Mom or enjoying her new freedom. Dad tried to help her decide by shutting down two of the four carburetors in Mom's powerful Delta 88 that Kat now drove to school, his best guess at how to parent a teenage girl. I tried to step in, but I was hardly an authoritative voice. In exile in Albuquerque, without a team, I too free-floated. "I'm here when you want to talk," I offered, trying to be a big brother and parent both, when really I was the one who needed to talk. Kat still wanted distraction, so she turned to her gaggle of girlfriends who were more concerned with making the drill team and shopping for makeup than dealing with repressed grief.

If I could've distracted myself until the edges wore down, I would have. All I knew to do was run, work, and party, none of which penetrated the shroud that draped over me. When "This Is It" by Kenny Loggins came on the radio, I cranked it up even though it made me feel worse, but also better because I didn't feel so alone.

It was easier for Kat to get in touch with her anger at Mom, so I joined her there. Why did Mom treat us as if she were always so disappointed? Were we really that bad of kids? Mom didn't know an iota of the crap I pulled in high school and college, so I figured I was unjustly judged based on her scant information. I mean yeah, I was guilty, but Mom didn't have proof, and so I was indignant. So we hunkered together at the kitchen table and complained at Mom's strictness and puritanical rigidity.

Dad told us that while he and Mom were in Stillwater to watch me run, he offered to take her to receive medical treatment. Although she knew she may not survive the breast cancer, and unimaginable suffering may lay ahead for her, she told him she'd rather stay true to her beliefs and live an eternity in heaven with her children, than betray herself and live another fifty years on earth.

That pretty much shut us up.

Bryan got me on at Rio Grande Metals in the South Valley, which provided metal to machine shops across the Southwest. I punched the clock each morning and entered the sawdust-and-oil smelling warehouse, fired up the forklift, and loaded the International Harvester for the day. Sometimes Bryan climbed onto the other forklift and we rammed each other like rutting bulls. Then I switched to the humming side loader and got slabs of shiny aluminum, brass sheets, steel pipes, and tread plate down off the massive racks, slid them onto the appropriate saw—band saw, plate saw, or shear—and cut the metal to the specifications ordered. The work was robotic, I an extension of the machines, a cog inside the cavernous warehouse, my hot grief more out of place than my cold boredom.

While at the top of twelve-foot racks, I took out my Magic Marker and wrote existential Kurt Vonnegut quotes on ton slabs of aluminum:

"'Why me?' 'Why you? Why anyone?' So it goes."

I wasn't thinking of the steel bar that broke my big toe before the La Luz Trail race, or that I worked in a warehouse when I wanted to be at school. No, I thought of Mom and struggled to understand what inside of me had also died. So I wrote my questions in secret places and hoped my pseudointellectual scat was so blatantly out of place that it highlighted my special status, if only in my mind. Someday my tidbits would be discovered by my replacement, I imagined, who'd frown and hope for the opportunity to beat the liberal out of whoever left such a thing at such a place. To him it would be like finding a human turd in the most unlikely of settings. I felt superior; although I poured myself into my role of warehouse man, I method acted, see, and in a single year my role would end because I wasn't *really* a warehouse man—I was a latent distance god.

Eventually John Lennon got shot, so I listened with especial poignancy to "Watching the Wheels" over the warehouse intercom as I poured gasoline into the trash barrel. I liked starting the barrel fire each morning. It expressed how I felt.

As a kid I lit matches in my bedroom—I liked the sizzle, the anger, the smolder—until Mom called me a "pyro" and made me toss out my matchbooks. Getting rid of the symptom was as close to getting to the cause as she knew, and similar to how I treat OCD today.

When the trash barrel didn't light, I added more gas, and with another match the barrel exploded. On fire from my thighs to my cap, I was on the verge of rolling on the ground before I managed to pat myself out. There were snorts as my cohorts observed me smoking, sans eyebrows or eyelashes. I grinned. Yeah. The college boy had another brain fart. That's how I made *them* feel superior.

Later that day I hid another Vonnegut quote and felt a little bit better about myself.

Bryan's distance-runner work ethic generalized to the warehouse, which earned him the ire of our coworkers because they looked lazy in comparison. By the time President Reagan got shot Bryan's industriousness won him the foreman position, which meant I now drove the two-and-a-half ton flatbed delivery truck. Now I sat in an air conditioned and heated cab and drove around town and throughout the Southwest, dropping off chunks of metal to beefy men with greasy hardworking hands. I waddled into their shops with sixty-pound hunks of metal held doublehanded at crotch level.

"Hey, *primo*," they greeted me. "Whatcho got fer me today?"

Uh, more metal....

"Looka this young buck just startin' out," they chuckled. "Only thirty more years to go, ese!"

Not thirty years. I counted the months.

It was better for me to drive, back in a solitary position similar to washing dishes at the Royal Fork Restaurant, standing at the back of the theater as *Moonraker* gave way to *The Muppet Movie*, or crossing the mesa on a long slow distance day. Although I could get along in systems, my introversion and distaste of compromise pressed me back into solitary situations, a constant rub between needing to connect and needing to withdraw.

It was no secret at Rio Grande Metals that I was a runner because the local papers and news stations often covered the road races I won on the weekends. Sometimes Henry Rono showed up, in his prime, along with some of the redshirted University of New Mexico African stars. For my name to appear in the results so close to Rono's felt like progress, as if the gap closed. The year before, when he won NCAA cross-country, I was 124th and three minutes behind him. When he beat me a year later in an Albuquerque fun run I was third and only a minute behind him. It badly distorted our talent differences in my favor, but it kept me going at a time when I needed the boost. Sure, I tucked myself away for a year, but it didn't mean I thought about becoming a distance god any less. No, I just took a breath between sobs, but would collect myself soon enough and continue the quest of becoming elite.

The owner of Rio Grande Metals thought I was already elite and so offered to sponsor me. It meant a lot to me, but still I explained how prickly the NCAA was about perks for athletes, how my coach held longwinded meetings on the topic, peered over his desk as he went over the minutiae of NCAA regulations. Timmie told of draconian measures and heinous consequences for innocent and not-so-innocent athletes who attracted the attention of the NCAA. I paid especially close attention to the anecdotes about athletes losing their eligibility. The cruelty of the NCAA suits appalled and terrified me. If Timmie's goal was to get my attention and educate me, then he won a gold medal.

So no, I would not wear a singlet with *Rio Grande Metals* across the front, but thanks for asking. Really.

The owner understood. He then said that three years of college also put me first in line to move up to sales, to settle into a career. I turned him down again. It was difficult to pass up though. Sales compared to warehouse work were like a finish line timer compared to dragging out the high jump pits. Thirty years at Rio Grande Metals? Uh-uh. Nothing against selling metal, but I'd toss myself off a bridge long before I got to thirty years. No, I'd return to KU and stay eligible in the meantime.

It puzzled me why people smirked. They didn't know that when I pulled the truck out of the bay and disappeared for the day, in my head I ran down distance gods and chanted "free beer!" with my running brothers in Lawrence.

I took a break from the grief and the dark cloud of isolation to visit Lawrence. When Timmie heard I was in town, he parked his truck beneath the massive oak tree in front of our mansion and told me to get into the back with him. For half an hour he tried to wrap his mind around why I had kept Mom's illness a secret, why I wouldn't let him or my buddies into my world.

How could I explain? Even though Timmie raised his eyebrows and stared at me as if a reasonable answer were about to pop out of my mouth, how could I give him the Christian Science Cliff's Notes, my family dynamics, and my personal psychology all while sitting in the sag wagon? I didn't have it figured out either. Although I was very self-aware, I did not have good insight. No, I was a late adolescent better known for my mercurial behavior and doggedness, and so I did not give Timmie what I have just spent tens of thousands of words explaining to you.

Timmie deserved more from me—an effort at least—but the whole mess confused me too. Still he nodded, patted my knee, and said he wished I had turned to him. Before he drove away, he said if I returned he'd give me a full-ride scholarship this time.

On Friday nights the warehouse guys met at the Moose Lodge. One man, who was bitter at having to work at Rio Grande Metals after getting kicked off the Albuquerque police force, liked to buy me beers and Kamikazes the night before races. The more noise I made about my race early the next morning, the more generous he became. After one such night I still reeked and spun after only three hours sleep. Only the winner of the local Pepsi Challenge 10K won the trip to the regionals in Omaha, Nebraska, so I hoped nobody good showed up.

John Esquibel of Adams State took us out hard and opened a gap by the first mile. Then he went straight when he should've turned left and ran into a dead end. He turned and held his hands out in a *which way?* gesture to me. I pointed to the left, down the bike path.

Not until recently did I consider that I might've handled it another way. Should I have waited for him? At the time it just looked like an opportunity for me seize the advantage. It was down-and-dirty Albuquerque road racing after all, so I didn't think anything else was expected of me. In The Tour de France, the bikers sometimes wait for their opponents, and as bizarre as that seems to me, it raises the kernel of doubt whether I did the right thing against Esquibel. I pointed the correct way to him, and then surged ahead. It was an excellent tactic to strike when he was thrown off his tempo and most demoralized. Hey, I didn't know how he prepared for the race the night before, whether he had been out until three a.m. doing shots with a disgraced ex-cop. So I tried to burn and bury him quickly so he wouldn't recover psychologically.

I won.

The poor guy who was an out-of-towner on a poorly marked course stomped around afterward. Similar misroutes happened to me over the years, so my attitude when it happened to Esquibel was *bummer, dude, but we all face the twists of fate in the fog of war.* Later I learned that Esquibel was an NAIA cross-country and track champion and would eventually be inducted into the Adams State College Hall of Fame. In the meantime I figured I did something that Pre might've done, so I didn't learn my lesson about staying out late partying even a little bit.

Kat tried to be a distance runner, but when a teammate stopped to tie her shoe, Kat stopped and waited. She didn't want the other girl to feel bad about falling behind.

OK....

Clearly cutthroat racing was my thing and not Kat's, who was known for her compassion and sweet disposition. She didn't like running in my shadow anyway. It's significant, our different approaches to racing, how she slowed down to join, and I sped up to put more distance between me and everybody else.

Kat became an artist like Mom but also had a day job. When Gentry was very young, I flew Kat out in the summer while I went to the office. When I returned home Pokemon characters were painted on Gentry's bedroom walls. Mom would approve, and when I saw Kat show Gentry artists tricks, such as turning the paper upside-down for a new perspective, Mom lived through them both.

Kendall and Schmidt visited me that redshirt year. We put on cowboy hats, rode the mechanical bull, and listened to Johnny Lee sing, "Lookin' fer love in all the wrong places...." OK, Kendall wouldn't put on a cowboy hat, ride the bull, or sing, but he made the effort to show up, which meant a lot to me, especially then. We snow skied, and Schmidt found the patience to coach me while Kendall faked enthusiasm until he straddled a tree. Later Kendall ate Captain Crunch mixed with tuna fish. Kendall and Schmidt, the oddest couple, Kendall the tuna, Schmidt the sweet cereal. They were so extremely different that I cherry picked parts from each to emulate. They met in the middle where I was, one arm around Kendall's shoulder, he twisting away and cringing from the touch. When I wanted to pull away and withdraw, when I felt like a misanthrope, when I just didn't want to put up with people's crap any longer, I felt like Kendall. My other arm was around Schmidt, his arm thrown back around my neck, the crook of his elbow pulling me toward him. He gave me an excuse to let go of my inhibitions, to be naughty for an evening, to give in to my immature and hedonistic impulses when work was done and it was time to play.

Besides winning the trip to Pepsi Regionals, I won fun stuff too—stuff that didn't pay back student loans: a pair of racing flats; an AM/FM cassette player; a ride in a hot air balloon. I only

197

won a medal for The Ann Gilliland Memorial Run, though, but it was the best award of all. Ann was one of the best female track-and-field athletes in the nation. She was a pentathlon champion, ranked fourth indoors all time for high school girls, and got second place in the high jump at the Junior USA-USSR Track and Field Meet. While boating with her family on a lake under a clear sky, the nineteen-year-old put a ski in the water and got struck by lightning. When I read about it in *Track & Field News*, I got a foreboding pit in my stomach; if someone as vital as Ann could meet a tragic end, then it became a possibility for me.

I won Ann's memorial race that set up a scholarship at the University of New Mexico in her name. Ann's best friend worked the race and saw me receive the inscribed gold medal. Six years later I met that best friend, Renni, who was still heartbroken and applying to medical school. If only she had been on the lake that day, if only she had the medical training, then Ann would still be alive, then Ann would one day stand in Renni's wedding as promised. I gave Renni that medal. Three years later we married, and Renni carried a photograph of Ann tucked in her garter.

My social-security survivor's benefits went straight to Dad. They covered my expenses, I figured, since I didn't want to be a burden. "Expenses hell!" Dad snickered. "It paid for loose women, fast cars, and good liquor, boy!" We were party buddies by then, so we high-fived. I wrote him a check for what he had lent me for school up to that point, and paid off my student loan. I wanted to say I put myself through college, that I understood it was every dog for himself. On Mom's first death anniversary I returned to Lawrence.

My redshirt year as a truck driver for Rio Grande Metals, 1981.

CHAPTER 22

MOST HALLOWED

Trenholm, Kendall, and an ex-decathlete named Jim Groninger, pooled their money and built The West Coast Saloon. I helped lacquer the long pine bar, and they gave me the quarters that fell beneath the machines so I could play *Space Invaders*. Later I tended bar—like Pre did in his day, I liked to think. When Dan Fogelberg songs came on the jukebox Kendall rejected them from a button behind the bar, declaring there was no need for anyone to listen to that crap. Then he put Elvis Costello's *Imperial Bedroom* on the stereo behind the bar, and when customers complained he flipped the album over and played the full B-side. Later Trenholm lined us up at the taps and told us, "One, two, three, chug!" and then we continued to serve our young patrons. By ten we banded together and tossed out drunk, aggressive frat boys and townies, and by eleven forty-five we flipped on the lights, shouted, "Last call!" and danced on the bar top to "New York, New York." Could it have been any better for a twenty-one-year-old college senior to return to school with a full track scholarship and three buddies who owned the hottest bar in town?

I also helped Timmie clear brush and build rock walls on his farm as the cross-country course emerged. I enjoyed working alongside Timmie, getting to know who he was besides my coach. He was a track fanatic, which I liked. He missed important birthdays,

201

anniversaries, and weddings to attend meets. He sat with me in the back of his truck and tried to figure me out when everyone else was too confused, afraid to ask, or unconcerned. When I asked him questions like "Who's the US five-thousand-meter champion?" he would say "Matt Centrowitz" without hesitation. He was always my coach, though, never a buddy. I can't imagine sitting on a tabletop with Coach Timmons and chanting, "Free beer!" or him dancing to "New York, New York" on the bar top.

Excited to be back, I wanted to prove to Timmie that his confidence in me was not misplaced. I feared he offered me the full ride not believing I'd really return and take it, like offering the last beer to someone and they're supposed to say, "No, thanks. Give it to someone thirstier." There was nobody thirstier than me; I took the full ride. Then I trained hard through the summer and took that trip to Omaha, Nebraska, for Pepsi Regionals. Bill Rodgers won ahead of Stan Vernon, Bob Wallace, Jon Eggers, and Ted Castaneda. I looked up the results on the Internet recently, and only the top five were listed.

I was sixth.

Still, I was ready to roar out of exile, and Timmie and I got excited for the upcoming cross-country season. I hoped I had a certain mystique, the Big Eight Two-Mile Champion* who disappeared for a year, back now, faster than ever.

As I removed a tree limb on Timmie's farm, I swiped my left knee with the chain saw. Timmie, the combat vet, remained calm, put me in his truck, and rushed me to town.

"Don't look at it," he commanded.

I nodded. That I understood. The gash went through my muscle almost to the bone, so there was the question whether I could run again. I could've told him to just take me home and I'll Know the Truth, but I hedged and said, "I don't want to go to the hospital."

I knew it was my Stillwater moment.

"You need stitches," he said. "I have to take you to the emergency room."

I nodded.

They say that murder gets easier after the first time you commit it. I assumed that also applied to rabbits, your opponent's motivation, and denial. When I laid on the table and they pulled the curtain around me, I had never had a stitch or a splint—not even an aspirin or vitamins. As the emergency physician sewed up my gory knee, I feared I had just lost both Christian Science and running.

Who would I be?

They put me in a splint, and I missed half of the cross-country season. I slowly came back, though, and by the Big Eight Conference, I got fifth, well behind Scrutton, who won, and just ahead of my teammate Schultz.

Now I knew I shouldn't compete against my teammates, and although I always did, usually it wasn't personal. I raced everybody, regardless of what uniform they wore. They could be my teammate, roommate, or best friend and I'd still try to set them down. If it was a relay, the team score, or an event I wasn't in, then I was all over the cheers, hugs, and "gimme some skin"— you know, the supportive teammate.

In a race I raced to the death.

In thirteen years of racing—fourteen if you count my big-ass comeback—nobody ever asked me, "How can I help *you* run faster today? Would you like to beat me today? I'll lay back for you; what the heck." Sure, I got a few, "Let's work together today, bro, take turns leading, and then it's war the last lap. Deal?"

When it came down to the end, nobody ever said, "You go on ahead; I've had my share of victories," or, "Let's hold hands and tie, my man." Never. Not even hinted at it. For starters I would've been offended, like they patronized me. I always went for the win, never the tie. Was it just me? Did I send off hostile vibes? Don't we line up, and regardless of uniform or relationship, we *race* when it's time to race? I didn't get that wrong too, did I? We're not supposed to wait for each other to tie our shoelaces, are we? Is distance running inherently every dog for himself and that's yet another reason it was such a good fit for me?

Sometimes I wonder if I took it too far, though. I remember this college eight hundred I witnessed while I was still in high school. Mike Boit controlled the race, intentionally boxed-in his opponent coming out of the final curve, and allowed his teammate to surge ahead. Then Boit sprinted for the win, so Eastern New Mexico University got one–two instead of one–three. See, if I had been as fast as Boit, I would've been so far ahead I would've broken the meet and track record, and my teammate would've gotten third. I'm no Mike Boit. Sometimes I wish I would've been though.

Schultz was an extreme recipient of my competitiveness because with him it was personal. Remember he was slightly younger than me, which unsettled me because it made it tougher to pretend I could age into a distance god. Schultz had been a high school distance god, which put him in my crosshairs, and he had beaten Scrutton when they both had good days in Big Eight cross-country our junior year, which piqued my jealousy. Schultz never said much to me through our years of running together, other than pointing out a mistake in the KU media guide our freshman year that cast me in a better light than I deserved. It read *National Junior Olympic* two-mile champion instead of *AAU age group* two-mile champion. Schultz was the National Junior Olympic two-mile runner-up and I wasn't the guy in front of him. But guess what? I didn't publish the media guide, but I did get the mistake corrected. Still, because the mistake was in my favor, his *tone* implied I had something to do with it and he had caught me, rather than the truth that some unknown proofreader made a mistake. I'm sure I made it all up, but still it meant I was almost as happy to beat him as I was to make All Conference cross-country. That was probably wrong too, but speaks to my respect of his running ability and my crowd's persnickety insistence on accurate reporting of running data.

My buddies at The West Coast Saloon trumpeted my conference finish in an ad in the school newspaper, highlighting that I was the first American finisher. Our team beat Colorado, albeit we lost to Iowa State.

A few weeks later at NCAAs, I thought my goal was reasonable: to make All American. I wasn't even close at 78th place. I'm a late bloomer, I told myself, but something not buried very deeply knew that future distance gods did better than that. Scrutton got fourth. Schultz beat me too; I suppose I should mention that. He didn't make All American either, and the mean part of me was a little bit relieved that I wouldn't have to live with the envy. That makes me sound petty, but I only admit it now because that's what I thought then, and I probably wasn't the only dickweed to have those thoughts. Of course it made no difference to my status how Schultz did, but I twisted things up in my mind to where if a high school distance god and member of the US Cross-Country Team at the Junior World Championships could fail to make cross-country All American, then I didn't suck quite as badly as I feared. I could still believe that my best races were ahead, perhaps on the track that spring. Worst-case scenario I'd bloom after college.

Afterward people asked if mauling myself with the chainsaw helped me run better toward the end of the season since I couldn't overtrain. It irritated me because it seemed like criticism of both Timmie and me. Also, I liked to pretend that I would've made All American if I hadn't hurt myself. Still, I asked Timmie if I could skip the morning runs through the indoor and outdoor track seasons. He considered it briefly, and agreed.

At the Nebraska dual indoors, four of us from KU took turns leading the mile. The other three guys—Greg Leibert, Tim Gundy, and Bob Luder—were younger studs busy developing into kickass milers. We had a blanket finish, with me winning, which is why I mention it at all. I rarely won collegiate races, especially at a distance as short as a mile, so when I did I made sure to overgeneralize the result to indicate how I teetered on distance god status.

My "archenemy" Schultz and I dueled in Big Eight XC, 1981.

Then I came back in the two-mile, my main competition my own teammates again, this time against Schultz, and Brent Steiner, an 8:46.9 high school two-miler and the national high school cross-country champion in 1979, which easily made him a high school distance god as well. When I called him a distance god he denied it. Chuck Aragon also denies it. I like their humility. I think they just remember all the runners ahead of them. I remember them ahead of me. Out of all of us, Steiner became an NCAA Cross-Country All American, and then postcollege an elite triathlete. Having Schultz and Steiner with me was like having Andy Martinez and Gary Louis on my team. Since they were fresh, I let them do the work as Timmie yelled at me to take a turn leading. I hated not doing exactly what Timmie told me to do, but I was too wiped out, I wasn't trying to be a scab. I was super-motivated for the reasons I've mentioned, so I went around Steiner, and the final two laps I taught Schultz to respect his elders. The Big Eight indoor Two-Mile approached, when I would take on Scrutton again to regain my title.

I wanted to run the two-mile at Big Eight fresh again; I didn't care what anyone said. Two years earlier when I stepped up to the top position on the awards stand, the second-place guy from Oklahoma sneered up at me and asked, "Did you run the three mile?" I shook my head, and unless it was my imagination, he thought he would've won if I had doubled like he did. I usually doubled and never made excuses, not out loud at least. So when I ran fresh I just called it good tactics. I wanted to run fresh, take my best shot to flabbergast everyone again, and remove the asterisk from Big Eight Two-Mile Champ*. Scrutton had won the previous year while I was redshirted, so there would be two champions in the race. Running out of my ass was called for. Lightening needed to strike. I would run the two-mile fresh again, I decided.

But Timmie decided we needed my points in the three-mile the night before the two-mile.

I ran well behind Scrutton in the three-mile and began to hurt, so I backed off for a half mile to recover. When I was passed by an Iowa State African and Schultz, it put me in seventh place and nonscoring. I didn't want to go to all the drain of racing three miles for nothing, plus I didn't want to give Schultz the satisfaction of beating me. So I honked it on, passed those two back, and finished fifth. Scrutton won again—he won every Big Eight race after being DQ'd against me—but my time broke the KU school record. It was another weak record, Kendall quickly pointed out, but it was mine and I was proud to have left my mark, weak or not, in Allen Fieldhouse, on the wall, beneath Jim Ryun's mile and two-mile records.

At the time I disliked the confusion, being in that transitional era when the US changed from yards to meters. In high school we ran miles in cross-country and track, but in college cross-country we sometimes ran miles and other times ran meters. Indoors we ran miles, but outdoors we ran meters. Get it? I liked to compare exact distances. I wanted to stay with miles, but realized that because the Olympics and the rest of the world used meters the change would happen. Too many splits in meters were meaningless to me. Quarters, halves, and miles I knew.

In the end it worked out in my favor because after I left college, the full transition to meters was finally implemented, which meant my three-mile record could not be broken and stands to this day. I don't delude myself that I was in the same league as other KU record holders—say, Jim Ryun for example—I'm just saying there were gaps to be filled by us chase-pack runners.

The next day I came back in the two-mile, but it was anticlimactic. The real story was about my teammate, Tyke Peacock, the World Cup champion in the high jump who had transferred to KU. He also played basketball for the Jayhawks, so after his game he was helicoptered to Lincoln, Nebraska, and won the Big Eight high jump and broke the school indoor record. Me? I rode the bus and finished fourth in the two-mile.

Tyke went on to get second in the World Championships, was ranked number one in the world, and was favored to win the gold at the 1984 Olympics. Yet he didn't attend the 1984 US Olympic Trials, just as I hadn't. I didn't attend because I didn't qualify, but he didn't attend because he faked an injury due to increasingly severe drug use. He didn't show up to an NBA tryout either, and did multiple stints in prison for stealing to support his addiction.

I once saw Tyke at a party at Jayhawker Towers, but I didn't talk to him. What would I say? You ever pee in the Gatorade? Could you see my failure-to-defend two-mile race from up in the clouds? I'm just venting again; I hope you know that about me by now. Truthfully I loved the view from the bus. I loved being on the bus, although I would've accepted a helicopter ride.

Outdoors at the Kansas Relays, I lined up in the exchange zone to anchor the distance medley. I was ready, my sweats pulled, so none of my teammates had to scream from the infield to kick my ass as my nemesis had done. Colorado led, with KU and Brigham Young University chasing. Scrutton wished me luck, grabbed the baton, and took off. I sucked in behind him, with Petersen from BYU just behind me. This was an important race for me, in front of my home crowd, against Scrutton, and now Petersen too, this dude who had been on my recruiting trip when Paul Cummings showed me around BYU. Cummings would've totally remembered Petersen. Petersen knew not to order iced tea at lunch or walk on the grass, plus, oh yeah; he was a 4:11 high school miler, so there's that. So now I thought how the BYU coaches would see whether they had chosen well. I wanted them to feel regret over not offering me a better ride, even though I kind of knew they offered me what I deserved, maybe even better. Books and freshman English with Marie Osmond wasn't such a horrible deal for a runner like me.

After three and a quarter laps, I made my move on the backstretch, shooting out of the turn just like Gary Louis showed me in the state two-mile five years before. The crowd went wild, as they say. Now, any crowd going wild for me would probably get me past an awful lot of really good runners, just not Scrutton. He matched my pace and kept me on the outside going into the final turn. I lost ground each step, tried to tuck in behind him, but now Petersen moved into the rumble seat and kept me outside. We came out of the turn one-two-three, me third, forced to watch Scrutton sprint away for the win. That made me the guy who missed the winning shot at the buzzer, struck out at the top of the ninth with the game-winning run on third, who got the baton second in front of his home crowd but finished third despite running a PR, albeit in a relay, which you should always admit.

Sometimes (but pretty much never) at dinner parties we talk about running, and someone asks what my mile time is. I'm uncomfortable because it's from a former life but also because I wasn't a true miler. Granted, I probably have a faster mile PR than the person I'm talking to—the guy who ran track in high school but can't remember either his times or the distances he ran. How do you not remember your event? I'm no idiot savant, but I remember many of my races and times. I might've forgotten what I ate the night before, but I remember who beat me. We remember what matters to us. The dude will say that a 4:07(r) mile is super fast or he won't have a clue; I can tell by how he nods and grins. I could say 3:51, and the nod and grin would be exactly the same. All the nuances I leave out—such as it would be fast for a high school boy, but I was a fifth-year college senior—would all be lost on this person who's just trying to make small talk until he can find a smooth exit to join the group of women discussing the best liposuction in Scottsdale (he will give them his card). He better escape soon, though, because I'm about to segue into my Chuck Aragon story, starting with, "It was a relay split, but I have a buddy who should've gone to the Olympics in the metric mile but...."

Perhaps if I had kicked sooner in the state mile my senior year I still would've gotten third. Perhaps if I had kept Gary Louis on the outside in the state two-mile like Scrutton did to me, I'd be a state champion and not be left sitting on Timmie's carpet. But then again, I was no Scrutton. Scrutton easily proved that had he not been DQ'd in the two-mile my junior year he would not have "lost" to me, as if that point needed repeated proving. Perhaps all the fawning over Petersen during our BYU recruiting trip was justified. He did kick my ass the one time we raced. Did he sit next to Marie Osmond in English 101? Perhaps my high school and college records were indeed soft. Perhaps my state age-group records were weak.

What do I do with all that? Does it mean it doesn't matter? Or does it come down to tending my own garden—that that should be enough? Is it really about no comparison—no judgment, no competition—as my hot yoga instructor says (and by *hot yoga* I mean that's the nomenclature of the class)? Is it really about what *I* get out of it, regardless of who I don't beat and what times I can't run? It's beginning to feel like it was about *me* the whole time, that in a way at least I got that one thing right. It was only marginally about the clock or the distance gods.

Timmie was right too. I'm a Timmie supporter. I refer to him whenever I get the chance. When Gentry had an archery unit in PE at his middle school whoever made a bull's eye did not have to run laps.

"Running isn't a punishment," I said. "I had a dear coach in college, and when I said, 'I *have* to run,' he always said, 'You *get* to run!'"

Gentry scrunched up his face.

Sweet, innocent boy.

As I reminisce here, I'm not feeling as bad as I thought I would about running in the chase pack. It feels kind of cool that I got to run at all.

I could've been forced to shoot arrows instead, I suppose.

If I can't claim winning the Big Eight indoor two-mile as the apex of my running career because I didn't win outright, then perhaps I can claim this next race. We flew to Eugene, Oregon, for a dual track meet, and I knew I was in a special place when miler Tom Byers of Athletics West came up to me in a pizza establishment the night before the meet while I played *Space Invaders*. "Hey man," Byers said, "let me show you how to beat that game," and elbowed me aside. He must've known that I recognized him, his long hair, and knew he beat Olympic 800 champion and 1500 world-record holder Steve Ovett the previous year. Now he did the same thing to *Space Invaders* as he did to Ovett, which was tear the testicles off the video game. I didn't stand there with my mouth open only because he ran a 3:50.84 mile. My mouth was open because he racked up more points and beat more screens than I thought possible. So yeah, I let him use my quarter. I didn't mind a bit. I probably got the quarter free from Kendall or Trenholm anyway.

Remember, I liked talking to fanatical runners, and here I was in Track Town, USA. I jogged on Pre's trail and recognized people I'd seen in magazines and on TV. I liked to get excited over obscure races, times, and splits, to name drop, talk about cross-country, indoors, outdoors, the roads, killer workouts, mountains we've run up, and marathons we wanted to run. Barring that, I was fine just playing *Space Invaders* with a distance god. If that made me guilty of being a track fanatic, then fine—I gladly wore the label. It put me in really good company.

The next day I was pitted in the five thousand against two-time Olympian Bill McChesney. The previous year he was ranked first in the US and fourth in the world at that distance, and the year I raced him, 1982, he was ranked third in the US in both the five thousand and ten thousand meters, and held Oregon's records in both those events. We were both twenty-two years old, and as I managed my anxiety in the staging area before the race, he wished me luck and shook my hand. He didn't seem afraid of me at all. Perhaps he focused on how badly he creamed me at NCAA cross-country in 1979 and again in 1981, but he hadn't yet heard about the distance gods who occasionally met misfortune while I gave chase.

Fine. I came to race, and we might see how lightning could strike, especially if I took him by surprise. I still believed that when preparation met opportunity odd things sometimes happened. I couldn't count on it, but always hoped. That was why we ran the race instead of just mailing in our times, right?

McChesney took it out hard, and I latched on behind. Please don't shake your head. Although I knew who he was, I planned to run out of my ass, and who knew, I might just need another asterisk. After all, Byers beat Ovett, and a couple times I sort of beat Scrutton. I wanted to suck in behind McChesney and let him pull me to a good time at least. I didn't *expect* to beat him—I had guile, not brain damage—but I'd beat him if I could, I promise you that. I'm not apologizing. I'd humiliate him in front of his home crowd if I could, just like Scrutton and Petersen did to me at the KU Relays. I never expected mercy, and never gave it. If that made me an A-hole then fine, I was an A-hole. If someone ran into a dead end I'd surge and worry about the ethics later.

Reasonably, though, I hoped to stay with McChesney for as long as I could, fade slowly, and get pulled to an NCAA qualifying time.

McChesney had other ideas. He went out in a sixty-four-second quarter, so OK, apparently he didn't believe in giving mercy either. Since he did all the work, I just held the tiger by the tail. Then he kept cranking out sixty-fours, and I got really irritated, really quickly, not to mention tired. What was he thinking? Yeah, right, we were gonna run a 13:20? OK, yeah, *he* could run that fast, but more likely he was flicking me off, which I thought was totally rude. Maybe he took me seriously after all. Maybe he knew that I wasn't afraid to lose so I'd challenge anybody. Maybe he just didn't need the hassle of this goofy Kansas guy puppying after him. How could he have known that I fantasized hanging...hanging...I'm a harmless puppy, Bill, look at my tiny milk teeth...and then crack! Deliver a figurative kick to his man berries. Oh, sorry, old boy, but was that the great Bill McChesney losing on the lean? To whom? A guy wearing *pink* shorts?

Seriously, though, I thought him burning me off early was unnecessary. He could cruise, win the race, and take me with him, right? He was no less an Olympian if I ran faster, right?

But, no.

So I let him go. What could I do? What could I freaking do?

McChesney opened a ten-second gap on me and stayed there. Then Oregon's second man came up and started messing with me. So we got into this big old hairy duel, and took turns leading every other lap, trying to burn each other off, drafting, dishing some pain, hanging on again, until I finally outkicked him, still ten seconds behind McChesney.

Second place was fine, I admit it. I've never felt bad about losing to distance gods. It wasn't like it was only me. It wasn't like last place, or even last pick. So as I walked around the grass infield with a new PR people in the bleachers stood and clapped. I looked to see what action I missed—a good high jump, long jump, or vault?—but no one was there, of course, because the meet wound down. They looked at me, those track fans, and not like I would be looked at in a year when I'd jump into the Marine Corps Marathon. So I jogged, and the spectators stood and applauded as I passed before they sat back down. I looked around again because I didn't want to be that guy who perked up and waved when the person was really waving at someone behind me. Nope. It was definitely for me. I don't want to sound like I'm bragging, but I don't know what else to call it other than a standing ovation at the most hallowed American track venue, Hayward Field. That's right. A standing ovation for an also-ran, chase-pack, wannabe distance god.

On Pre's track.

In Pre's race.

Against Pre's heir apparent.

Just another dual-meet win for McChesney was arguably the highlight of my running career.

I heard Kendall's voice in my head like my own, pointing out it was a *sympathy* ovation—at best a *nice-try* ovation—and so could not be counted as a true standing O, not the kind that Pre or McChesney got. I'd agree too—to a degree. I've stood and cheered the McChesneys of the world countless times myself, but I've also stood for the Dick Beardsleys, which made it a possibility for me.

As I jogged in front of the bleachers, I didn't know if I should wave like Pre and shout, "I love Oregon!" I felt sort of numb, like it couldn't really be happening because I didn't win.

Maybe the view from the bleachers was they appreciated the way their number-two man and I worked together. They didn't know I did my best to shake the guy but couldn't. They thought I was being cool, when really I was up to my old tricks of trying to burn and bury their boy.

Could it have been that Oregon track fans were so knowledgeable and fanatical as to appreciate me *trying* to stand up to their distance god? Everybody except me knew I didn't stand a chance against McChesney, so perhaps they identified with me the way you identify with that poster of an owl, talons outstretched, swooping down upon a mouse as the mouse flips the finger in defiance.

I like to think it was the spirit of Pre that the Oregon fans appreciated. Even though I couldn't run as *fast* as Pre, I could still run *like* Pre. Even if Pre couldn't beat McChesney, he still would've tried. I'm really certain of that.

Ten years after I tried to pull down Bill McChesney, I coached a state champion sixteen-hundred- and thirty-two-hundred-meter runner at Manzano High School. I told him to enjoy the ride, that it was fleeting. "You *get* to run again today," I told him, and one day, too soon, it would end. Then I walked up the La Luz Trail with a girl who believed in unicorns, and the following day I took away her fantasy. That year, in October 1992, the great Bill McChesney, sadly perhaps also in the spirit of Pre, died in a car accident. He was thirty-three years old, the same age as me when I tossed out even more of my running paraphernalia, which, as I've mentioned, I now regret. Especially the running logs and pink and blue meet uniform I wore when I raced McChesney and later broke the school ten-thousand record. It wouldn't mean much to anybody else, but would mean a lot to me, and now I'm thinking that matters a lot and always did.

Artist and track star Greg Leibert drew this for me in college. Renni advised me not to include it here; it makes me seem too full of myself. Still, I had to. I just had to.

CHAPTER 23

THE OLD GUARD

Kendall and Groninger sold their share of the bar to Trenholm, and then the three of us moved to Arlington, Virginia, to join our old teammate Bruce Coldsmith and live The Runner's Life. Kendall lasted a few months, decided there was no need, and split. I only lasted a year and a half, but as you already know, I had much frustration trying to run with the distance gods while supporting myself by waiting tables. So when I didn't qualify for the Olympic Trials, I searched for another way to stay on the roads. I heard the army liked runners, so I drove back across the country to Santa Fe where Dad lived with his new wife. He swore in a dozen young men and me at the Recruiting Center in Albuquerque, and in the middle of the night, I flew to Fort Benning, Georgia.

Was this move a stroke of genius that would push me up to the distance gods or just another brain fart, but of marathon proportion?

At basic training they shaved my head and gave me battle-dress uniforms; the irony was striking that I spent my youth trying to be visible and unique and now was pressed into invisibility and sameness. It spoke to my psychic conflict between my press for uniqueness simultaneous with my press to belong to something larger than myself.

I was inoculated for the first time in my life. After waiting in line for an hour at parade rest for my eye exam, the optometrist snarled, "You're not trying!" and sent me to the back of the line to wait another hour. Falsely accused of shredding my bunk sheets, they took the money out of my pay. The armorer pulled me in from the field and said I had the dirtiest weapon ever. It wasn't *my* M16, I explained, but since he had stripes and didn't want to hear anything he didn't already think, I stayed up all night cleaning an unassigned weapon. They returned me to the field during a rainstorm, and as I finally got dry and sleepy somebody yelled, "Whose Leather Personal Carrier is this?" Mine, of course. The downpour had dug the sand out from beneath my shelter half and carried my boot downstream. So I spent the night digging a trench and finished about the same time we broke camp and force-marched to a new location.

I stood out in some good ways, though. I was a bit older at twenty-four, had a college degree, and my father was a full-bird colonel. When they discovered I could run I was picked to represent my platoon on the obstacle course.

Last getting to the rope climb because I couldn't sprint since my Achilles chronically hurt by then, I also struggled because my hands were wet and sandy. The humiliation continued when I lost my grip on the parallel bars for the same reason, which put me dead last. Trainees from the other platoons whooped at my failure as their own representatives disappeared into the woods. So I low-crawled under barbed wire and sprinted into the trees after them. There I caught the slower, gasping trainees, and then plunged into the swamp. Parts were waist deep with roots catching my feet, but other parts were open, and that's where my running background roared into actuation.

The perception was of a guy badly out of the race going into the woods and almost winning coming out. It was a *Rocky* kind of thing to my fellow trainees. Of course they didn't know my history and that I almost blew it. So I got permission to train for a Fort Benning road race, easily won it, and so found myself standing out in this new milieu that stressed blending in and teamwork.

Just before graduation was the big-ball competition, a rough game where the object was to push an enormous rubber ball over the other team's goal line. It was platoon against platoon, and since the numbers weren't even, there were sides chosen. My old grade-school PE feelings resurfaced. Do we ever really get over such things?

The unpicked trainees equaled a few plus me.

Let's review: High school Athlete of the Year? Check. Two records at a Division I university? Check. Ran semipro on the roads? Check. Squad leader? Older? College degree? Check, check, and check. Veiny, beefy arms that swayed from my shoulders like sides of beef? Uh-oh.

Finally, to graduate we had to do a minimum number of push-ups and sit-ups. I easily maxed out the sit-ups, but did the minimum number of push-ups. We also had to run two miles in a minimum time.

Two miles, you say?

So in the last two-mile fitness test, I ran far ahead, but the drill instructors failed to pay close attention to their watches. They said I tied the army basic-training record, but who knows? I think nobody knows, but I hang onto it twenty-eight years later not because it mattered to anybody, because it obviously didn't, but because it still matters to me.

My contract promised to station me in West Germany so I could participate in the Cold War. It was the best I could do since I wanted to be in a war with plenty of horror—a young man's quest to be sure, one that concerns me today when I look at my son. I not only positioned myself as a fair-game combatant, but as someone looking for trouble. I had unresolved feelings around vulnerability and death, you see, so I hunted screaming rabbits, bought a motorcycle, and visited graveyards as a hobby. I yearned to be tougher, *safer*. Death brushed past me, as close as a first-degree relative, so I needed exposure to the carnage to take its power away. An infantryman in war seemed like a good way to do that.

Then the Old Guard recruited me out of basic because of my test scores and how tall and thin I was. They wanted infantry-trained soldiers who followed orders and looked good in dress blue uniforms. It was elite duty, they said, like Rangers, Delta Force, and Special Forces. It sounded lots better than living in a hole in West Germany, which I discovered in basic was not as glamorous as advertised.

The 3rd US Infantry, the Old Guard, was the Presidential Honor Guard and stationed at Fort Meyer, Virginia. Although my barrack was just blocks from the house where I lived The Runner's Life, it was a whole different world. Now Georgetown and Alexandria doormen saw my high-and-tight haircut and wouldn't let me into their clubs, and restaurants seated me in empty rooms in dark corners. Girls laughed at me, but older men and women thanked me for my service. I wondered if I told them about the abuse if they would feel as proud. I just smiled grimly. People really don't want to know what's in their sausage.

In Delta Company I was in the same squad as *Gardens of Stone* author Nicholas Proffitt, only twenty years later. Our job was to do parades in Washington, DC, ceremonies at the Tomb of the Unknowns, go on bivouac for weeks aggressing the 82nd Airborne at Fort Bragg, North Carolina, and practice Command and Control in case there was a riot in DC. Mostly, though, I buried veterans in Arlington National Cemetery. I followed the

horses and the caisson that had carried JFK into the "boneyard."
Eight of us slid the casket off the caisson and carried it to gravesite,
and as we held the flag taut between us over the casket a religious
man said something religious. Finally seven riflemen fired three
cracks, the bugle played "Taps," and we folded the flag. I was the
guy who handed the tight triangle to the officer, saluted, and as
he presented it to the widow and began, "On behalf of a grateful
nation…," I turned smartly and marched away, back to the bus,
back to prepare for the next drop. I was moved throughout the
service, especially during Taps. It always mattered to me because
it seemed more real than a parade or endless training. It mattered to the country, and certainly to the grieving family. Of all
the possible places to be buried in America, I think Arlington is
the best; Old Guard soldiers are the best ones to do it, and that's
coming from a guy with a bad attitude.

I again received special permission to run on my own during physical training. So when my squad played basketball or
touch football, I ran on the same routes as before I enlisted.
However, I had less time to train, and was on my feet more
than when I waited tables. On the days my squad "ran" (i.e.,
jogged), I was obligated to run with them, which was a warm
up for me and I got no benefit. If you bench-pressed three
hundred pounds, did it benefit you to rep ninety pounds?
When I was allowed to run, I sped far ahead, around the
Iwo Jima Memorial and back to my barracks where George
Washington's troops once stayed.

My idea of what training was needed and what my superiors
thought was generous time to train, were not in synch. I trained
after duty hours for the most part, after standing in formation
and marching all day. If not that, I was out in the boonies where I
couldn't run at all. At the end of yet another long day of mindless
work and getting dogged out by the NCOs, I had to sit idle in the
bay area and wait for "the word" to come down from battalion
that we were off. The platoon sergeant told us, "Smoke 'em if you
got 'em," the soldiers BS'd for an hour or two as the sun set, and
my run was put off as it got darker and colder and I stewed over
the inefficiency of the military and how it certainly wasn't better
than The Runner's Life I had given up.

So to answer the earlier question about genius or brain fart: brain fart.

I was chosen for the US All-Military Cross-Country team that competed in the World Military Cross-Country Championships in Portugal, 1985. It was my first and only international team, and I was thrilled to wear *USA* on my chest. Representing my country as a runner felt like the most authentic way I could express my patriotism. The team voted me flag bearer for the opening ceremony. I was in the middle of acting all humble, when Captain Bret Hyde, a graduate of the Air Force Academy and ranked eighth in the United States in the steeplechase that year, and nationally ranked for nearly a decade, said I was chosen because of my Old Guard experience. Well, OK. If that's what put me over the top then fine, but the inside scoop is that holding a flag and walking isn't really all that difficult. Even a grunt can do it, right? Still it was a huge honor, even though it was defaulted to me by more humble runners. Afterward Bret asked if I had dipped the flag when passing our host nation, I replied, "No," but feared him asking was an accusation, so I left out the "sir" part, being passive-aggressive as usual.

It was always a bit confusing for me when officers, NCOs, and enlisted men mixed in these running settings. We went on a first-name basis in Portugal, which was to my advantage and the officers' disadvantage. It was up to them to enforce boundaries, and up to me not to overstep them, so of course I overstepped them because I always felt that people were equal. I saw everyone on the team as a successful hardcore distance runner and rank as a distraction, and didn't like the distance it created between us. It felt weird to have those boundaries when we did the most passionate thing of all together, distance running. Of course that's coming from the lowest guy in the pecking order. I'm sure worms would be all for equality with birds if they could manage it.

Today in therapy I try to close the distance that titles create. Doctor. Senator. Mr. Mrs. I ask what they want to be called, and they *always* say to use their first name. It makes it their responsibility, see, so they don't feel disrespected. They can call me whatever they need to. If they need the formality of *Doctor*, that's what I am to them. If they need a more intimate and equal relationship, *Tim* is just fine. Dr. Tim is especially common. The main thing is they feel safe enough to open up and work.

So no, I did not dip the flag; I carried it proudly and then finished sixty-sixth in the race. I mostly only remember a cluster of kick-ass runners ahead of me. There were many Olympic runners from other countries who in reality were paid professionals supported by their government, so I didn't stand a chance. I appreciated the experience, though, and hanging with the heroes on the American team.

Bret Hyde died of ALS in 2001, also known as Lou Gehrig's disease. So here's yet another distance god who died horribly and young. He not only ran first man on our team, but cared whether the flag was dipped or not. I wish I had called him *sir*— he deserved it whether he was an officer or not.

After the race a Portuguese runner insisted we trade uniforms. His was too small for me, but he wore mine beaming with pride. That's another uniform I gave up, but somehow letting it go in the spirit of being an ambassador for America felt right and a whole lot better than putting it in a Goodwill truck.

Then I returned to life in the fishbowl—the Old Guard. We were the soldiers looking soldierly when President Reagan's motorcade drove past—the impeccable blue men who picked up bodies at Andrews Air Force Base and buried victims of terrorism in Robert E. Lee's rose garden. We had to be perfect in dress and manner, and mustered an entire company of tall, fit soldiers in finely creased uniforms who marched in precision, presented arms in perfect unison, and then marched away without committing a single discernible mistake to the public eye—yet a cataclysm of errors in the eyes of the sergeants.

Over a hundred men moved as one.

Which all came at a high price, of course.

I shined brass in my four-man room for hours, placing each ribbon and award on my uniform *exactly*, measured with a ruler, as the Scorpions sang "Still Loving You," and The Grease Man kept my sagging spirit just above hopeless.

The door banged open, and my squad leader glared at me from the doorway.

"At ease!" I shouted and sprang to my feet at parade rest. The spindly buck sergeant scowled as he strutted into the room. I kept still as if on a starting line, my hands on the small of my back. The sergeant reveled in the power his stripes gave him, and used it to abuse, taunt, and harass me. He told me on the day I reported to duty, "You shoulda got anyone else besides me because I'm telling you right now, I'm an asshole." He was a bully almost without limits, and made me do pushups on the hot asphalt until my hands blistered.

He glowered, his bowling-ball head wobbling in a perpetual state of indignant mortification at whatever it was I tried to get away with that he hadn't yet caught me doing. His legs spread with hands on hips, he said he hoped I looked him in the eyes and gave him the excuse to bite my face off.

Bite my face off?

I'm confused here, I thought. *We're all elite and special to The Old Guard. We're the face of the US Army and represent America. He wouldn't treat Bill McChesney this way, would he? Aren't we the good guys? I'm treated as if I attended a communist rally. Is this how* patriots are treated?

"Playtime over now, flat dick," he snarled.

"Yes...*Sergeant.*"

"What? What? You gotta attitude, Private?"

"No, Sergeant." Actually I did.

"Oh, you do," he said, "cuz you mad-doggin' me, boy. I'll butt-stroke you to the head, knock yo' teef out."

"Yes, Sergeant." *I volunteered for this?*

"'*Yes, Sergeant,*'" he mimicked. "Tay', you one get-over bitch." He pressed his face close to mine so that I endured his fecal breath. And that's all I did. I endured it.

Everything from my past was meaningless; stripes were the only thing that mattered now.

Think of everything that proceeded this, review the previous couple hundred pages, and then imagine me standing there taking crap from this guy. Does this chapter seem somehow out of place? It doesn't fit, does it? *I* didn't fit.

Lookin' good but hatin' life. The Old Guard, 1986.

My powerlessness had peaked. I couldn't say, "Suck it, Sergeant!" or fight him at the bus stop. I couldn't twist my mouth up, fold my arms, and say, "I'll accept your apology now." I couldn't ignore him or go on a run. For the first time in my life, I had to remain engaged and not react. The best I could do was use shoe edge dressing to write *TOGS* (The Old Guard Sucks) on the bottom of my shoes, a rebellion that was strangely tolerated throughout our company. On maneuvers we fantasized about trapping our sergeant in his mummy bag, beating him into docility and regret, and then slipping away to feign sleep and innocence. Since nobody felt like going to Leavenworth Penitentiary, scheming was as far as it got. When I didn't externalize my predicament I internalized it, and envied the soldiers who were rumored to have suicided by pouring edge dressing into a plastic bag and affixing it over their heads. Somehow it now seemed reasonable. Soldiers routinely got Dishonorable Discharges and I envied them their freedom, but I would not emulate them. I swore to serve two years. I would not dishonor my father, who was on the verge of becoming a Brigadier General, or myself. So when I couldn't escape via special running assignments such as the World Military Cross-Country Championships or the Boy Scout Jamboree, I coped in this twisted reality where my commander called formations to praise the NCOs for their professionalism and we grunts for our high moral. Even more confusing was when the same guys who complained the most reenlisted. When I complained I meant it, just like now. I'm reliable that way.

The Old Guard put on a race that was only for Old Guard soldiers, so everybody had to either run or cheer. My whole company cheered for me and chanted my name at the start. Pumped up and psyched to show off, I went out hard like John Esquibel at the Pepsi Challenge in Albuquerque five years earlier, when he lost the race because he ran into a dead end. I didn't run into a dead end though. I demolished the field and was so far ahead that the guy on the course directing runners didn't know I was in the race and directed me off the course. I ran an additional half-mile, and by the time I got back on course I was in tenth place. I sprinted up to second but was humiliated. It still hurts to think about. The race itself wasn't important or competitive, but I wanted to show my fellow soldiers what I could do, why I missed so much duty, that their picking up the slack for me was all worth it because I was so freaking awesome. When I think about it I still feel horrible.

I know, I know. I can hear Trenholm's voice in my head saying, "Well, if that's the worst thing that's ever happened to you...." His father had recently died, which put things in perspective. We flew kites on the beach for Mr. Trenholm.

I'm reminded of another Trenholm insight: "Suppose you've got a turd," he'd say. "You can polish it and polish it, but in the end you've still got a turd."

I shared this story as open self-disclosure, an exposure to something that pains me, and hoped for greater resolution. However, I think I've just polished another turd.

So I wasn't always the beneficiary of other runners' misfortune; it went both ways, you see.

When the other soldiers went to the Arlington bars at the end of the duty day, I went on a run. A handful of times soldiers expressed how much they respected me for my running. They said they were drinking at such-and-such bar and saw me run past. I liked that people felt that way about what I did, but of course they didn't know that I had to do it. They thought I had a choice. The unhealthy aspect of my running showed if you were looking for it.

For example, there was a two-mile race on the mall for soldiers and marines from other DC area battalions. We were required to wear combat boots and battle dress trousers, and although The Old Guard had a team, I ran alone far ahead of everyone, marines on the sideline shouting that I had to stay with my team-mates. But I had entered solo and wasn't on anyone's team. And when I won I won alone and celebrated alone.

Back at my barracks there was growing resentment towards me, beginning in my squad, then my platoon, and finally compa-nywide. Whenever I got sent on a temporary duty assignment to run, the soldiers I left behind were one man short. It didn't mat-ter how fast the missing man could run when all it meant to those left behind was they had even more tiny American flags to poke into the Arlington National Cemetery graves on Memorial Day.

Similar to the KU students who saw me as a prima donna for trying to use my King's X card to get into closed classes, the soldiers saw me as treated special while they suffered. Yet again I saw myself as deserving special consideration because of all the extra work I did at running. They liked me to wear *ARMY* across my chest, but then didn't give me adequate time to train, by the standards of the distance gods anyway.

The Old Guard running-club leader was Lieutenant George Burdick, a good guy, always kind and respectful to me, and I was glad to have another officer as an ally. We went to local races together, which I typically won. He was so impressed that he took my trophies and stopped by the battalion commander's house and showed him, and the colonel had to feign interest. Then Lt. Burdick took my trophies to my company commander, Captain Brian Evans. Captain Evans called a company formation, announced business, and at the conclusion called me out of formation and presented the trophy back to me. The troops didn't know the difference between an award from a local fun run or the Cherry Blossom Ten-Miler, so everyone was impressed.

So I kept taking my trophies to Captain Evans. I thought the self-promotion empowered me, that I'd get more time to train. Finally Captain Evans called another formation, and the entire company, over a hundred men, who were on their own time, stopped whatever they did, dressed in the uniform of the day, hurried up and waited in the weather in stiff company formation until Captain Evans came out, called us to attention, and presented me with another trophy.

Company dismissed.

Of course it was greatly resented, and I fell out of favor with most of the company. The one guy who remained was my buddy Evan Campbell, a nonrunner who carried our squad's sixty-caliber machinegun. Out in the boonies we snapped our shelter halves together and shared Tabasco and M&Ms. When he finally finagled a transfer to a ranger battalion it left me to drape my shelter half over a bush and shiver alone beneath it.

I laid low after irritating my company, hiding my awards, making more of an effort to blend in and be green instead of gold.

Finally I was sent to The Presidio in San Francisco for two months to run on the All Army track team. My barrack was within a quarter mile of the Golden Gate Bridge in a park-like setting, and other than morning and afternoon formations and two workouts a day, my time was my own. This was what I had in mind when I heard the army liked runners.

When I showed up, I wasn't in *real* shape and fought to round into condition quickly. Sergeant Mike Haywood pulled me aside and asked me if I thought we were training too hard—shouldn't we come together to persuade the coach to scale back the workouts? You know me. I shrugged and said to go on ahead. I didn't want to compromise his training, but since these workouts weren't dick to me, I planned to scale them *up*.

For the first time since college, my job was to train twice a day, and I planned to take full advantage of it.

I did my morning 10K slow run, and then I either isolated myself in the post library or got together with army track buddies and walked down to Fisherman's Warf. Later we loaded onto the vans and went to the track for speed workouts. Afterward it was chow and watch movies. Except for the formations twice a day my life was close to perfect.

Which, in retrospect, was like a very sick patient who gets significantly better the night before he dies.

At the All Military Track and Field Championships, I ran the ten-thousand meters. The race broke into a lead pack of three with an officer named Mark "Steve" Littleton, a cross-country and track All American from the University of Pittsburgh at Johnstown running for navy, and an air-force officer named Joe Sheeran, who probably had the worst day of everyone because it was his race to lose. He was an All American out of Eastern Illinois University who beat me badly in the military world cross-country championships in Portugal. He's currently the best fifty-plus distance runner in the nation, but back then he fell off the pace and left the race to Littleton and me. I had an off day as well because of my sore Achilles, which caused me to run stiffly, and my heels blistered on the hot, hard, asphalt track. I should've dropped out, but wouldn't. I feared what people would say. Oh, that flat dick left for two months for the army track team and *dropped out* of the only race that mattered? No way. I was prideful too. So Littleton sat on me until the last lap. He even waved to his buddies, I saw his shadow and the thumbs up from his teammates, and then he outkicked me. I couldn't walk afterward, so my buddy piggybacked me to the bus.

When I got back to Ft. Meyer, I went to see the medical chief warrant officer even though army doctors generally treated me with the care and bedside manner of a pathologist. As he drained blood and pus and picked skin and fat out of my heels he commented to his minion, "This guy will never run again."

Having read this far into my memoir, let's pause a moment and let that sink in—not because it was so insensitive, but because for the next twenty-five years it was so accurate.

*All Military Track and Field Championships, 1985. Mark "Steve"
Littleton, me, and Joe Sheeran race the ten thousand as
I incur my career-ending heel injury.*

CHAPTER 24

RAGE

From 1985 to 2009, I didn't consider myself a runner. Oh sure, I was a big-time *ex*-runner, but I didn't crow about the passion and angst. A new life took shape, the Berlin Wall came down, and I held the front page up to my tenth graders and said, "If you only remember one thing from this class, remember this." On 9/11 my brother was supposed to be high in the second tower, but his secretary misrouted him to Chicago. The great recession and housing meltdown caught Renni and I with three properties we couldn't unload. See, I had become a husband and coach, a teacher and father, and eventually a clinical psychologist, but no, not a runner—not anymore. Yeah, I jogged every now and then, but it ended in pain and never with the commitment of my youth. It hurt too much, and as you perhaps now understand, I'm not only talking about physical injuries.

Then at forty-nine years old, a photograph taken of me on the beach cast me into the role of the stereotypical middle-aged guy with a potbelly. Later that night I awoke at 2:00 a.m. with the realization that I did not want to be *that* guy.

Groomsmen, 1989. The popular Ralph Clark, my nephew Terry, Kendall Smith, me in the middle (as usual between Kendall and Schmidt), Tim Schmidt, my brother Tom, and my junior-high track buddy Bryan Nelson. Shaun Trenholm's sister was married the same day, so he missed my wedding.

You see I was most vulnerable and neurotic when I awakened in the middle of the night. The thoughts I repressed in the sunshine rose when I awoke in the darkness bare-chested, barefoot, and in my underwear. It wasn't sleep and it wasn't wakefulness that threatened me, but the twilight in-between that allowed dread to surface.

Renni breathed heavily beside me as we lay in bed at our Mexican villa on the Sea of Cortez, one of those properties we couldn't unload when Mexico relapsed to her role as the North American relative that insists on chronic dysfunction. It was July 2009, and I became viscerally aware. Fifty wasn't some far-off hypothetical age anymore but three months away. Granted it was "just a number," just as a four-minute-mile is just a number, and 26.2 is just a number, but it meant to me that although I had successfully navigated half a century, I was now not only on the cusp of becoming "elderly," but also closer to death. Time had sped up, and *time left* was even more precious because of its scarcity. I was in the shadow of things once distant, and the emotional realization struck in the middle of the night, that's all I'm saying.

Of course there were no traps set or sprung. Aging and death had merely methodically stalked me just as every age and life-stage does for those of us who live. Now twilight approached, the horizon drew nearer, and growing old wasn't as hypothetical anymore.

My point is I had defended myself better before that photograph and before I awakened that night.

See, for me aging was the disagreeable cousin of death, the slow piling on of mileage before the career-ending injury. I knew it approached even when I held my father's knife to my heart at four years old and when I witnessed the horror of the slaughterhouse at ten. Yet it was cerebral then, as a boy, and I didn't *feel* my decline and impending mortality as poignantly until that night. Whereas it had been neuroticism before, at 2:00 a.m. some July morning in 2009, it became real as my denial was temporarily caught off guard.

Yes, I was intimidated to climb high on a ladder and step upon tree limbs while building a tree house for my son; I didn't bounce the way I did when I ran the steeplechase. Sometimes I let myself go, and sometimes I did not. Would I become the gnome-like guy who answered simple questions with non sequiturs, who people smirked patronizingly behind his back (which he wouldn't notice), who turned to his wife for a reiteration of the conversation in progress, who was patted on the back like a boy, had doors held open for him like a woman, whose best friend was the TV, and who kind of looked like a zombie if you wanted to be mean about it?

Taken a step further, I awoke viscerally conscious that I would die sooner than I wanted, but not young. I would grow old because I was not struck by lightning at nineteen like Ann Gilliland and because I did not die in a violent car accident like Steve Prefontaine at twenty-four or Bill McChesney at thirty-three. I wasn't eaten alive from the inside out at forty-one like my mother or incapacitated like Bret Hyde of Lou Gehrig's Disease at the same age. I wasn't drowned in a horrible boating accident at forty-eight like Paul Cummings. All that dying young business was nonsensical worry, because I did not die in any case, not in a war purposefully sought, or in a bizarre or tragic accident.

Here I am.

So I have lived but always with the oppressive knowledge that death makes life precious. Didn't I suck the marrow out of life in acknowledgment of inevitable death? Hadn't I pursued distance-god status not only to bolster my self-esteem, but also to increase my vitality and thus cheat death? The hotter I burned and juicier I lived, the more *alive* I was, and the more certain I was of continued life—or so I concluded when my magical thinking wasn't intruded upon by distance gods' and loved ones' early demise.

My subconscious distortions finally gave way at two in the morning. No, I would not die young; I would instead grow old.

I would become the *opposite* of a distance god.

Back in 1986 while still in the army but injured, I was too close to my loss to be able to see that I was in a period of initiation as I struggled to move to the next level of personal development. I was a new nonrunner for the first time in thirteen years, which was half my life. I had less angst when I sat in the bay area at the end of the duty day and wasted time. Hurry up and wait was still the inefficient and fatty life of an enlisted man, but now rather than smolder with impatience, I relaxed. There was no run to get in.

Two months before my discharge, they sent me to the Primary Leadership Director's Course, PLDC, in Fort Knox, Kentucky, to learn how to be a noncommissioned officer even though I only had double-digit days before a wake up. All army specialties attended PLDC, but being infantry-trained I knew how to do the combat skills, and being in the Old Guard I knew what it took to do the ceremonial skills. So I easily took care of my own business, and then helped the other soldiers, who were desk jockeys and mechanics and were rusty. I felt important, but a sweet side effect was popularity, the opposite of my experience at Delta Company back at Fort Myer. Socially similar to my old high school buddy Ralph, I had my most direct experience of the consequences of being my best self, similar to today when I do psychotherapy.

When I returned to Fort Meyer, I was promoted to corporal, the lowest NCO, and made a team leader. A new private stood at parade rest in front of me as I growled, "You shoulda got anyone else besides me because I'm telling you right now, I'm an asshole." Just kidding. I considered it but then didn't. Instead I felt sorry for the fresh meat, just beginning his life-in-the-fishbowl "perfect" years. I became less selfish and began to connect.

So I lay in bed in the middle of the night in our villa in old Mexico, listened to the surf, and had the gut-twisting realization that my youth was spent and now I would become old. Not hypothetically but literally. Admittedly I was a bit premature in my old age lamenting, but I like to think of it as far-sightedness rather than neuroticism. When I was young I did not see men my age as a threat. "Go to the corners of the dirt playground," I now think. "You have been unpicked."

I'll be petulant, and it will be cute—an old man with colic. I'll yowl at the lions at their kill, but they will tolerate me. We are civilized after all, but they will secretly wish I'd wander off into the desert, marbled meat for scavengers.

It's their turn now, I remind myself. I had my turn; I did not waste it.

Still I rage against the dying of the light, yet I can't act it out as excellently anymore. Sure, I can talk, but we all know that talk is cheap, and I don't want to be that guy either.

So I was to become invisible again and await the boot.

Was my only recourse to scream?

Or could I turn to running to save me again?

CHAPTER 25

MAXIMUM STEADY

It was blatantly absurd for a one-time wannabe distance god to start with a meager mile, but there I was *jogging* and wearing an iPod. Ignoring the pain in my left heel from my army injury, my Achilles grew sore again. Still, after I accepted that I'd run with pain it didn't seem to be a deal-breaker, just the price. It was all-or-none by then, since I had no running career to lose, no races to miss.

Running felt alien, unnatural, and awkward. *Creaky. Clumsy.* It reminded me of the things beginning runners said to me, and I nodded and advised them to build slowly, trust it would come. The difference for me was I knew it would come if I could manage my injuries.

Renni reminded me there was medication for me now. I hadn't thought of that and was surprised when it helped. Sometimes when things are pointed out to me, such as there's help to relieve suffering rather than merely Knowing the Truth, it's still a bit miraculous to me. Many of my clients also overlook things that are obvious to the rest of us. We all have blind spots, and sometimes just saying it can be one of the most powerful interventions.

You are not a bad person; you just didn't know any better at the time.

Forgive yourself.

Let it go and move on, as difficult as that may be, especially when other people do their best to keep you stuck with them.

I'm sometimes asked *how* I move on. I say, "First become aware, then make the decision, and then keep doing it the new way you choose to do it. It will become habitual, and then you've changed."

So I added longer runs on weekends and experienced conditioning I hadn't felt in twenty-five years. As my mileage increased, Timmy Two-Mile emerged, rubbed his eyes and suggested—shyly at first, like a freshman, then more forcefully like a fifth-year senior—that I run further and faster. It was also Timmy Two-Mile who, one Sunday morning, thought it was fine to have coffee and doughnuts before a fifteen-miler in the heat without water. Of course I got into trouble. It's obvious, right? Why *wouldn't* I get into trouble? At a car wash I slurped water from the grimy bathroom faucet and then sat with the customers. In that hour I realized I wasn't the same on the *inside* either, that I couldn't do running the same way as before. I had to pay attention to my body, its needs. Finally I walked home with my new habit.

I built up to Sunday twenty-two-milers, rediscovered the joy of running effortlessly and fast, and caught more glimpses of Timmy Two-Mile. He liked to assert himself when I ran swiftly and nothing hurt for a while, when I cruised along at maximum steady pace and floated over the Scottsdale bike paths.

"Oh, yeah," Timmy Two-Mile said. "I'm back, baby!"

When I started, Gentry couldn't recognize me from my high school yearbook. Then I dropped from 195 pounds to 165, only 15 pounds heavier than Timmy Two-Mile.

"You should *race*," Timmy Two-Mile goaded, which sounded like a good idea to me too.

There's another theory in psychology that says our relationship with God is similar to our relationship with our parents. When I was young, my parents were godlike, all-powerful and omniscient. They laid out the rules I was to follow, which were as incontrovertible as gravity, and I followed them or suffered the consequences. I had the choice to walk or run, was free to fall, but was expected to pick myself up and continue on. My life was mine from the beginning, and I've always been grateful to my parents for that.

However, there was something missing. As I mentioned earlier, the missing thing is often the most difficult to identify. Although I couldn't articulate it then, still it became a profound message and feeling to me as young as nine years old.

While in the front yard my dog snarled at the mailman. In Albuquerque 1969, dogs and children often ran loose. The mailman tossed a broken brick at my dog, and I feared I was his next target, but he settled for chewing me out. Terrified and humiliated, I tearfully went inside and discovered Mom listened on the other side of the door the whole time. I was small and on my own, so naturally the feeling was anxiety.

Today I look at Gentry and imagine him terrified, believing he is alone, having to toughen up to get through life. I want to run to him, hug him, let him know that life does not have to be that way, that he's never alone even if sometimes I can't be there. I want to make it easier for him.

Humans have a drive for autonomy but also connection, and somehow we must balance the two. I was given food and shelter until I graduated high school, but I was otherwise independent and could not expect to be rescued. I could collapse or harden myself.

How this generalized to my relationship with God was that he laid out the rules of the universe, and I maneuvered through life on my own and did not expect an omniscient being to rescue me. I didn't pray to God for help because it would be like praying to alter gravity. I didn't pray to alter the weather, nor did I pray to alter the laws of physics. No, I prayed to actualize my speed, strength, endurance, and tactical skills. God was as real as gravity to me, but just as cold and ruthless if I failed to understand the metaphysical laws. Consequences were my own fault for not Knowing the Truth. When Mom died this paradigm imploded for me, not because it was not theoretically true, but because it was not practical. I fell away from the belief that prayer resulted in divine intervention, although psychological well-being was doable, which had a wonderful side effect of improving my life.

Considering my family system and my religious worldview, was it any wonder that I was a determined but lonely little boy who found a family among distance runners? When that family was taken away by injury I was forced to grow in other ways, and I built a new family with Renni and Gentry, who saved me after my injury better than any two-mile ever could.

Renni, Gentry, Toffy, and me at the Sea of Cortez, 2010.

I trained for a marathon because that burned the most calories. So I needed a tune-up race and ran a half marathon in Scottsdale. I went out too fast and died just after the 10K split. It was a rookie mistake, but I had a good reason. See, in my head I'm frozen at a 1:06.01 half-marathon, so although I knew I wasn't going to run that pace exactly, I certainly didn't expect to trot along at 1:30 pace. Nor did I expect a woman who looked an awful lot like Oprah Winfrey to power by me. I drafted until I couldn't hang on any longer and then let her go.

Steve Scott wrote in his memoir that he felt like a bridesmaid because he never medaled in the Olympics or got a world record, even though he had the US mile record and went to three Olympics. Steve Scott a bridesmaid? Relatively that makes me the flower girl. No, the guy outside parking cars. There's a lesson there too, something about running and racing having to be more than just about times and place for the rest of us who aren't Steve Scott. It's something about it not being about winning so much, as being a winner, as trite as that sounds, and as difficult as it is to live up to.

Then a thirteen-year-old boy winning his age group ran past me. Little dude came up to my chest—he was me circa 1973—but it was an absolutely intolerable situation when reversed. So I tried to go with him too, embarrassed to lumber behind and breathe hard the way people used to do to me. I used to sniff at their absurdity before I burned them off. I let him go as well. He's probably a future distance god anyway.

Finally a man with one of those Oscar Pistorias legs churned past.

Oprah, a kid, and a one-legged man?

This comeback thing was going to take some recalibration.

I ran the Rock and Roll Marathon in Phoenix, my first serious marathon since 1983, in 3:18.47 and discovered I had qualified for Boston. I could return exactly twenty-eight years later to the day. OK then, who am I to go against fate?

"Was there any question, bro?" Timmy Two-Mile said, a bit chagrinned at not having broken three hours, but choosing to focus on the positive. "I mean, there was no question, was there, providing there was no kryptonite out there, right? Am I right?"

So I ran shorter races as speed work to prepare for my bust-out race at Boston.

I won a tiny 10K, which felt a lot like winning an eighth-grade time trial.

Then I ran The Zoo Run, which was a two-loop 5K within the zoo. I alternated the lead with some young buck, but when we went into our second loop, we began to lap mothers with strollers and small children. I shouted *Track!* but they didn't know what I meant, and I came up quickly and brushed past the surprised walkers and toddlers. The other dude didn't slow down either, he still tried to burn me off, determined to win, screw the collateral damage, it was war after all. We crashed, bumped, and zigzagged through the thickening crowd. I've been in some very big races, and in some very competitive ones as well, but this race was neither. Still he smashed through the civilians in a fun-run fundraiser, and when he glanced back to see if I still hung on, I saw in his eyes that he would not slow down.

"Burn and bury this poser, this wannabe, this aging frat boy!" Timmy Two-Mile screamed at me. "Go, man, go! We're running subsix pace, for heaven's sake, not subfive!"

My head told me it wasn't worth it, though, and surprisingly my gut agreed. I let the guy go. Consciously. Premeditated. Did I quit? Was it shameful considering I was not broken? I think not. It wasn't worth it to me to crash through mommies with baby strollers. I also understood he needed to win in a way that I no longer did, and I didn't judge or blame him. On the contrary, I liked that road racing hadn't changed in that way.

The thing was, I had changed.

There were other races: a 10K where two young guys ran far ahead but took a wrong turn and so I won, a few age-group wins, and a few high finishes overall, which I savored. Black shorts and singlet was my trademark, like the Colorado guys, to intimidate. Before long, though, I fell apart and had to sit out the hot summer months. I tried to build up my mileage over the winter but couldn't, and as spring and Boston approached, I couldn't run at all due to the reasserting injuries, which led to new injuries, and then I was done.

"This sucks," Timmy Two-Mile moped.

"You look like a broken runner," Gentry said.

"Why even go to Boston if you're injured?" Renni asked.

Why drink beers in Georgetown with the national five-thousand-meter champion? Why try to join the distance gods? Why indeed. I would go because I had qualified.

CHAPTER 26

BOSTON MARATHON 2011

They say that nothing is really forgotten; we forget what we want or need to forget. At Boston 2011 I forgot my Garmin watch and sunglasses. Worse still, I forgot to eat. I caught the early shuttle from my hotel to wait in the impossibly long line that ran serpentine through the Boston Common in the chilly morning to get on the bus to take me to the start. It didn't occur to me that I hadn't fueled up. *Unbelievable*, I thought. But then I thought, *No, very believable*; that's how I did it the first time in 1983. So I waited in Hopkinton with only a belly-ful of Starbucks coffee, knowing I hadn't run in over a month. And I now wore training flats because of my horrific Achilles, my Air Nikes heavy as combat boots compared to my sleek racing flats.

Why did I need to forget the important things?

Perhaps I needed to feel OK about running slowly. Perhaps it was decades-old bad habits.

Conditions were almost identical to 1983, which was near perfect. Since I had a red number, I was in the first wave, one of nine thousand other red bibs. But soon after the start, I was gradually overtaken by second-wave white numbers. I ate oranges and GU along the course and tossed my old race T-shirts to women in lawn chairs in the back of pickup trucks. Instead of going inside myself to get into the zone, I enjoyed the spectacle as we passed through each enthusiastic town.

I think about Sebastian Coe. He was the 1500 Olympic champion and world-record holder in my day. Today he is Lord Coe, member of Parliament and president of the Organizing Committee for the London Summer Olympics 2012. Seb Coe is long past the height of his athletic ability, but he has moved on to other domains and is excellent today in other ways. The same is true for Alberto Salazar, who has developed into a great coach. Billy Mills and Bill Rodgers are great ambassadors for distance running. This dynamic continues with Dr. Chuck Aragon. When a man collapsed in front of his house Chuck saved his life. Chuck is an anesthesiologist now with progeny who outstrip his feats at the same age, his daughter Dani running the eight hundred in Barcelona at the World Junior Championships in 2012. Dani and her older sister, Alexa, both made All American in 2013 for Notre Dame, and their younger sister, Christina, might be even faster. The torch is passed and then we morph from our physical prime into something less physical but just as intense. It still feels like progress and full living. The compulsiveness and competitiveness we directed into distance running now serve us in other endeavors. It's growth regardless of age. That's what I'm trying to do now as a psychologist, husband, and parent.

I thought running was about times and kills when its true value was what it taught me about myself and how I ran my life. Whether I competed at the junior-high level or semiprofessionally, the feelings, lessons, and personal victories were worthwhile. What I put into running came back to me, not always the way I wanted, but it came back manyfold and enriched my life. It was about how I dealt with being a distance runner that mattered, how I dealt with the challenge of putting one foot in front of the other faster and further, against whoever showed up—sometimes they were distance gods—against whatever challenge, whatever quirky thing happened.

In the end it was about me, after all. I thought the early maneuvering didn't matter—only the finish, time, and kills. I had that backward, though; the maneuvering was what mattered most. How I trained and raced mattered. The process mattered, and how I handled life as a runner mattered. What happened along the way mattered, and in the end that was all I really had—the present. All the fortune telling—predicting a future I feared I wasn't big enough to cope with—caused unnecessary anxiety. It fades and we age.

I stopped a few times to pee out that Starbucks coffee—once in a field and again in a porta potty, not an elevator. It was the first time I'd ever stopped in a race. I also stopped at Wellesley when Renni, Gentry, and our local friends cheered for me while holding homemade signs of encouragement. People didn't make signs for me back when I was competitive. If they had, I would've blown past and wouldn't have seen them anyway.

At twenty-one miles I remembered how I blew up after Heartbreak Hill in 1983, having gone out too hard and not properly fueled myself. This time I kept my legs moving, albeit slowly, and made a point to not walk. Instead of the Boston College crowd "bullying" me like when I was twenty-three years old, now they looked very young, and their cheers, smiles, and energy lifted me up. That's what they did back then too, of course, but I wouldn't accept their help. This time rather than run in the middle of the road to try to claw back into the zone, I ran close to the Boston College kids and got countless high fives.

I often assign journaling to clients. It's a more concrete way to process the thoughts that waft through our brains. Language imposes structure on our thoughts, encourages specificity, and leads to clarification and better understanding of what we think and feel. Writing it down is especially structuring and revealing. I've discovered that the answers I sought are not a clear intervention or catharsis, but a gentle acceptance of who I've been, who I am, and how I move ahead by expressing the qualities of a distance runner today in other domains.

I see the grudges I made up and held, my defensiveness, and the uselessness of it. Paul Schultz wasn't really my archenemy; he was a runner I respected who helped bring out the best in me. He didn't reveal much to me, so he was the blank slate, and I projected my deficiencies onto him. The two times I went to the NCAAs, it was because the *team* qualified, and without Schultz and the other studs, I wouldn't have experienced two of the most important and highest-quality races of my career. I undermined myself and now wonder what could've been.

I see how I've isolated myself over a lifetime and that others weren't always shunning me. I see now that by doing these exposures, both in imagination via recall and in vivo via returning to the roads and to Boston, I am both embracing and moving away from the past.

I came across the eulogy for Olympian Paul Cummings. It seems he was very quiet and not one for conversation. He was an exceptional person, someone who led by example and was always taciturn.

Taciturn: reserved or uncommunicative in speech; saying little.

Cummings didn't disrespect me or deny my existence at the Jacksonville River Run postrace party in 1983. He was *shy*.

Oops.

Of course it was never about Paul Cummings but about my self-imagined deficiencies. For all I know, Cummings may have felt ashamed for not winning that race and couldn't bring himself to accept my attention. It's more likely that Cummings just didn't know what the heck to say when he was relaxing with his friends and some guy just walked up and started talking about how he was recruited to BYU by Cummings years earlier. So he nodded and looked down at the floor the same as I would.

I should've practiced a little bit of grace back then, to others and myself. That's what I gave myself for my fiftieth birthday—grace—and it's what I give to others today, every day, whether they know it or not. Sometimes I falter, and that's when I hope they give a bit of grace to me.

The distance gods were far ahead at Boston, and I still wanted to run with them. If I were able to run with the distance gods today, I would—I promise you that. Even Joan Benoit didn't run with the distance gods. At fifty-three years old, she didn't come up behind me in a media bubble, surrounded by sirens. She was already far ahead, busy winning her age group.

By the time I approached the finish, third-wave, blue-bibbed runners showed up around me. Still I didn't gut it out; I was too injured for that. Haglund's deformity, it's called. It's a scary way to describe a genetic growth of bone behind both Achilles tendons. I would have surgery after Boston, which would finally correct the lifelong problem, but there is no correcting being a man in his fifties. The young guy who put on my cast attended college at Bowling Green State. I asked him if he'd heard of a guy named Dave Wottle. He hadn't, but said he'd ask his dad.

The truth is that I enjoyed the run to the finish line and let the thousands of spectators cheer for me. I didn't berate myself for running 4:27.32. I was glad to be there.

A man in the eighty-plus age group ran 4:26.25.

I also got beat by four blind guys.

The next year Galen Rupp got second in the Olympic 10,000 in London and was immediately heralded as the next Steve Prefontaine.

EPILOGUE

I wanted to be a distance god, to run so far ahead of even the elite runners that I raced alone, detached, my awesomeness confirmed, my mortality denied.

Instead I was an also-ran, another wannabe in the chase pack.

So I didn't get my wish, but I got something better: I got connection.

And I got to run.

Keep the passion, bro.

Me, Coach Bob Timmons, and Tim Schmidt at KU Relays reunion.

27252078R10138

Made in the USA
Lexington, KY
04 November 2013